Genders and Sexualities in the Social Sciences

Series editors
Victoria Robinson
Centre for Women's Studies
University of York, York, UK

Diane Richardson
Sociology
Newcastle University
Newcastle Upon Tyne, UK

The study of gender and sexuality has developed dramatically over recent years, with a changing theoretical landscape that has seen innovative work emerge on identity, the body and embodiment, queer theory, technology, space, and the concept of gender itself. There has been an increasing focus on sexuality and new theorizing on masculinities. This exciting series will take account of these developments, emphasizing new, original work that engages both theoretically and empirically with the themes of gender, sexuality, and, crucially, their intersections, to set a new, vibrant and contemporary international agenda for research in this area.

More information about this series at
http://www.springer.com/series/15001

Peter Robinson

Gay Men's Working Lives, Retirement and Old Age

Foreword by
Humphrey McQueen

Peter Robinson
Arts, Social Science and Humanities
Swinburne University of Technology
Hawthorn, VIC
Australia

Genders and Sexualities in the Social Sciences
ISBN 978-1-137-43531-6   ISBN 978-1-137-43532-3   (eBook)
DOI 10.1057/978-1-137-43532-3

Library of Congress Control Number: 2017937144

© The Editor(s) (if applicable) and The Author(s) 2017
The author(s) has/have asserted their right(s) to be identified as the author(s) of this work in accordance
with the Copyright, Designs and Patents Act 1988.
This work is subject to copyright. All rights are solely and exclusively licensed by the Publisher, whether
the whole or part of the material is concerned, specifically the rights of translation, reprinting, reuse
of illustrations, recitation, broadcasting, reproduction on microfilms or in any other physical way, and
transmission or information storage and retrieval, electronic adaptation, computer software, or by
similar or dissimilar methodology now known or hereafter developed.
The use of general descriptive names, registered names, trademarks, service marks, etc. in this
publication does not imply, even in the absence of a specific statement, that such names are exempt
from the relevant protective laws and regulations and therefore free for general use.
The publisher, the authors and the editors are safe to assume that the advice and information in this
book are believed to be true and accurate at the date of publication. Neither the publisher nor the
authors or the editors give a warranty, express or implied, with respect to the material contained herein
or for any errors or omissions that may have been made. The publisher remains neutral with regard to
jurisdictional claims in published maps and institutional affiliations.

Printed on acid-free paper

This Palgrave Macmillan imprint is published by Springer Nature
The registered company is Macmillan Publishers Ltd.
The registered company address is: The Campus, 4 Crinan Street, London, N1 9XW, United Kingdom

In memory of Roger Horton

Foreword

'Work! Consume! Die!' remains salutary about the nullities to which life can be reduced in the absence of fulfilling relationships across its every sphere and at each stage. We become what we do, as individuals and as a species. If we do nothing, we become nothing. The fate of Sebastian in Tennessee Williams' *Suddenly Last Summer* (1958) is a metaphor for idleness relieved by preying on the poor, who eat him.

Peter Robinson's third instalment from his study of gay males takes us beyond reported experiences of work and retirement into his reflections and on to those of his interview subjects. As ever, we are left questioning how to make sense of a universe indifferent to our existence yet amenable to our needs and hopes through the social effort we too narrowly call 'paid work'.

*

Most of us, much of the time, remake ourselves in such jobs where estrangement and alienation can turn work to a near-life experience.

Allowing for the fact that earning a quid has always been compulsory for the 99%, the prime attraction in going to work used to be to socialise. The fragmentation of the application of labour since the 1980s has stripped away much of that enrichment. Finding enough paid work

viii   **Foreword**

each week to survive is not going to get any easier in competition with robotic automation. Moreover, precarious employment all but excludes the promise of paid work that enriches our individuality through the quality of our relationships.

Higher rates of joblessness and the fractured future for such work as will be on offer are not specific to any strata of the workforce. However, in a buyer's market for labour, the petty prejudices that would otherwise be inoperative add to the chances of gays being passed over, a discrimination doubled if the application is both gay and not quite white.

Gay liberation had hardly got underway when the long trough in unemployment ended in the mid 1970s. The 1980s saw two more whacks with the restructuring of work and HIV-AIDS. In a world where a majority of otherwise sensible people fail to distinguish a cold from the flu, it is hardly surprising that the facts about the limited means for transmitting the AIDS virus has still not eradicated the panic about breathing the same air let alone sharing a toilet seat, as the experiences of the New Zealand teacher testify.

The discrimination against a HIV+ lawyer depicted in *Philadelphia* (1993) was nasty yet Hollywood's portrayal of his final days was more glamorous than the fate of the tens of thousands of his fellow US citizens who died impoverished in a polity where a halfway decent health service remains an impossible dream.

*

'Unemployed at last!' exalts 'Tom Collins', the narrator of Joseph Furphy's *Such is Life* (1903) in one of the most arresting opening lines in literature. Tom is looking forward to writing up his diaries. Good luck to him. For most of us, to be out of paid work even for a week or two means a financial crisis. Long-term unemployment causes relationships to sunder and results in homelessness. Once again, those outcomes are not extremes. In recent years, millions have been denied their entitlements because of corporate and state bankruptcies. The unravelling is far from over, and may even have not begun if the Bank for International Settlements is right in alleging that the measures taken by governments since 2008 have done no more than postpone the day of reckoning while making its impact worse. Nest-eggs might hatch vulture funds.

Foreword   ix

To retire early on a package is not the same as getting the sack before ending up on a disability pension in one's 50s. In any society which thrives on structured inequalities, Sophie Tucker knew of what she spoke: 'Ah's been rich an' ah's been poor, and believes me, rich is best.' In societies like Australia, the age pension guarantees frugal comfort—if one is out of the commercial rental market, does not need to drip-feed Big Pharma and has no calls for big-ticket outlays, say, for home repairs. People are now being made to wait till they turn 67, and encouraged to keep working beyond those years while being told that you are too old at 40.

The economic imperatives that exacerbated the insecurities inherent in working life during the 1980s are reaching into retirement, indeed, are in pursuit of the money we cannot take with us. The secular stagnation that persists from the implosion of capital expansion late in 2008 impels its agents of capital to seek fresh sectors from which to garner profits by colonising hitherto sheltered realms, notably education, health and aged care. Just as the Mad Men of marketeering learnt to chase the Pink Dollar, their equivalents in the corporatised service sector are now buying up retirement homes, a take-over in which the churches are complicit, selling-out their caritas to the likes of Lend Lease and Stocklands. Is this oncoming wave of elder abuse designed to meet the compensation payouts for decades of institutionalised child abuse? We all now have as much to fear from corporates that are profit-blind to sexual orientation as from religious Fundamentalists who see little else.

The business plans vary according to the targeted facility. For one very expensive ex-Anglican property, the aim is capital gain from renovating the unit after its current owner's departure. At an ex-Roman one intended for welfare tenants, the scheme is to replace its blocks of motel-type rooms with spaces reminiscent of Japanese capsule hotels, while dispensing with the trained staff who dispense the medications. The luxurious and the slack will be promoted as providing flexibility and freedom of choice, two of the Big Lies behind which corporates retain their sovereignty over us as consumers.

An alternative of modest guesthouses is hinted at by the interviewee who plans to take in a couple of boarders to make his own ends meet. Why not a B&B element to vitalise the talk at the shared breakfast table? Single men used to wash up in inner-city boarding houses until gentrifiers knocked down those cheap and cheerless refuges. Today's bad used to be a lot worse, and still is across most of the world, and will not improve anywhere without campaigns to match those around securing decent responses to HIV-AIDS.

In keeping with the American way of death, US firms bought up municipal cemeteries around the world, pushed up the price of burial sites and cold-called families to shame them into spending thousands on graves in need of 'renovation'. We can escape their clutches by bequeathing our cadavers to anatomy schools. Being old does not make all our bits obsolete and so it is worth bequeathing any still functioning parts for transplant.

*

Several decades ago, Dennis Altman surprised an academic seminar that he had come to understand more about himself from novels than from the social sciences. Since no one was interviewing gay men about their lives—other than Hirshfeld and the Kinseys into sexual practices—creative writings, and responses to them, call for sensitive rereadings, not grubbing for data but seeking what Raymond Williams calls 'structures of feeling', for a start, to appreciate which kinds of work were deemed appropriate for homosexual men.

Vautrin is Balzac's master criminal and anything but the fop, although his mastery of disguise could doubtless have extended to full drag had a crime demanded it. Patrick White's *The Twyborn Affair* (1975) portrays its protagonist as a jackeroo in the Snowy Mountains. His character was inspired by the oil portrait of Herbert Dyce-Murphy, a trannie espionage agent, one of the kinds of work that earned queers a bad name as traitors.

Fiction can take us into tabooed territories, though their frontiers are as permeable as presumptions about what queers should do for a living. Stereotypical occupations of hairdressing and ballet-dancers provided a cover for gay soldiers and scaffolders, one which the coming out of footballers and Olympic Gold Medallists has removed so that anyone can now be 'sus', but none more so than men of any persuasion who work with young children. In the backwash from the exposure of the institutional cover-ups of abuse in schools and orphanages, students are aware of their power to accuse. These interflows between reform and fresh forms of repression remind us that there are few gains without some losses.

Lillian Hellman's play, *The Children's Hour* (1931), and the 2012 *The Hunt* traverse the disasters from children falsely accusing teachers of deviance or molestation. Steve J. Spears's internationally renowned play, *The Elocution of Benjamin Franklin* (1975), about a sexually aware pubescent boy and his besotted speech instructor, went where few would now dare to tread, even though nothing happens. Far more circumspect is Kenneth Mackenzie's *The Young Desire It* (1937) about the friendship between a repressed teacher and a straight 15-year-old student.

George Turner's career as Commonwealth Employment Officer in the large Victorian city of Wangaratta in the 1950s provided the materials for his close observation of blokey behaviour. His *Waste of Shame* (1965) explores the alcohol-fuelled violence between the homosocial and the homophobic in a rural sawmill. Alcoholism just one of the addictions not touched on by the interviewees as a means to cope with workplace stress or the loss of structure in retirement.

*

To conclude with a scatter of responses to some of what's not obvious from the interviews.

Since we seem never to find the time to do in retirement half the things that we imagined we would, it is superfluous to think up what else gay men might do. The frequent references to volunteering around AIDS suggest opportunities to extend a gay Meals on Wheels beyond to those with HIV-AIDS. There is a gay LifeLine, so why not a service to draw up living wills?

No one talks about being part of a 'Men's shed'.

There is only one very passing suggestion about voluntary euthanasia despite overwhelming public support for its legalisation in some form. More is involved here than release from physical torments. A decision to go while the going is good is not a disease in need of medication and therapy.

To knowing what music the interview subjects would choose for their memorial services does more than 'round out' our assessment of their other answers. There is no mention of an afterlife—or reincarnation—and none of cryogenics, that ultimate vanity of vanities. Those silences should not lead us to assume that all the respondents are atheists for it seems as likely that those who do retain a shy hope of a life everlasting have been secularised in how they speak about the lives they lead on earth. Perhaps that loss explains the emotional roller-coaster of how we do nowadays react to the deaths of those closest to us, as portrayed in Tony Ayres's 2002 feature, *Walking on Water*.

The moment of death is not mentioned. Fear of dying has displaced the fear of no longer existing. An acquaintance who bought a unit facing Moreton Bay dealt with his being woken early by an enlarged prostate by slipping across the street to sit on a park bench and enjoy the sunrise. Regular joggers exchanged greetings with him until one morning he could no longer respond. That exit might not be perfection but it was much, much better than most of us can expect. Sherwin Nuland's *How We Die* (1993) dispelled most of my fears about how the end would overtake me by spelling out that few of us will die of this or that disease, since dying, not unlike living, is a process but one in which each afflicted body part disrupts others until the system shuts down. Nuland is not a cheery read but a reassuring one in ways that total ignorance cannot maintain when our time comes.

The loss of heavenly rewards has not abolished the fear of hell on earth, manifest in the concern at ending up a prisoner in a homophobic institution. Those who want a quiet life might revert to passing as straight. Why does none of the activists embrace the chance to carry the message of liberation to a new audience? The fear that the 'Out' hairdresser as stereotype would be in for a rough time from the fellow occupants has to be set against how elderly women will have had long relationships with their own gay hairdressers, and how much they will welcome the proximity of someone to provide the tactile pleasure of a warm mauve rinse for a lot less than the going rate down the road.

As I key in these words in my own unit at the top of 64 steps, I can still afford to sound fussy about where I might end up. Without allocating each fear to a circle of hell, the first that comes to mind is where the pinnacle of intellectual activity is bingo night and the communal television is fixed to a shopping channel. The thought of an all-gay retirement village is not without its own terrors. Being at the mercies of bossy queans jostles the despair at being condemned to the company of people who think Puccini the world's greatest composer.

*

After an 88-year-old woman friend haunted an exhibition of Yves Klein's blue canvases she said: 'The older I get, the more I value silence.' At the same time, she sought out new or rare operas: 'I don't have time left for what I already know.' Between serenity and impatience seems as good a spot as any to close these remarks and to end one's days.

Canberra, Australia
December 2016

Humphrey McQueen

Acknowledgements

At the Alfred Hospital, Caulfield, I thank Ms. Sally Costar for her support and the warmth and humour she brought to our many coffee morning meetings in Balaclava and the work we did together with Alfred Health, Melbourne while I wrote this book. As well, I thank a former colleague from RMIT University, Dr. Helen Marshall, for the keen eye she brought to proofreading the manuscript and her injunctions to find the energy to put more time into undeveloped ideas which if left to my own devices I would most likely have left for another time.

At Swinburne University of Technology, I thank Prof. Linda Briskman, Prof. Brian Costar, Dr. Scott Ewing, and Dr. Julie Kimber for their friendship and encouragement while I worked on this book and its predecessor. It is rare nowadays to find friendship in academia, so competitive has it become, but these four colleagues gave it without hesitation and I am grateful for its sustaining influence during lean times. I would like also to acknowledge here the kindness of our Dean of Arts, Social Science and Humanities, Prof. Robbie Robertson and the Dean of Health, Prof. Janet Hiller, both of whom were encouraging and egalitarian in their relations with me.

xvi   **Acknowledgements**

Thanks also to my undergraduate students, among whom were Mr. Joe Jackson, Ms. Rachel Maguire, Mr. Nick Pelley, and Mr. Zac Rhode and my postgraduate student, Mr. Sam Teague. All heard about the travails of the research/teaching academic in the modern-day university and were kind enough to give honest feedback whenever I read them excerpts from the chapter I was wrestling with.

I was grateful for receiving a number of strategic research grants from the Department of Social Sciences at Swinburne, which helped with literature reviews for some of the areas covered in this book. I was grateful also to Mr. Sam Teague, whose Ph.D. research I was supervising at the time of writing this book, for his help as my occasional research assistant and sometime marking assistant. And to Prof. Michael Leach, my boss for his frank and thoughtful advice along the way.

At Palgrave Macmillan, Basingstoke, I was very fortunate in having Dr. Philippa Grand as editor for this and my two previous books. She gave me good, clear advice and was ever supportive. I was fortunate also in having Roger Horton as friend and colleague—to whose memory I have dedicated this book—who helped bring the manuscript of my first book to the attention of the then commissioning editor at Palgrave Macmillan, Ms. Melanie Blair, and who introduced me to the work of W.G. Sebald. Roger took his own life in 2013 and I have included in the Appendices an article he wrote of his time in the Australian army where in my view he was brutalised. While it speaks for itself, it will also give readers some idea of the long-term effect of institutional racism and homophobia, underlining similar accounts of interviewees which can be found in Chaps. 2–4. For her assistance with this book, I thank Ms. Beth Farrow at Palgrave Macmillan, London.

Finally, I thank Humphrey McQueen for agreeing to write the Foreword to this book and his interest in and encouragement of my research interests and writing ambitions over more than 30 years. It was he who first introduced me to the idea of the 'world of work' and I hope I have shown some understanding here of how three generations of gay men engaged with it over the course of their working lives and how it shaped them.

Contents

1	Scope and Content	1
2	Working Lives of Men Aged 60 and Older	37
3	Working Lives of Men Aged 45–60	85
4	Working Lives of Men Aged 45 and Younger	125
5	Old-Age Fears or Concerns	161
6	Old Age Plans	215
7	Conclusion	253
Appendix 1		267
Appendix 2		269
Appendix 3		271

xviii Contents

Appendix 4   273

Appendix 5   277

Appendix 6   279

Appendix 7   281

Index   287

1

Scope and Content

I like working with people and when I say, 'people' I mean the people with disabilities and [my university] students ... There is a lot of talk about collegiality but ... I find workplaces very unnatural ... There are a lot of people in workplaces—and this has to do with the conditions of work, not the individual—who really do not want to be there but if they were not there they would not know what to do with themselves.
(Callum, aged 43, Melbourne)

Introduction

This book follows in the wake of two books I wrote on gay men's lives, which Palgrave Macmillan published in 2008 and 2013. The first book, *The Changing World of Gay Men* (2008) looked at the changing circumstances under which gay men from three different generations shaped their sexual identity and lived their lives. It was based on interviews with 80 Australian men aged 20–79. Its central idea was that gay men's social/sexual lives were shaped by varying levels of social tolerance for non-heterosexuals and were therefore historically contingent. The second book, *Gay Men's Relationships Across the Life Course* (2013)

© The Author(s) 2017
P. Robinson, *Gay Men's Working Lives, Retirement and Old Age*,
Genders and Sexualities in the Social Sciences,
DOI 10.1057/978-1-137-43532-3_1

examined how age and ageing affect gay men's relationships, including their intimate relationships, friendships, fatherhood, cohabitation and marriage, and HIV.

This third book uses unanalysed data collected for *Gay Men's Relationships Across the Life Course* and examines the shape of their careers, their working histories, and how they anticipate retirement and old age. There are special circumstances such as being 'out' in the workplace and growing old with HIV that are mainly the lived experience of gay men and will affect their working lives, retirement and old age, the analysis of which is likely to make this book of interest to scholars and teachers in the fields of health studies, gerontology, sociology and anthropology, labour studies, nursing, medicine, and business studies, for example.

One of the book's chief benefits is that it provides a special focus on the work histories and careers of a sub-group of men whose presence is often overlooked when politicians, public servants and media commentators speak of the male workforce, male occupations, the 'breadwinner' and other heteronormative terms used to distinguish between workers on the basis of gender. Thus, one of the stories the book tells of men at work is that not all men who work are heterosexual or have families to support in conventional settings. And for this reason, it provides additional evidence to support an argument that men of all varieties gain from the patriarchal system because of the 'masculine dividend'.[1] It is unique also because like *Gay Men's Relationships Across the Life Course*, it is based on an international sample aged 18–87. A slightly modified sample was used for this book. On the advice of the publishers' reviewer, I removed indigenous men who had been recruited in Hong Kong and Mumbai, that is, Chinese Asians and Indians. Expatriates living in Hong Kong were not removed. The rationale: because the main focus of this book is on work, retirement and old age as understood in post-industrial, western societies, it was not possible to include the stories of indigenous men from Hong Kong and Mumbai. First, almost all the terms used in relation to working lives referred to recent western economic history, for example, economic rationalism, casualisation, privatisation and international corporate-professions as well as other western, workplace terms and practices, such as career, pension, superannuation, work-place rights. Secondly, the way in which ageing is conceived in this book assumed western or Anglophone understandings which do not translate to the broad context of ageing in Hong Kong or Mumbai.

Another of its benefits is that it allows a different set of males to speak about their experiences in the work force, a cohort which until now has not been asked to speak or has chosen not to speak (up) or distinguish itself from the generality of men. Analysis of the data the 82 men provided on their working lives showed not only that gay men's working histories were differently shaped than those of the traditional or hegemonic male—for example, some might begin later because of the temptation to spend time in their early 20s exploring their new identity or immersing themselves in the gay world, or are more fragmented because of the effect of homophobic workplaces—but also that they corresponded with those of the traditional or hegemonic male—that gay men are just as ambitious, just as capable, just as ruthless as the hegemonic male in the world of big business, high finance or international diplomacy or that gay men are just as vulnerable to the vagaries of highly casualised workplaces that are typical of conditions experienced by lowly paid or low-skilled workers.

To my knowledge, no book that considers the effect of sexuality on working lives and careers has been published since the 1970s when North American researchers Alan Bell and Martin Weinberg published their analysis of gay men and lesbians.[2] In their study, they devoted a chapter (of eight pages) to the effect being non-heterosexual had on job satisfaction, job stability, and careers of gay men and lesbians. A great deal of published research exists on male working lives, changes in employment practices since the 1970s, and the effect these have had on families, careers of men and women, and heterosexual relationships. Apart from journal articles, very little published research exists on the effect changes in employment practices have had on gay men or on the shape or nature of their working lives.

Interviews of working people and their work histories were included in the work of Studs Terkel and Pierre Bourdieu's collaborative study of the social effects of the new capitalism.[3] As well, scholars such as Humphrey McQueen, Richard Sennett and Loïc Wacquant have written about the work-place as it has been transformed to meet the needs of the neo-liberal economic agenda.[4] No one has studied or written about the work histories of gay men, however, or considered them a separate population requiring investigation, and herein lies one of the unique features of this book.

This book completes unfinished work that I said I would undertake in my second book but put to one side when I realised its increasing focus on gay men's relational life. Having written a book on generations and the historically contingent nature of the gay identity,[5] and a second book on gay men's relationships,[6] this third book will complete the circle by examining gay men's working lives and how they anticipate and are living life after work and in old age.

Language, Terminology

The reformulation of previous sexuality acronyms and terms such as 'gay and lesbian', 'gay, lesbian, and bisexual', 'gay people' and the original acronyms, 'GLB', and 'GLBT' and the creation of LGBT, LGBTI and LGBTIQ represents a reordering and rewriting of historical and lived experiences of same-sex attracted people and in particular of gay men who physically (often with their lives) bore the brunt of social censure and opprobrium from the early fifteenth century as well as the stigma, exclusion and high death toll of HIV-AIDS in the 1980s and 1990s.[7] Over the last two or more decades, activists and researchers in western countries have sought to include in public campaigns for greater acceptance the claims of transgender and intersex people, not always with their approval.

These actions have not been without controversy and the politically strategic grouping together of all 'non-heterosexuals' misrepresents the lived experience of each sexual minority. A female-male transgender person, a leather queen and a working-class lesbian have very little in common except that they are unlikely to be attracted to the opposite sex and some shared sense of exclusion but even the latter would be open to debate. This is an old complaint but I would simply ask that gay men's long involvement in social change not be relegated or erased, which can be the effect of the constant rewriting of the sexual acronyms and reordering of sexuality and gender among sexual minorities, which leads to the following note on terminology used in this book.

In this book, 'GLB' is used because it represents the group of non-heterosexuals whose lived experience most closely mirrors that of the gay men's lives examined in the following chapters. I have no knowledge of transgender or intersex people and for this reason I believe it would be presumptuous to speak on their behalf and for that reason have not done so. I have also heard anecdotal evidence from my undergraduate students at Swinburne University of Technology that their transgender friends prefer to remain apart, keep their identity separate from other sexual minorities because they have been mistreated and marginalised by feminists, lesbians and gay men as much as by straight people. In conclusion, the terms 'camp', 'gay', 'homosexual' or 'same-sex attracted' are used as adjectives or nouns in the book. A note about 'camp' men: the term 'camp' designated a personal style or a type of personal or public performance as well as mannerisms with which people were aware from the 1890s—when without knowing it Oscar Wilde was its author—till the present.[8] In Australia, camp was also the term that same-sex attracted men used for and among themselves in the 1940s, 1950s and 1960s until it was superseded by gay. Complicating under-standings even more, an organisation known as CAMP (Campaign Against Moral Persecution) was set up in Sydney in 1970 to fight homosexual oppression.[9]

In the sections that follow, accounts are provided of the age cohorts used in this book and their composition. After these, there are brief discussions of narrative-analysis method, how work is understood and then how ageing is understood here, and then, to finish, an outline of chapters.

Three Age Cohorts

My preference has been to use age cohort in preference to generation when dividing a sample by age groups so as to analyse and discuss their broad characteristics.[10] The three age cohorts used in this book—old, middle and young—roughly coincide with generations identified by

6   P. Robinson

the Australian Bureau of Statistics and are explained below in each age-cohort section.

The majority of men interviewed for this book came from middle-class backgrounds. 'Middle class' is used in this book and the previous ones in the same sense as Thomas Piketty: 'people who are doing distinctly better than the bulk of the population yet still a long way from the true "elite"'.[11] In Australia, for example, in 2016 the average income was AU\$79,000.[12] A university lecturer earning AU\$100,000 per annum could be said to be doing better than many and, even if it is moot whether s/he was 'doing distinctly better than the bulk', I would argue s/he belonged to the middle class.

A small number had working-class jobs: some self-declared, others by nature of their jobs with, for example, state railways or as unskilled labourers. A minority of interviewees were low-income earners and some were poor. Quite a number had experienced poverty in their childhood but were not poor at the time of interview and the high-income earners in the sample had salaries that were four or five times average incomes. Some interviewees had spent short periods of time on unemployment benefits and a couple had experienced long-term unemployment. A few at the top-end of the sample received an old-age pension and a small number of Australian interviewees at the bottom-end of the sample received tertiary student benefits known as Austudy.

One odd usage needs explanation before going any further and that is 21 to mark the 'coming of age'. In the 2010s it appears an old-fashioned, almost redundant term and it could be argued was so well before now: in the 1950s, for example, driving licences were granted to 15-year-olds in Idaho, USA.[13] The decision to use 21 as the marker for adulthood was made almost two decades ago when I began my Ph.D. Planning to interview men across the life course, I had to decide how to refer to an age when men born in the 1920s and 1930s could have become sexually active homosexuals, when it would be reasonable to assume they had achieved a degree of relative independence from their parents. They would have called themselves camp; their sons' generation called themselves gay and their grandsons' generation, queers, same-sex attracted gender diverse or LGBTI.

As French historian Philippe Ariès argued, childhood did not exist in the Middle Ages and children as young as seven entered the world of work doing the work of small men and women, so in a sense then, adulthood began very early, though possibly not sexually.[14] And in times of war, such as, for example, in Australia in World War I, young males (16–17) did manage to enlist in the Australian Imperial Force even though the official enlistment age was 21 or 18 with the permission of parent of guardian.[15]

Most of the boy soldiers who died and for whom there are records were aged between 17 and 18. There were also, however, quite a number of 15- and 16-year-olds.[16] In the Vietnam War, when conscription was introduced in Australia for males aged 18, there was, by contrast, no eagerness among young males to enlist before their time and considerable public opposition to the use of the conscription to raise an army and the manner in which the selective ballot was organised.[17]

Twenty-one was chosen because it made sense for the old cohort and at a stretch it could be argued also made sense to men born in the 1980s, although the work of sexologists and the case notes of medical practitioners and reports of police and law courts for more than a century have long shown that sexual and social maturity do not go hand in hand, that people from all classes can have had plenty of sexual experience with the same sex or opposite sex before they turn 21. Once the decision was made, however, there was no turning back and in all three books I have used 21 as the marker for adulthood.

Next, each of the three age cohorts is briefly sketched. The old cohort comprises 25 men aged 60 and older; the middle cohort 28 aged 45–60; and the young cohort 29 aged 45 or younger.

Old Cohort

Twenty-five men comprised the old cohort (aged 60 and older). Six of these men were in their 80s, nine were in their 70s, and ten were in their 60s. With the exception of two men, these interviewees were Anglo Saxon or Anglo Celtic. The two men who were not were a South Asian in his 60s from London and an African American from New York who was also in his 60s.[18] Almost as many men from this cohort left school when they could and got a job ($n = 13$) as went to university ($n = 12$).[19] Of the men who left school and did not go on to university

8   P. Robinson

which was a fairly common decision for men who became adults in the period between 1945 and 1967, the majority had been to secondary schools. A minority of four men had been to trade schools and one left school when he was 11 and went to neither secondary school nor trade school. By class, seven men were from lower-class or lower-middle-class backgrounds, sixteen were from middle or upper-middle class backgrounds and two were upper class. One man was HIV positive.

Born as they were between the mid 1920s and late 1940s, these men came of age in the 1940s, 1950s and 1960s during the long boom in the West and belonged to the pre-gay-liberation cohort of gay men.[20] In terms of conventional, generational identity, they belonged to what the Australian Bureau of Statistics (ABS) calls the 'Lucky' and 'Baby Boomer' generations.[21] More than half the age cohort were in relationships. Eleven men were single at the time of interview and five men had previously been married to a woman. These men belonged to a generation when it was not uncommon for gay men to marry and come out later in life when the time for expressing sexual difference was more propitious. Many who had same-sex relationships managed them quietly and discreetly, conducting their intimate life like their heterosexual counterparts—in something akin to a companionate marriage.[22]

Despite growing up and becoming adults in a time of relative hostility towards homosexuality, 14 men or almost half of those from this cohort were in relationships when interviewed in 2010. Eleven of the men were in relationships which have elsewhere been described as 'long lasting', that is, were relationships of more than 10 years in duration. Ten of the men were in relationships of between 25 and 42 years in length.[23] Half of the 14 men were in their 60s, while the remaining seven were in their 70s and 80s. Of the single men from this age cohort, five were in their 70s, three were in their 80s and three in their 60s.

Middle Cohort

The middle cohort comprised 28 men aged 45–60. Born between the early 1950s and early 1960s, they belonged to the 'Baby Boomer' generation. Many 'Boomers' were involved in or affected by the period of intense social-political change, which included gay liberation, in the late 1960s and early 1970s in Australia, England and the United States and other countries like them.[24] Eighteen of the men from this age cohort were in their 50s and ten were in their 40s at the time of interview.[25] The majority of men from this age cohort were white. There were three non-whites: two African Americans from New York and a South Asian from London. All but four men from this age cohort of 28 interviewees had university degrees. Of the four who did not, two had left school when legally permitted to do so and got jobs and the other two went to trade schools.

That the overwhelming majority of men from this age cohort had been to university was a function of when they were born and came of age, which being the early 1970s was when countries like Australia, England and New Zealand embarked on significant expansion of tertiary education, making a university degree available to children from lower-class families as well as children from the middle and upper classes. None of the men from this age cohort was retired at the time of interview. In terms of occupations, nine worked in business, either for corporations or for small businesses, seven worked in education, and the remaining twelve men worked in middle-class occupations such as media, public service and welfare agencies. Unlike the old cohort, the men from the middle cohort were without exception middle class or upper middle class. Their class position was estimated on the basis of the information they provided regarding their income and education backgrounds. At least two men from this age cohort were very rich.

Eleven of the men were in long-lasting relationships, which I have defined elsewhere as ten years or longer.[26] Four men were in relationships of between three months and seven years, and thirteen men were single. Nine men from this age cohort of twenty-eight interviewees were or had been in a gay civil union of one sort or another. Five men were in civil unions and four men were gaily married, that is, married in jurisdictions that permitted marriage equality.[27] As well, there were three men who were divorced from former wives, two of whom had children by them, and one man had an adopted son. Six men were HIV positive. Four were in their 50s and two in their 40s. All had come of

10 P. Robinson

age between 1975 and 1984, the time of greatest risk of infection for gay men in western countries, which would explain why the greatest concentration of men living with HIV-AIDS was found in this cohort. The older and younger cohorts each had one man who was HIV positive.

Young Cohort

This age cohort comprised 29 men aged 45 and younger. Eight of the men were in their 40s, ten were in their 30s, nine were in their 20s and one was aged 19 and one aged 18 at the time of interview. The majority of the men from this age cohort belonged to Generation X and Y born (1966–1986) as defined by the ABS and only eight of them belonged to i-Generation (born 1986 and after). Most of the men were white, Anglo-Saxon or Anglo-Celtic. The men who were not comprised an Aboriginal Australian from Melbourne, an Indian Australian from Sydney, two African Americans from New York, an Asian American from Los Angeles and two Maori from Auckland.

The majority of men from this cohort were employed—only one man was unemployed at the time of interview—and in jobs that were white collar such as business, education and retail. In this regard, they were no different from the men from the middle cohort, except, as to be expected, there was a group of university students, eight of whom were undergraduates plus one postgraduate. More than two-thirds of the men had university degrees, which is less than the proportion of men from the middle cohort where 85% were graduates. The remaining one-third of men from this age cohort had either trade- or secondary-school qualifications.

Seventeen or more than half the young men had partners. Two were in long-lasting relationships, that is a relationship of ten years or more. And nine men were in relationships of more than three years' duration. The remaining eight men had relationships of 12 months or less. Interviewee's age and length or relationship were not strongly related except that the group of men in relationships of more than three years was equally divided between men in their 30s and men in their 40s and the group of men in relationships of 12 months or less were almost entirely aged in their 20s. One man was HIV positive. The ages of the 12 single men from this age cohort were fairly equally divided between men in their 20s, 30s, and 40s and included the 18-year-old.

Narrative Analysis

Narrative analysis underpins the understandings drawn from interviews in this book. At the heart of narrative analysis is the idea Alasdair McIntyre proposed regarding the self as constituted in the stories individuals tell about themselves.[28] Accepting this to be true, the narrative analyst investigates life stories to identify what narratives (private or public) his/her interviewees rely on to explain how they see themselves. My work here and elsewhere has drawn also on that of Margaret Somers and Gloria Gibson who argued that we may understand our actions and our actions may be understood as part of a collection of narratives that reach back into our collective past and individual past and stretch forward into the future that we expect will unfold.[29] The repertoire of narratives from which an individual may choose is finite: for what is available to people is always 'historically and culturally specific'. Somers and Gibson argued that it is through the process of telling stories that we come 'to know, understand, and make sense of the social world'.[30]

Pierre Bourdieu identified one possible failing in this approach arguing that when related in an interview a life story will always tend towards a coherent narrative, to justify or present as logical steps in the individual's life course: 'to make consistent and constant, through the creation of intelligible relationships ... which are thus turned into *steps* of a necessary development'.[31] In 2016, a Mumbai reviewer wrote that a weakness in *Gay Men's Relationships Across the Life Course* was the possibility that interviewees might not tell the truth when recounting their life story.[32] This is partly what Bourdieu was hinting at: that instead of unconsciously drawing on narratives from the repertoire available—the argument of McIntyre and Somers and Gibson—individuals will knowingly create an autobiographical narrative to suit their own purpose.

> The autobiographical narrative is always at least partially motivated by a concern to give meaning ... And the more the interviewees have an interest, varying in relation to their social position and trajectory, in the biographical enterprise, the more do they have an interest in coherence and necessity.[33]

Everything that Bourdieu said is true in the context of biographies written for and about public figures. While I accept a similar inclination might be present for ordinary gay men who volunteered to answer questions about their lives—that is, to embroider, to overlook mistakes, to present only part of their story—I was convinced at the time of interview and later when transcribing that most if not all of them provided faithful accounts of their lives. I had no way of checking and offer an analysis of the stories I collected in good faith. I leave it to the reader to judge the quality of the material collected and the sense I made of it.

There are also structures in place, however, to reduce the likelihood of interviewees consciously shaping their autobiographical narrative to the extent that Bourdieu warned. To begin, they know that their full identity will not be revealed once the researcher agrees to collect material from them anonymously. Even if they might be able to identify themselves in the published work—for example, from their date of birth, age at time of interview, location—it is highly unlikely that people who know them could do the same. An opponent of narrative-analysis method might argue that anonymity allows an even greater temptation to provide a fictional or cosmetically enhanced autobiographical narrative. This is a risk researchers of life stories take. My answer would be that, as those interviewed are not doing so to promote or engage in discussion about themselves or their achievements, aside from their identity as gay or same-sex attracted men, they have little to gain from embellishing or fictionalising their autobiography. And as well, in almost all cases, I never had reason to doubt the coherence or integrity of the autobiographical narratives I collected from interviewees.

One other unintentional safeguard exists in the device known as the interview schedule. Some researchers provide their subjects with a copy of the questions in advance or at the start of the interview. On a few occasions, I have done the same in order to ease an interviewee's nervousness. I would argue that a structured or semi-structured set of questions, on topics as general as, for example, world of work, coming out, relationship history, age and ageing, makes it harder to maintain a fictional life story. Others could argue the opposite: that set questions in fact make it easier because they encourage interviewees to provide the answer they think the researcher seeks. As I said, this has not been my experience as, on the whole, I have been convinced by the coherence and integrity of the personal narratives provided in interview.

Understanding Work

The changes that occurred to the world of work since the 1970s were significant for two reasons. First, for the effect these changes—which were based on a rejection of Keynesian economics and an embrace of neo-liberal fundamentals—had on the working lives of large numbers of ordinary people working in developed and developing economies. Secondly, it is significant because it coincides with the time when the men from the old cohort were in the prime of their working lives, those from the middle cohort were beginning and consolidating theirs, and into which the men from the young cohort were born, who grew up knowing nothing of the welfare state, its rationale, or the advantages of government provision of goods and services. Also in this section, there is a brief analysis of the effect of sex and sexual activity on gay men's approach to the world of work, which builds on the work of Georges Bataille, Michael Pollak and Edmund White.[34]

Major changes occurred in work practices in the West since the era of full adult male employment in the 1960s and 1970s, also known as the 'long boom'. The oil crisis of the mid 1970s was followed by a period of intense inflation which gave rise to a radical shift to the right and a marked shift in power from labour to capital. In one of his last books, Pierre Bourdieu argued that the economic imperative to 'down size', to reduce wherever possible the minimum number of workers required to staff operations in firms and business organisations of all sizes created a sense of uncertainty and precariousness that flowed through to every aspect of people's lives: 'With "downsizing" a constant threat, the whole of life of wage earners is placed under the sign of uncertainty.'[35]

Zygmunt Bauman developed a similar argument: that insecurity, uncertainty and lack of safety, which he saw as the 'human predicament' of people living now in the western industrialised world, affected all aspects of their social, emotional and material life.[36] The features of insecurity, uncertainty and lack of safety had come, argued Bauman, to characterise the lives of workers in countries he described as 'the highly developed, modernized and well-off part of the globe' because of an economic ethos that required no job or position could be permanent or for the term of anyone's working life, as had once been common practice in all sectors of industrialised economies. The effect of this was 'unnerving and depressing because it is new and in many ways unprecedented'.[37] Never before have so many workers been employed so precariously. A 2016 report revealed that four and a half million people, or one in six workers, in England and Wales were in insecure work.[38]

Emphasising the human cost of the last 30 years of economic change, Richard Sennett asked whether in times of constant change individuals could feel sufficiently certain of the future to make long-term plans. He argued that in the past human beings had adjusted to change. For example, in living memory, they adjusted to the upheavals of two world wars: 'People have accepted the fact that their lives will shift suddenly due to wars, famines, or other disasters, and that they will have to improvise in order to survive.' What was different now, however, about the change we now live with is that it has become part of the everyday: 'it exists without any looming historical disaster; instead it is woven into the everyday practices of vigorous capitalism. Instability is meant to be normal.'[39]

New 'flexible' terms and conditions of work sound appealing—and let's not forget the power of the mantra that is a constant today: that freedom, which is what flexibility sounds like, is better than regulation—and difficult to resist when wily employers promote its advantages to, for example, females with children. For these workers, flexible employment is promoted as allowing them to care for their children and earn an income but, as women frequently find, it is the employer and not the worker who dictates the flexible hours and they are not permitted to arrange flexible hours to suit their child-minding needs.

> It is claimed ... flexibility gives people more freedom to shape their lives ... In fact, the new order substitutes new controls rather than simply abolishing the rules of the past—but these new controls are also hard to understand. The new capitalism is an often illegible regime of power.[40]

In a society 'composed of episodes and fragments,' argues Sennett, a human being cannot 'develop a narrative of identity and life history', for 'the conditions of the new economy feed instead on experience which drifts from time to time, from place to place, from job to job'.[41] The narratives that he speaks of are invaluable because they are more than 'simple chronicles of events; they give shape to the forward movement of time, suggesting reasons why things happen, showing their consequences'.[42] They are what make us human and give meaning to our lived experience and it is Sennett's belief that the values and practices of the 'new economy' leach them from us all.

Sex and Work

When I came out at 27—relatively late then and now—I was enrolled in a postgraduate degree in history at Oxford University It was the early 1980s and I chose to study overseas as an excuse to escape a fiercely homophobic Australia where homosexuality was hardly spoken of except derisively or violently, and gay men were the subjects of horrific hate crimes.[43] Formed from a reading of the novels of E.M. Forster and Compton McKenzie, my imaginary view of English society was of a more tolerant place where, despite the cruel press attacks on Jeremy Thorpe and what was done to Oscar Wilde a century before, it might be possible to meet people more like me than I had found in Melbourne. On the whole, my imaginary was proved right except for the stories my first boyfriend told me of conditions in his native Ireland and when a postgraduate student from Scotland told me how gay men were then treated in Glasgow—the 1967 Sexual Offences Act had decriminalised

16   P. Robinson

male homosexual acts between consenting adults (over 21) in England and Wales but not in Northern Ireland or Scotland.[44]

When I began to explore London's gay clubs and discotheques, like Bang in Shaftesbury Avenue or the slightly intimidating Coleherne in Old Brompton Road, I noticed that gay nightlife seemed to be arranged in opposition to the norms of the rest of society. From memory, Bang went by another name for the rest of the week except on Monday when it was gay. How then, I wondered on my first and every other visit, did all these men hold down jobs? That might seem a silly question but in the gay world then, no one would be seen lining up for entry before 10 pm, and 11 pm was the smart time to arrive. Closing as it did then at 1 pm (again, from memory), it seemed to me a struggle to leave Bang at 1 pm and be at work the next morning at 8.30 a.m or 9 a.m. One possible explanation was that the men had part-time jobs, another that they were mainly hairdressers but the last explanation made sense only in Australia where hairdressing salons were traditionally closed on Mondays, not Tuesdays. I never discovered whether hairdressing salons in London closed on weekdays. In Oxford (memory again) they closed on Wednesday afternoons so as to compensate staff for working Saturday.

On returning to Australia I found that the really big night for going out was Sunday. The clubs were full of energy on Sunday nights and bouncing like at no other time of the week. Unemployed or in part-time work in the mid 1980s, I explored dance clubs in Melbourne and Sydney. No matter how often I went, I still could not help wondering who all the people were and if all of the men in the club were in fact hairdressers and could use a holiday Monday to sleep off a big night out. That mystery remained with me for decades and explains the impetus for the part of this book that looks at gay men's working lives: because I wanted to understand if it were possible to combine a standard working life with full engagement with the gay scene.

When I began to investigate published research on the working lives of gay men, I found very little. There was a stimulating, insightful chapter by Michael Pollak in a book edited by André Béjin of the Annales school in Paris which began to provide some of the answers that I was looking for. In it, Pollak outlined what he argued were principal features of gay men's lives, in particular their social and sexual practices.[45] Even though the research is dated, it was useful for what it suggested about gay lifestyles before the onset of HIV-AIDS, which, for almost two decades, overwhelmed all other considerations of gay life and identity.

North American writer Edmund White approached the question of gay employment in an early book where he toured on a state-by-state gay communities in the USA.[46] It was a fascinating glimpse into the variety of lifestyles and life experiments that gay men were leading in the late 1970s, just before so much of it was wiped out. When in San Francisco, White asked the editor of a gay and lesbian newspaper to describe gay men's lives. His response was that gay men roughly fell into two groups, community leaders—men in their 30s who had always lived in San Francisco—and newcomers, young men who came to San Francisco to escape small-town America and who were experimenting with new ways of living. About the second group of men, the editor said the following:

> The Castro Street group is a really rough culture. Their relationships are brief, they don't work but live off welfare, they hang out like teenagers, they drink too much, they take too many drugs, they fuck day and night, they are scattered—and of course radical politically. They act like kids in a candy store. San Francisco has an unusually large educated white male population on relief. I oppose the gay obsession with sex. Most gay men have their lives led for them by their cocks. In return for ten minutes of pleasure they design the rest of their day.[47]

Here was one possible explanation to the mystery that had been troubling me since I first walked into Bang in 1981: perhaps a lot of the men who devoted so much energy to dancing on Monday nights (in London) or Sunday nights (in Melbourne or Sydney) were living a life on unemployment benefits or part-time jobs so that they could immerse themselves in disco and sex. And in so doing they unintentionally helped create a gay culture in the suburbs and neighbourhoods of cities like Amsterdam, Berlin, London, Manchester and Sydney, which were then called ghettos, without shame or judgement. White was not critical of the views the newspaper editor expressed but he did argue for greater compassion:

> I am … suspicious of those who denounce others for having 'too much' sex. At what point does a 'healthy' amount become 'too much'? There are, of course, those who suffer because their desire for sex has become compulsive; in their cases the drive (loneliness, guilt) is at fault, not the activity as such. Almost everyone is willing to draw the line somewhere—that is, will draw it for others.[48]

In saying this, White was challenging a strongly held belief, which still exists in the 2010s, that gay men are sex obsessed or have greater opportunity or capacity for casual sexual encounters. There is no single agreed view on the sexual practices of gay men. What views that exist range from a heteronormative belief—which prevailed until countries began amending marriage legislation in the early 2000s to allow gays and lesbians to marry—that gay men had more sex because they could not marry,[49] that men are naturally more sexual, have higher sex drives and this is borne out in gay men's sexual practices,[50] to a libertarian narrative, which says that the sexual explosion of the 1970s was gay men's response to decades of repression and social hostility.[51]

Interest in the relationship between sex and work is not a recent thing: in 1939 Norbert Elias wrote that it puzzled him that sexuality needed disciplining in order for 'occupational work … [to become] a general way of life'.[52] But sex and work are linked and according to Georges Bataille it was because they represented the twin poles of our human-ness. In his critique of Kinsey's 1950s research, Bataille argued that energies devoted to work deplete energies available for sexual activity and vice versa.[53] Kinsey and his team had measured the frequency of orgasms among groups of men and noted a stronger weekly frequency occurred among labourers and unskilled workers over white-collar workers. Although Bataille mocked this work, he drew on parts of it to develop his argument about the reciprocal relationship between sexual energies and energies required to engage in work. 'There is nothing arbitrary in sexual restrictions: each man has only a certain amount of energy and if he devotes some of it to work he has to reduce his sexual energy by that much.'[54]

Bataille's proposition that human energy divided between the sexual and non-sexual helped explain how some gay men could combine a life of dance and sex while living on part-time work or unemployment benefits but it was not the full story, for not only was there that other group the editor described, the community leaders, but also a third emerging group of gay men. Over time, an increasing number of gay men came out who had ordinary jobs in, for example, agriculture, business, education, and manufacturing and who had to work normal hours, week-in, week-out. A life of frequent if not regular dance and sex was incompatible with the demands of the structured working week. The working lives of this third group were similar to those of everyday people and are represented in the sample interviewed for this book. As hard as I tried, I could find only a small handful of men who had dedicated their lives to dance and sex in the way described by Edmund White's newspaper editor. They exist and their work histories are discussed in Chaps. 3 and 4 on the working lives of men aged 45–60 and those aged 45 and younger.

One final point concerns the type of work that attracts gay men. Michael Pollak argued that we were *not* naturally sensitive or artistic and that these traits did *not* explain our over-representation in occupations such as hairdressing, the arts or diplomacy. Instead, he argued:

> the logical compulsions of social life and the milieu dictate the encroachment of sexual strategies on professional careers. The sensitivity specially attributed to homosexuals is nothing but a form of clear-sightedness derived from continuous role playing, a distancing from themselves, in reaction to an ever-present, though unstated, feeling of being excluded.[55]

And his argument was mostly borne out in a report of the Australian Bureau of Statistics (ABS) on the ten most common occupations of men in same-sex relationships compared with those in opposite-sex relationships (straight men).[56] The contrast was marked. For gay men, the five most common occupations were in white collar or service sector and included two areas where women have long found work: sales assistant and registered nurse (the latter requiring a university qualification).[57] The second group of five comprised the stereotypical gay occupation, the hairdresser, two occupations requiring university qualifications (accountant and solicitor), and one fairly gender-neutral occupation, general clerk.[58]

20   P. Robinson

The five most common occupations for straight men were, with one exception, in blue-collar occupations or trades; the one exception was retail manager.[59] The second group of five consisted of two more in blue-collar occupations (construction manager and motor mechanic), two occupations notorious for rewarding aggressive behaviour (sales and advertising) but also one where females increasingly dominate, public relations, and four requiring university qualifications (construction manager, advertising, public relations and accounting).[60]

The most obvious contrast between jobs gay and straight men favoured was their gendered nature. While straight men showed a preference for blue-collar work—truck driver, electrician, metal fitter and machinist, carpenter and joiner—where large numbers of men are employed and which have little appeal to women, gay men preferred white-collar jobs in offices and department stores or shops. There was little evidence of gay men gravitating to occupations where females dominated or that had been feminised. The three exceptions were (in order) sales assistant, registered nurse and hairdressing. Finally, jobs requiring university qualifications were evenly represented for occupations in both groups.

Ageing[61]

The work of two foundational sociologists and one historian underpin understandings of ageing and old age used in this book. The sociologists are Simone de Beauvoir and Norbert Elias, and the historian Philippe Ariès.[62] Beauvoir was 60 when she wrote *Old Age*. In it, she examined how old age was constructed according to the worth the elderly had in society, which she argued was most often a function of their class position. The more material resources they had at their command, the greater their worth and the power they could exercise or, when the reverse is true, ageing brought vulnerability if an elderly person surrendered control of their material resources or had little in their own name, which is still the case today.[63]

Philippe Ariès wrote how understandings of death have changed since the Middle Ages such that it now terrifies and Norbert Elias wrote how old people now mostly die alone and anonymously in hospital wards. While now there is greater understanding of the importance of social and emotional contexts of ageing and aged care, an individual's material resources or social class continues to be the single most important factor in determining how well a person will experience old age and the duration of that experience.

More recently, understandings of old age have broadened to take account of changes in material class and social capital of retirees in the West. Writing before the global financial crisis of 2008–2009, Chris Gilleard and Paul Higgs wrote that in the last decades of the twentieth century there was a consistent growth in the material and socio-cultural well-being of elderly citizens in advanced western societies. 'Those retiring now are not only richer, better educated and more culturally active, but they are also fitter than previous cohorts of retirees.'[64] While much of what Gilleard and Higgs argued was mostly true for many retirees in the West, in the years following the 2008–2009 global financial crisis, billions of dollars were wiped from retirement funds and the cohort that appeared so materially fortunate is now less so. As well, the picture Gilleard and Higgs painted of healthy, well educated, active senior citizens ignored aged people who had never been employed or well educated and showed up in only a handful of accounts provided by those interviewed for this book.

A less optimistic outlook was forecast by Ulrich Beck and Elizabeth Beck-Gernsheim, who argued that increasing rates of individualisation will have serious effects for ageing populations. First, that as more women enter the work force and domestic gender relations are renegotiated, fewer women will be willing or able to perform care work for elderly family members. Secondly, underlining the work of Beauvoir, that class would have a greater effect on an individual's experience of old age: 'the rich [will] simply purchase good and expensive care themselves on the "senior services market", while the less well-off receive no help because they cannot pay for it'.[65] Ageing literature has developed over the 45 years since Beauvoir first drew attention to her own lived experience of old age and historical analysis of its social construction to include more nuanced understandings of how material class, social capital, relationship status, gender and sexual difference can affect the individual.

With the exception of the early work of British scholars such as Ken Plummer, Diane Richardson and Jeffrey Weeks, research in the field of GLB ageing was slow to start, mostly getting going in the mid to late 1990s and early 2000s, that is, after the worst of the AIDS crisis in the West was over.[66] In her work on lesbian communities in the USA, Arlene Stein argued that, as the lesbians she studied grew into middle age, their attachment to the lesbian sub-culture changed.[67] I found a similar pattern in the stories of gay men's long-term relationships—of moving away from the gay world and relying on it less for social/sexual relations, while in his work on Manchester's gay village, Paul Simpson argues that middle-aged gay men were capable of both submitting to and rebelling against gay ageism.[68] This book continues the work of the early scholars of gay and lesbian ageing as well as that of contemporary scholars working in the field and I hope also creates some interest in the working lives that sustain gay men.[69]

Chapter Outlines

The book is in two parts. The first part, comprising Chaps. 2–4, examines the working lives of the three cohorts beginning with the old. The second part concerns retirement and old age: Chap. 5 considers the old-age concerns or fears of the sample by cohort and Chap. 6 the interviewees' retirement plans, also by cohort. The contents of each chapter are now briefly summarised.

Chapter 2 focuses on the working lives of the old cohort (25 men aged 60–87), examining their work stories on the basis of three principal narratives that were identified: work as work, care and creativity, and social or political change. Those whose work histories were explained by work as work regarded work as something they did and had to do. They had no illusions about it, expected nothing from it by way of personal improvement or meaning. Care and creativity encompassed work histories of men involved in caring occupations such as nursing or counselling and creative work such as in the arts or craft movement. Social or political change represented the work histories of a small group who understood a secondary purpose in their work, which was to assist progress towards a more egalitarian society. Included in this chapter is a section on the effect of their sexuality on the working life of three men. Two remained closeted because they feared the consequences if their sexuality were made public. A third, who worked in entertainment, a field where gay men were accepted, if not vital for its functioning, experienced no ill effects because of his sexuality. In Chap. 3, the working lives of the middle cohort (28 men aged 45–60) were analysed as were those from the old cohort: according to principal narratives identified in the men's work histories. Four principal narratives were found: care, travel, work as work, and social or political change. Three were similar to those from the old cohort and one new narrative, travel, helped explain the men's work histories. Notable was the change in order: whereas work as work was the primary narrative for the old cohort, care was the primary narrative for the middle cohort. There were two reasons for this: first, the baby boomer generation that comprised most of the middle cohort were more at ease working in care occupations than the older cohort and benefited from an expansion in the 1970s of jobs in care occupations; secondly, many of those from the middle cohort were drawn to work in care roles during the HIV-AIDS pandemic. Travel work was more important for them than for the other cohorts and a substantial number sought work in travel-related industries (airlines, shipping companies) or to combine work with travel opportunities such as in trade delegations, diplomacy, multi-nationals. Three men included accounts in their life stories of how sexuality affected their work life. One of the stories represented a harrowing account of ostracism by a small-town community in rural New Zealand, a story which could just as easily have come from another man's experience in a rural town in Cumbria, New Mexico or Tasmania. The man survived and was reunited with his children when they became adults. The third chapter devoted to work histories, Chap. 4, examines those of the young cohort (29 men aged 18–45). Those from the cohort turned 21 in 1986–2000, an important period in gay social history for the waning of the HIV-AIDS pandemic in the West and growth of gay-marriage movements in liberal democracies. Analysed as were those from the older cohorts, their working lives were organised around five principal narratives: creativity, which was important for this generation, care, social or political change, work as work, and travel. The most noticeable change in narratives being the change in the rank position of travel: from primacy for the middle cohort to minimal for the young. The section on being out in the workplace showed that, while homophobia can be less virulent now, it has not disappeared and continues to affect the lives of gay men. Where those it affected in the workplace in the 2010s have an advantage over previous generations is from legislation that now forbids discrimination on the grounds of sexuality, in place in many advanced western democracies. The empowering effect of this structural change was illustrated in the case of one man who was able to confront a homophobic manager with the support and approval of senior management and win the day.

Chapter 5 looks at the concerns or fears interviewees held in relation to old age. These ranged from grave fears about the loss of a lifelong partner or having to return to the closet because of homophobia to milder concerns about having to rely on neighbours for home help or having an unwanted sibling at their death bed. The stories were examined by age cohort, beginning with the old where the most worrying concern related to homophobia they might find in aged accommodation. Of interest was the fact that despite fairly widespread fears about a homophobic environment no one said he would refuse to move into a nursing home because of it. The middle cohort were also worried about the possibility of homophobia in aged accommodation. Their greatest worry was being socially isolated in old age—a universal fear and one they shared with the other cohorts. Whether or not others resort to the same solution only time will tell, but some from this cohort said that their solution would be to continue sexual adventurism for as long as they were able to do so. For different reasons, social isolation in old age was a concern also for the young cohort. Arguing that the absence of children explained why gay men would be socially isolated they were also conscious of gay community inaction to support elderly GLB people. The other gay community absence they noted was provision of gay-specific aged accommodation, which they regarded as axiomatic. The second chapter on ageing, Chap. 6, considers the plans and preparations the men had made or, in the case of the young cohort, believed they would make for their retirement and old age. Four important findings arose from the analysis. The first was that a notable minority from the old cohort said that they would work 'till they dropped', in other words, intended to continue working either in voluntary work or a different type of paid employment than their life's work until they could no longer work. The second was a significant number of men from the old and middle cohorts had well-structured retirement plans. The third significant finding concerned a group of men living with HIV-AIDS: two from the old cohort and four from the middle. The stories they related suggested first, that illness can be the reason people take good care of their retirement plans and secondly, that no single account told the story of how men living with HIV-AIDS plan for their old age, for the evidence from this sample showed some had extremely well-structured retirement plans while others who were both precariously employed and well employed, had no retirement plans to speak of and partly because they had not expected to have an old age. The fourth finding related to the assumptions of a small group of privileged men from the young cohort who explained that they were unconcerned about their material needs in old age because of financial arrangements made for them by their families.

Notes

1. R. W. Connell (2002) *Gender* (Cambridge: Polity), p. 202 (Connell 2002).
2. M. P. Bell and A. P. Weinberg (1978) *Homosexualities: a study of diversity among men and women* (Melbourne: The Macmillan Company of Australia), pp. 141–148 (Bell and Weinberg 1978).
3. S. Terkel (1975) *Working* (Harmondsworth: Penguin Books Ltd.); P. Bourdieu (1999) *Weight of the World: Social Suffering and Impoverishment in Contemporary Society*, trans. P. P. Ferguson (Oxford: Polity Press) (Terkel 1975; Bourdieu 1999).
4. H. McQueen (2011) *We Built this Country: Builders' Labourers & Their Unions, 1787 to the Future* (Adelaide: Ginninderra Press); R. Sennett (2006) *The Culture of the new Capitalism* (New Haven: Yale University Press); L. Wacquant (2009) *Punishing the Poor: The Neoliberal*

Government of Social Insecurity (Durham and London: Durham University Press) (McQueen 2011; Sennett 2006; Wacquant 2009).

5. P. Robinson (2008) *The Changing World of Gay Men* (Basingstoke and New York: Palgrave Macmillan) (Robinson 2008).

6. P. Robinson (2013) *Gay Men's Relationships Across the Life Course* (Basingstoke and New York: Palgrave Macmillan) (Robinson 2013).

7. Robinson *The Changing World*.

8. S. Sontag (2009, 1961) *Against Interpretation and Other Essays* (London: Penguin Group), pp. 275–292 (Sontag 2009, 1961).

9. R. French (1993) *Camping by a Billabong: Gay and Lesbian Stories from Australian History* (Sydney: Black Wattle Press), p. 111 (French 1993).

10. For fuller explanation of this approach, see Robinson *Gay Men's Relationships*, pp. 8–9.

11. T. Piketty (2014) *Capital in the Twenty-First Century* trans. A. Goldhammer (Harvard: Harvard University Press), p. 251 (Piketty 2014).

12. Equivalent in other currencies: AUD 79,000 = GBP 46,180, HKD 440,050; NZD 82,370; USD 56,600, see: https://www.google.com.au/webhp?sourceid=chrome-instant&ion=1&espv=2&ie=UTF-8#q=1 AUD to GBP accessed 26 December 2016.

13. See J. Gerassi (2001) *The Boys of Boise: Furor, Vice and Folly in an American city*, with a foreword by P. Boag and a new preface by the author (Seattle and London: University of Washington Press), p. xxiv (Gerassi 2001).

14. P. Ariès (1973) *Centuries of Childhood* (Harmondsworth: Penguin Books), p. 295 (Ariès 1973).

15. Australian War Memorial, 'Boy soldiers', https://www.awm.gov.au/encyclopedia/boysoldiers/ accessed 4 December 2016 (Australian War Memorial 2016).

16. Australian War Memorial, 'Boy soldiers on the Roll of Honour for the First World War', https://www.awm.gov.au/encyclopedia/boysoldiers/first/ accessed 4 December 2016.

17. J. Beaumont (2014) 'Australians and the Great War: Battles, the Home Front and Memory', *Agora*, v. 49, n. 4, 46–54; http://search.informit.com.au/documentSummary;dn=787141053971605;res=IELHSS> ISSN: 0044-6726 accessed 4 December 2016 (Beaumont 2014).

18. Four were from Auckland, one was from London, three were from Manchester, nine were from Melbourne, two were from New York, and six were from Sydney.

19. See Appendix 1.
20. For more on the long boom, see S. Macintyre (1999) *A Concise History of Australia* (Melbourne: Cambridge University Press), pp. 214–224; regarding features of pre-gay liberation lives, see Robinson *The Changing World*, pp. 17–35 (Macintyre 1999).
21. Throughout, the Australian Bureau of Statistics definition is used of post-World War II generations, where a member of the 'Baby Boomer' generation is defined as someone born between 1946 and 1966, 'Generation X and Y' as someone born between 1966 and 1986 and 'i-Generation' as someone born between 1986 and 2006 and which in the media is also being referred to as 'Millennials'. The generation preceding the Baby Boomers the ABS called the 'Lucky' generation. See Australian Bureau of Statistics (2006) 'From Generation to generation' in *A Picture of the Nation* (Canberra: Australian Bureau of Statistics): http://www.ausstats.abs.gov.au/Ausstats/subscriber.nsf/0/FCB1A3CF08 93DAE4CA25754C0013D844/$File/20700_generation.pdf accessed 4 January 2017 (Australian Bureau of Statistics 2006).
22. Robinson *Gay Men's Relationships*, 63–71.
23. Robinson *Gay Men's Relationships*, 66–82.
24. See Robinson *The Changing World*, pp. 36–53.
25. Four were from Auckland, six were from Hong Kong, four were from London, three were from Los Angeles, two were from Manchester, two were from Melbourne, six were from New York, and one was from Sydney.
26. Robinson *Gay Men's Relationships*, pp. 62–82.
27. For more on gay marriage and civil union, see Robinson *Gay Men's Relationships*, pp. 100–120.
28. A. MacIntyre (2003, 1981) *After Virtue*, 2nd edn. (Notre Dame, Indiana: University of Indiana Press) (MacIntyre 2003, 1981).
29. M. R. Somers and G. D. Gibson (1994) 'Reclaiming the Epistemological "Other": Narrative and the Social Construction of Identity' in C. Calhoun (ed.) *Social Theory and the Politics of Identity*, Oxford: Blackwell, pp. 38–39 (Somers and Gibson 1994).
30. Somers and Gibson 'Reclaiming the epistemological "other"', p. 74.
31. P. Bourdieu (1987) 'The Biographical Illusion' trans Y. Winkin and W. Leeds-Hurwitz in R. J. Parmentier and G. Urban (eds) *Working Papers for the Centre of Psychosocial Studies* (University of Chicago), p. 2; emphasis in the original (Bourdieu 1987).

32. On 1 March 2016, a review in Hindi of *Gay Men's Relationships* was published in *Galaxy*, Mumbai, a magazine for India's queer population. The editor was unable to provide a translation but this is the link to the review: http://www.gaylaxymag.com/hindi/book-gay-mens-relationships/#gs.GX8fxk0 accessed 18 Aug 2016.

33. Bourdieu 'The Biographical Illusion', p. 2.

34. G. Bataille (2001, Eng. trans 1962, orig. 1957) *Eroticism*, trans. M. Dalwood (London: Penguin Books with introduction by C. McCabe); M. Pollak (1986) 'Male Homosexuality–or Happiness in the Ghetto' in P. Ariès and A. Béjin (eds) *Western Sexuality: Practice and Precept in Past and Present Times*, trans. A. Forster (Oxford: Basil Blackwell), pp. 40–61; E. White (1980) *States of Desire: Travels in Gay America* (London: Pan Books Ltd.) (Bataille 2001; Pollak 1986; White 1980).

35. P. Bourdieu (2003) *Firing Back: against the tyranny of the market 2*, trans. L. Wacquant (New York: The New Press); p. 29 (Bourdieu 2003).

36. Z. Bauman (2001) *The Individualized Society* (Cambridge: Polity Press), p.154 (Bauman 2001).

37. Bauman *Individualized Society*, pp.154–155.

38. K. Allen (2016) 'Nearly one in six workers in England and Wales in insecure work', *The Guardian*: http://www.theguardian.com/money/2016/jun/13/england-wales-zero-hours-contracts-citizens-advice-insecure-work, accessed 13 June 2016 (Allen 2016).

39. R. Sennett (1998) *The Corrosion of Character: the personal consequences of work in the new capitalism* (New York: W.W. Norton & Company), p. 31 (Sennett 1998).

40. Sennett *Corrosion*, pp. 9–10.

41. Sennett *Corrosion*, pp. 26–27.

42. Sennett *Corrosion*, p. 30.

43. In 1980s and 1990s a large number of gay men appeared to take their own lives in the vicinity of well-known gay beats on coastal headlands in Sydney. For more than 30 years, the New South Wales police refused to investigate these 'suicides', which were later found to have been murders carried out by teenage gangs and off-duty police. For more, see A. Blue (dir.) 2016 *Deep Water–The Real Story* (Sydney: Blackfella Films for SBS, with major production investment from Screen Australia); see: http://www.sbs.com.au/programs/deep-water-the-real-story/article/2016/09/27/

deep-water-real-story-crime-documentary-pulls-no-punches accessed 7 January 2017 (Blue 2016).

44. J. Weeks (1990, 1977) *Coming Out: Homosexual Politics in Britain from the Nineteenth Century to the Present* (London: Quartet Books), p. 176 (Weeks 1990, 1977).

45. Pollak 'Male Homosexuality', pp. 40–61.

46. White *States of Desire*.

47. White *States of Desire*, p. 37.

48. White *States of Desire*, pp. 37–38.

49. One argument being that marriage is and has been 'an important device for taming sexual desire'. See, for example, R. A. Posner (1994) *Sex and Reason* (Cambridge, Mass.: Harvard University Press), p. 302 (Posner 1994).

50. See, for example, G. Hekma (2006) 'Sade, Masculinity, and Sexual Humiliation', *Men and Masculinities*, v.9, n.2, pp. 247–248 (Hekma 2006).

51. J. Weeks (1985) *Sexuality and its Discontents: Meanings, Myths & Modern Sexualities* (London: Routledge & Kegan Paul), p. 221 (Weeks 1985).

52. N. Elias (2000, 1939) *The Civilizing Process: Sociogenetic and Psychogenetic Investigations*, trans. E. Jephcott with some notes and corrections by the author, ed. E. Dunning, J. Goudsblom and S. Mennell, rev. edn (Oxford: Blackwell Publishers Ltd), p. 176 (Elias 2000, 1939).

53. Bataille *Eroticism*.

54. Bataille *Eroticism*, p. 158.

55. Pollak 'Male Homosexuality', p. 50.

56. Australian Bureau of Statistics (2013) 'Same-sex Couples' in *4102.0—Australian Social Trends* (Canberra: Australian Bureau of Statistics) (Australian Bureau of Statistics 2013).

57. In order: retail manager; sales assistant; advertising, public relations and sales manager; registered nurse; contract, program and project administrator; Australian Bureau of Statistics 'Same-sex Couples', pp. 7–8.

58. The most common occupations in the second group of five were in order: contract, program and project administrator (presumably in private and public works); hairdresser; general clerk; café and restaurant manager; accountant; solicitor; Australian Bureau of Statistics 'Same-sex Couples', pp. 7–8.

30   P. Robinson

59. In order: truck driver; retail manager; electrician; metal fitter and machinist; carpenter and joiner; Australian Bureau of Statistics (2013) 'Same-sex Couples', pp. 7–8 (Australian Bureau of Statistics 2013).

60. In order: construction manager; accountant; advertising, public relations and sales manager; motor mechanic; sales representative; Australian Bureau of Statistics (2013) 'Same-sex Couples', pp. 7–8 (Australian Bureau of Statistics 2013).

61. Some material in this section appeared in P. Robinson (2016) 'Ageing fears and concerns of gay men aged 60 and over' *Quality in Ageing and Older Adults*, v. 17, n. 1, pp. 6–15 (Robinson 2016).

62. S. de Beauvoir (1977, 1970) *Old Age*, trans. P. O'Brien (Harmondsworth: Penguin Books); N. Elias (1987) *The Loneliness of the Dying*, trans. E. Jephcott (Oxford: Basil Blackwell); P. Ariès (1991) *The Hour of Our Death*, trans. H. Weaver (New York: Oxford University Press) (de Beauvoir 1977, 1970; Elias 1987; Ariès 1991).

63. K. F. Balsam and A. R. D'Augelli (2006) 'The Victimization of Older LGBT Adults: patterns, impact, and implications for intervention' in D. Kimmel T. Rose and S. David (eds) *Lesbian, Gay, Bisexual, and Transgender Aging: Research and Clinical Perspectives* (New York: Columbia University Press), p. 111; C. Phillipson (2013) *Ageing* (Cambridge: Polity Press), pp. 136–141 (Balsam and D'Augelli 2006; Phillipson 2013).

64. C. Gilleard and P. Higgs (2005) *Contexts of Ageing: Class, Cohort and Community* (Cambridge: Polity Press), pp. 14–15 (Gilleard and Higgs 2005).

65. U. Beck and E. Beck-Gernsheim (2008) *Individualization: Institutionalized Individualism and Its Social and Political Consequences* (London: Sage Publications), p. 133 (Beck and Beck-Gernsheim 2008).

66. K. Plummer (1981) 'Going Gay: Identities Lifecycles and Lifestyles in the Male Gay World' in J. Hart and D. Richardson (eds) *The Theory and Practice of Homosexuality* (London: Routledge & Kegan Paul), pp. 93–110; J. Weeks (1981) 'The Problems of Older Homosexuals' in Hart and Richardson *The Theory and Practice of Homosexuality*, pp. 177–184 (Plummer 1981; Weeks 1981).

67. A. Stein (1997) *Sex and Sensibility: Stories of a Lesbian Generation* (Berkeley: University of California Press) (Stein 1997).

68. Robinson *Gay Men's Relationships*, pp. 62–82; P. Simpson (2013) 'Alienation, Ambivalence, Agency: Middle-aged Gay Men and Ageism in Manchester's Gay Village', *Sexualities* 16: 297 (Simpson 2013).

69. See, for example, A. Cronin (2006) 'Sexuality in Gerontology: a heteronormative presence, a queer absence' in S. O. Daatland and S. Biggs (eds) *Ageing and Diversity: Multiple Pathways and Cultural Migrations* (Bristol: The Policy Press), pp. 107–122; B. Heaphy (2009) 'The stories, complex lives of older GLBT adults: choice and its limits in older lesbian and gay narratives of relational lives', *Journal of GLBT Family Studies*, 5: issue 1–2, 119–138; M. Hughes (2009) 'Lesbian and gay people's concerns about ageing and accessing services', *Australian Social Work*, 62(2), 186–201; A. King (2016) *Older Lesbian, gay and bisexual adults: Identities, intersections and institutions* (United Kingdom: Gower Publishing); S. Neville, B. Kushner and J. Adams (2015) 'Coming our narratives of older gay men living in New Zealand', *Australasian Journal on Ageing*, v34, 29–33; P. Simpson, K. Almack and P. Walthery (2016) '"We treat them all the same": the attitudes, knowledge and practices of staff concerning old/er lesbian, gay, bisexual and trans residents in care homes', *Ageing & Society*, doi:10.1017/S014468X1600132X; S. Westwood (2016) *Ageing, Gender and Sexuality: Equality in later life* (Abingdon: Routledge); P. Willis, T. Maegusuku-Hewett, M. Raithby and P. Miles (2016) 'Swimming upstream: the provision of inclusive care to older lesbian, gay and bisexual (LGB) adults in residential and nursing environments in Wales', *Ageing and Society* 36(2), 282–306 (Cronin 2006; Heaphy 2009; Hughes 2009; Hughes 2009; King 2016; Adams 2015; Simpson et al. 2016; Westwood 2016; Willis et al. 2016).

References

Allen, K. 2016. Nearly One in Six Workers in England and Wales in Insecure Work. *The Guardian*. http://www.theguardian.com/money/2016/jun/13/england-wales-zero-hours-contracts-citizens-advice-insecure-work. Accessed 13 June 2016.

Ariès, P. 1973. *Centuries of Childhood*. Harmondsworth: Penguin Books.

Ariès, P. 1991 *The Hour of Our Death*, trans. and ed. H. Weaver. New York: Oxford University Press.

Australian Bureau of Statistics. 2006. From Generation to Generation. In *A Picture of the Nation*. Canberra: Australian Bureau of Statistics. http://www.ausstats.abs.gov.au/Ausstats/subscriber.nsf/0/FCB1A3CF0893DAE4CA257 54C0013D844/$File/20700_generation.pdf. Accessed 4 Jan 2017.

Australian Bureau of Statistics. 2013. Same-Sex Couples. In *4102.0— Australian Social Trends*. Canberra: Australian Bureau of Statistics.

Australian War Memorial. Boy Soldiers on the Roll of Honour for the First World War. https://www.awm.gov.au/encyclopedia/boysoldiers/first/. Accessed 4 Dec 2016.

Balsam, K.F., and A.R. D'Augelli. 2006. The Victimization of Older LGBT Adults: Patterns, Impact, and Implications for Intervention. In *Lesbian, Gay, Bisexual, and Transgender Aging: Research and Clinical Perspectives*, ed. D. Kimmel, T. Rose, and S. David, 110–130. New York: Columbia University Press.

Bataille, G. 2001, 1957. *Eroticism*, trans. and M. Dalwood. London: Penguin Books with Introduction by C. McCabe.

Bauman, Z. 2001. *The Individualized Society*. Cambridge: Polity Press.

Beaumont, J. 2014. Australians and the Great War: Battles, the Home Front and Memory. *Agora* 49(4): 46–54: http://search.informit.com.au/document Summary;dn=787141053971605;res=IELHSS. Accessed 4 Dec 2016.

Beck, U., and E. Beck-Gernsheim. 2008. *Individualization: Institutionalized Individualism and Its Social and Political Consequences*. London: Sage.

Bell, M.P., and A.P. Weinberg. 1978. *Homosexualities: A Study of Diversity Among Men and Women*, 141–148. Melbourne: The Macmillan Company of Australia.

Blue, A. dir. 2016. *Deep Water—The Real Story*. Sydney: Blackfella Films for SBS, with major production investment from Screen Australia. http://www.sbs.com.au/programs/deep-water-the-real-story/article/2016/09/27/deep-water-real-story-crime-documentary-pulls-no-punches. Accessed 7 Jan 2017.

Bourdieu, P. 1987. The Biographical Illusion, trans. and ed. Y. Winkin and W. Leeds-Hurwitz. In R.J. Parmentier and G. Urban (eds.). *Working Papers for the Centre of Psychosocial Studies*. University of Chicago, p. 2; emphasis in the original.

Bourdieu, P. 1999. *Weight of the World: Social Suffering and Impoverishment in Contemporary Society*, trans. and ed. P.P. Ferguson. Oxford: Polity Press.

Bourdieu, P. 2003. *Firing Back: Against the Tyranny of the Market 2*, trans. and ed. L. Wacquant. New York: The New Press.

Connell, R.W. 2002. *Gender*. Cambridge: Polity.

Cronin, A. 2006. Sexuality in Gerontology: A Heteronormative Presence, A Queer Absence. In *Ageing and Diversity: Multiple Pathways and Cultural Migrations*, ed. S.O. Daatland, and S. Biggs, 107–122. Bristol: The Policy Press.

de Beauvoir, S. 1977, 1970. *Old Age*, trans. and ed. P. O'Brien. Harmondsworth: Penguin Books.

Elias, N. 1987. *The Loneliness of the Dying*, trans. and ed. E. Jephcott. Oxford: Basil Blackwell.

Elias, N. 2000, 1939. *The Civilizing Process: Sociogenetic and Psychogenetic Investigations*, trans. and ed. E. Jephcott with some notes and corrections by the author, eds. E. Dunning, J. Goudsblom, and S. Mennell, Rev. (edn). Oxford: Blackwell Publishers Ltd.

French, R. 1993. *Camping by a Billabong: Gay and Lesbian Stories from Australian History*. Sydney: Black Wattle Press.

Gerassi, J. 2001. *The Boys of Boise: Furor, Vice and Folly in an American City, with a Foreword by P. Boag and A New Preface by the Author*. Seattle: University of Washington Press.

Gilleard, C., and P. Higgs. 2005. *Contexts of Ageing: Class, Cohort and Community*. Cambridge: Polity Press.

Heaphy, B. 2009. The Stories, Complex Lives of Older GLBT Adults: Choice and Its Limits in Older Lesbian and Gay Narratives of Relational Lives. *Journal of GLBT Family Studies* 5 (1–2): 119–138.

Hekma, G. 2006. Sade, Masculinity, and Sexual Humiliation. *Men and Masculinities* 9 (2): 236–251.

Hughes, M. 2009. Lesbian and Gay People's Concerns About Ageing And Accessing Services. *Australian Social Work* 62 (2): 186–201.

King, A. 2016. *Older Lesbian, Gay and Bisexual Adults: Identities, Intersections and Institutions*. United Kingdom: Gower Publishing.

Macintyre, S. 1999. *A Concise History of Australia*. Melbourne: Cambridge University Press.

MacIntyre, A. 2003, 1981. *After Virtue*, 2nd ed. Notre Dame, IN: University of Indiana Press.

McQueen, H. 2011. *We Built this Country: Builders' Labourers & Their Unions, 1787 to the Future*. Adelaide: Ginninderra Press.

Neville, S., B. Kushner, and J. Adams. 2015. Coming Our Narratives of Older Gay Men Living in New Zealand. *Australasian Journal on Ageing* 34: 29–33.

Phillipson, C. 2013. *Ageing*. Cambridge: Polity Press.

Piketty, T. 2014. Capital in the Twenty-First Century, trans. ed. A. Goldhammer. Harvard: Harvard University Press.

Plummer, K. 1981. Going Gay: Identities Lifecycles and Lifestyles in the Male Gay World. In *The Theory and Practice of Homosexuality*, ed. J. Hart, and D. Richardson, 93–110. London: Routledge & Kegan Paul.

Pollak, M. 1986. Male Homosexuality–or Happiness in the Ghetto. In P. Ariès and A. Béjin (eds.). *Western Sexuality: Practice and Precept in Past and Present Times*, trans. ed. A. Forster, 40–61. Oxford: Basil Blackwell.

Posner, R.A. 1994. *Sex and Reason*. Cambridge, MA: Harvard University Press).

[Review of] Robinson, P. 2013. *Gay Men's Relationships Across the Life Course*. Basingstoke: Palgrave Macmillan. *Galaxy* (2016). http://www.gaylaxymag.com/hindi/book-gay-mens-relationships/#gs.GX8fxk0. Accessed 18 Aug 2016.

Robinson, P. 2008. *The Changing World of Gay Men*. Basingstoke: Palgrave Macmillan.

Robinson, P. 2016. Ageing Fears and Concerns of Gay Men Aged 60 and Over. *Quality in Ageing and Older Adults* 17 (1): 6–15.

Sennett, R. 1998. *The Corrosion of Character: The Personal Consequences of Work in the New Capitalism*. New York: W.W. Norton & Company.

Sennett, R. 2006. *The Culture of the New Capitalism*. New Haven: Yale University Press.

Simpson, P. 2013. Alienation, Ambivalence, Agency: Middle-Aged Gay Men and Ageism in Manchester's Gay Village. *Sexualities* 16: 283–299.

Simpson, P., K. Almack, and P. Walthery. 2016. "We Treat Them all the Same": The Attitudes, Knowledge and Practices of Staff Concerning Old/er Lesbian, Gay, Bisexual and Trans Residents in Care Homes. *Ageing & Society*. doi:10.1017/S014468X1600132X.

Somers, M.R., and G.D. Gibson. 1994. Reclaiming the Epistemological "Other": Narrative and the Social Construction of Identity. In *Social Theory and the Politics of Identity*, ed. C. Calhoun, 37–99. Oxford: Blackwell.

Sontag, S. 2009, 1961. *Against Interpretation and Other Essays*. London: Penguin Group.

Stein, A. 1997. *Sex and Sensibility: Stories of a Lesbian Generation*. Berkeley: University of California Press.

Terkel, S. 1975. *Working*. Harmondsworth: Penguin Books Ltd.

Wacquant, L. 2009. *Punishing the Poor: The Neoliberal Government of Social Insecurity*. Durham: Durham University Press.

Weeks, J. 1981. The Problems of Older Homosexuals. In *The Theory and Practice of Homosexuality*, ed. J. Hart, and D. Richardson, 177–184. London: Routledge & Kegan Paul.

Weeks, J. 1985. *Sexuality and Its Discontents: Meanings, Myths & Modern Sexualities*. London: Routledge & Kegan Paul.

Weeks, J. 1990, 1977. *Coming Out: Homosexual Politics in Britain from the Nineteenth Century to the Present.* London: Quartet Books.

Westwood, S. 2016. *Ageing, Gender and Sexuality: Equality in later life.* Abingdon: Routledge.

White, E. 1980. *States of Desire: Travels in Gay America.* London: Pan Books Ltd.

Willis, P., T. Maegusuku-Hewett, M. Raithby, and P. Miles. 2016. Swimming Upstream: The Provision of Inclusive Care to Older Lesbian, Gay and Bisexual (LGB) Adults in Residential and Nursing Environments in Wales. *Ageing & Society* 36 (2): 282–306.

2

Working Lives of Men Aged 60 and Older

When I was 17 ... I got a job as a cadet reporter on the [newspaper] and was a journalist in Toowoomba for about ten years. I got hugely involved in the first World Refugee Year ... Although I had not at 17 started off with any social conscience, somewhere in my 20s I developed one ... and [in the 1960s] became preoccupied with the refugee issue.
(Drake, aged 77, Melbourne)

Introduction

This chapter examines what the 25 men from the old age cohort, aged 60 and older, said about work and their working lives. The jobs the men had over the course of their working lives are explored as are their experiences in the workplace and whether being homosexual had any effect on their jobs or careers. The two chapters that follow examine also what the men from the two younger age cohorts felt about work and their working lives. The two younger age cohorts are the middle cohort comprising men aged 45–60 and the young cohort comprising men aged 45

© The Author(s) 2017
P. Robinson, *Gay Men's Working Lives, Retirement and Old Age,*
Genders and Sexualities in the Social Sciences,
DOI 10.1057/978-1-137-43532-3_2

and under. Together, these three chapters provide a basis for comparing and contrasting generational effects on gay men's experience of work.

Born 1924–1957, the men aged 60 and older reached their social/sexual maturity between the mid 1940s and the late 1970s.[1] According to the definitions used by the Australian Bureau of Statistics (ABS), this age cohort included men from three generations. In the ABS's nomenclature, anyone born before 1926 belonged to the 'oldest' generation and in this cohort there was one such man. Anyone born 1926–1946, belonged to the 'Lucky' generation and here there were 16 men. And anyone born 1946–1966, belonged to the 'Baby Boomer' generation of whom there were eight.[2] The bulk of men in the cohort belonged therefore to the lucky generation and the eight youngest to the baby boomers.

Because of their relative old age, many of the men from this cohort can provide a retrospective account of a completed working life, which is different from the narratives the men from the younger age cohorts provide in the next two chapters. Also, the working histories of these men aged 60+ offer a perspective on change—both a changing social world and the changing world of work, about which there is more discussion later in this chapter and the next two chapters.

The work histories of these men included being at work during wartime and in the 'long boom' that followed the end of World War II when western countries experienced an extended period of relative high rates of full-time, male employment. During the long boom, governments rewarded procreating married couples and the nuclear family by way of tax advantages and other subsidies.[3] The period coincided also with the outbreak of the Cold War and a decade of acute homophobia when, for example, gay men in Australia, England the USA and other western countries were excluded from working in 'sensitive' occupations, the bureaucracy and media, or were hounded from them if already employed.[4] At that time and until the advent of the gay liberation movement in the early 1970s, same-sex attracted men were called and referred to one another as 'camp'.[5] This term is used interchangeably with 'gay', 'homosexual', and 'same-sex attracted' in this chapter.

The era during which these men aged 60 and older developed their careers, that is, the 1950s, 1960s and 1970s included the period that saw the creation of the women's movement, Black power, the anti-War movement, and the gay liberation and environmental movements. They were young adults, therefore, in a period of marked social change. Their work histories are of particular interest not only because they had to shape them in the context of two quite different periods, the first being a period of relative social repression that followed the end of World War II and the second being a period of marked social change and liberation that occurred in the 1960s but also because they shaped them during the long boom when permanence and security were principal features of work and the workplace.

Most of the men from this cohort were middle class. Seventeen men had incomes ranging from the equivalent in 2009 terms of US$10,000 to US$50,000; four from US$50,000 to US$70,000; and four from US$70,000 to US$200,000 per annum.[6] In other words, more than two thirds of the men's incomes were spread between low income and low-middle income.

There are two sections to this chapter. The first looks at the work histories of the men aged 60 and older and the second is a case study of three men's experience of being 'out' at work. As mentioned in Chap. 1, historians and sociologists have argued that in the 1950s and 1960s gay men's working lives could be negatively affected by repressive social mores and this lessened as social tolerance increased. In the first section, the men's working lives were examined for any evidence that they were affected by the repressive period that followed the end of World War II or the more tolerant period in the late 1960s and 1970s in the West. Three principal narratives were identified in the men's work histories and they are: 'work as work'; 'care or creativity'; 'social or political change'. Work as work referred to an approach to work that saw it as the accepted transition from childhood (or teenage) to adulthood, which, in the case of most men, meant greater independence as a result of engaging in paid employment. Care or creativity combines two fields of work where gay men have found work.

While occupations included in the care field (counselling, nursing, teaching) have little in common with those in the creative field (acting, architecture, poetry, tapestry weaving), the connection was based on an assumption that these fields were more welcoming to women and gay men, less affected by sexism or homophobia.[7] Social or political change referred to work that intentionally or coincidentally contributed to social change or political justice. And like work-as-work, social or political change could just as likely explain the working lives of straight men as those of the men interviewed for this book.

In the second section, the work histories of three men from the all-Australian sample are examined for what they said about how easy or difficult it was for camp men to manage their public self in the workplace. I drew on the all-Australian sample because it was only there that I found men who referred to their sexuality when telling the story of their work life. None of the men did so who belonged to the 60-and-older age cohort from the international, Anglophone sample. The fact that none did underlines another argument in this chapter, which is that the repressive period in which the men came of age and lived their lives as young adults did not permit any open expression or discussion of sexuality, especially from sexual minorities. In relation to the three from the all-Australian sample whose stories are examined below, none was out to workmates when young men. Two came out in later life, the other did not. And their accounts say a great deal about the effect homophobia has had on the working lives of same-sex attracted men in western liberal societies.

Work Narratives

The old cohort comprised 25 men who were aged 61–87. Principal features of this age cohort were as follows. Almost half the cohort had university qualifications and thirteen had secondary school or trade school qualifications. More than half the men were retired at the time of interview and one man was HIV positive.

Their working lives were mostly spent in education or retail and small business. Eight men worked in education, which included school teaching and teaching at universities. The next largest group was a group of seven men who worked in retail or small business. After these, were smaller groups comprising, for example, two men who worked in transport, two men who worked in human services and two men who had clerical jobs.[8]

2 Working Lives of Men Aged 60 and Older   41

All the men interviewed for this book were asked the same question: 'Please tell me the story of your working life and what you enjoyed about work'. Almost without fail, the men provided a semi-structured narrative when they answered the question, starting with their first job and ending with their final job or account of the start of retirement. Not every man included in his narrative what he enjoyed about work but was able to do so when prompted. The men provided meaningful work narratives of the type that Richard Sennett argued were typical of working people's lives before the transformation that occurred in the 1990s under new capital and marked the beginning of the period of acute precariousness, which I would argue is now affecting people's working lives more than before.[9]

Analysis of their answers was guided by a desire to understand how the men regarded work, its purpose in their lives, and what they enjoyed about it. Looking for the meaning, purpose and enjoyment in work might seem an odd conjunction but the men's work histories revealed multiple dimensions of work and being a worker. These included, for example, work as identity (teacher, train driver, concrete pourer), emotional/physical investment ('just a job' or 'my life's meaning'), pains and pleasures (dealing with other people, raising consciousnesses).

The analysis yielded three principal narratives regarding work's purpose or value, which were as follows. First, the stories that a group of twelve men related about their working lives suggested a pragmatic, nononsense approach to employment. This narrative was known as 'work as work' and represented the approach to work of people who understood work as a transition from school or university to paid employment and became the means of supporting the individual and his/her partner and/or family. Secondly, a group of ten men related stories about care work or creative work where they had made their careers. Care or creativity is the name for this work narrative. In this age cohort, it represented the work histories of men who worked in caring occupations such as nursing or counselling or jobs requiring pastoral care such as teaching at school or university as well as those of men who worked in creative occupations such as in the arts or crafts. Thirdly, three men related how work provided them with an opportunity to improve the lot of other citizens, help bring about social change and greater social

42   P. Robinson

justice. This was the third work narrative. The three work narratives are examined in order.

Work as Work

The work histories of the twelve men examined in this section had one thing in common: how the men saw or understood work. For them, it was simply something they did and had to do. They did not look for or expect to find anything special in their work day or working life and accepted work as a normal fact of life. It does not mean the men would do anything, nor that they did not seek enjoyment. It does mean that they do not identify themselves with their job. And as well, as the discussion shows, the work they did could be meaningful and often was because of the relationships they developed in the workplace.

The men's occupations included bricklayer, electrician, librarian, photographer, psychologist, sales representative and store man, in other words, a combination of working-class and middle-class jobs. Four of the men were from Auckland, four from Melbourne, two from Sydney, one man was from Manchester, and another was from New York. Two were in their 80s, six in their 70s, and four in their 60s.

A breakdown of the group according to how many jobs they had over the course of their working life showed that half the group had many jobs, four men had had one job only, and two men had had a couple of jobs. There are two reasons for using the number of jobs interviewees had over their work histories as a means of distinguishing between the men in this group. First, it is a rough measure of career consistency and secondly, it is a rough measure of the type of work histories camp men and men who were same-sex attracted shaped during World War II and the post-war decades.[10]

The term 'career' has middle-class connotations but does not apply only to middle-class workers. For example, a man from this group was a bricklayer all his life, so it could be argued that bricklaying was his career while another man from the group had at least nine different jobs in five different countries before settling on psychology as a means of earning an income in late middle age. The fact that many men from this

2 Working Lives of Men Aged 60 and Older

age cohort were able to change jobs easily and to shape their working lives around different jobs was more a measure of the economic climate that prevailed when they were young men and middle-aged men than it does about their sexuality. In the next section, the work histories of the men are examined in the following order. First, the six men who had many jobs and secondly, the four men who had one job only and the two men who had a couple of jobs.

The men whose work histories comprised many jobs were born between 1927 and 1943. If the oldest from this group had his first job at 16, he would have started work during World War II and the youngest would have done so in the late 1950s. Their working lives began, therefore, during or on the cusp of a significant period of employment and development in Australia, which historian Stuart Macintyre called the 'Golden Age':

> There were jobs for all men who wanted them. People lived longer, in greater comfort. They expended less effort to earn a living, had more money for discretionary expenditure, greater choice and increased leisure.[11]

Two of the men from this group were in their 80s, three were in their 70s and one was in his 60s and they were from Auckland, Melbourne and Sydney.[12] Their experience of 'work as work' is represented here by accounts from two 82-year-olds and a man aged 70.

In 1927, two of the oldest men from the international sample were born, one in Sydney and one in Melbourne. Each had a varied working life with many jobs. Amery, the Sydneysider lived and worked most of his life in Sydney, moving from job to job until in the late 1950s he settled into the state public service of New South Wales, remaining there until retirement in 1988. Herbert lived in Melbourne but spent many years travelling overseas and changing jobs. Another Melbournian with an extremely varied working life was Arran, aged 70, whose life included a lot of what I have called 'love travel', that is, travelling or changing jobs in pursuit of a love interest and which I would argue is something camp men in the 1950s were relatively free to pursue because they were less often bound by ties to mortgage, wife or children.

One other possible reason for the appeal of 'love travel' is contained in this interview extract from Reginald, aged 79 who came from Melbourne:

> I worked in the advertising department of [a department store] ... I was not terribly happy there because of the feeling that I had that they did not much care for somebody like me. I decided to leave there and I went to work as a food waiter in a hotel.

> I would go down to the docks each morning to see if I could get on a ship ... to work my passage. That was something that a lot of us were doing in those days.[13]

It is difficult to know if what Reginald expressed is an example of class unhappiness or sexual unhappiness or both. He did find a boyfriend when he eventually got to London in the 1950s. Since those times when Reginald would go down to the docks looking for a cheap passage to Europe, love travel has become more widespread and affordable and considerably less wrenching, not just for gay men but for whole generations of young Australians seeking self-fulfilment or enlightenment abroad.[14]

When asked what he enjoyed about work, Amery said: 'I think I suffer from the Protestant work ethic. If I am not doing something, I tend to feel guilty'. When he left school, he was not able to go to university—even though he had successfully Matriculated—because his parents were, in his words, 'not in a position to let me go'.[15] His first job was as a receptionist for a commercial photographer who he later discovered was a starting-price bookmaker.[16] When the police raided the back office with its eight phones and scribblers, his first job came to an end. Through a connection of his father's, Amery was offered a job as a trainee manager at a large, department store in George Street, Sydney. Shortly after, he decided that he wanted to go to university and joined the New South Wales public service where part-time studies were not regarded as unusual. Amery finished his degree in 1956, the year of the Melbourne Olympics, and transferred to the Registrar of Births and Deaths. He briefly flirted with work in private enterprise as an account secretary but then returned to the public service where he worked until his retirement in 1988. The main feature of his working

2 Working Lives of Men Aged 60 and Older   45

life was flexibility. Through good luck or good skills of negotiation, he was able to move between the public and private sectors, chiefly it would seem because of flexible arrangements available to public servants in New South Wales at the time. The post-war decades were the heyday in Australia for employment in the public service when it offered life-long security with a good state-funded pension at the end.[17] Since then, public servants have been subject to casualisation of work in much the same way as employees in the private sector.

Herbert's working life reflected a similar degree of flexibility and movement as Amery's but in Herbert's case it included lots of foreign travel and work abroad inspired at times by love travel. Before his love travel, Herbert worked first as a telegraph messenger for the GPO and then as a clerk with an insurance company, 'gradually moving from job to job' until he found employment with TAA.[18] He then went to England and this is a short account of his love travel:

> I met an old lover in London and lived with him in London for a lit-tle over two years. Eventually, I came back to Australia. Before I had left to go to London, I had met a Dutchman in Melbourne and he was still single when I came back and we resumed the friendship and that lasted 50 years.

Love travel was inferred from Herbert's account and he was not asked during the interview if he went to London knowing he would meet his old lover there. The relationship that began with the Dutchman on his return for Melbourne did provide travel opportunities but not at first. His Melbourne-based working life resumed when he found a job as a clerk with a lighting company. This was the early 1960s and Herbert had begun buying and selling houses, 'which was terribly easy in those days'. How he raised the capital to begin his property entrepreneurship is not clear and he was not asked to elaborate but what it did provide was money for travel:

> We went to Holland to see [partner's] family and that became a pattern from then on. Every few years, we would go to Holland, buy a car and drive around Europe. Life was pretty good.

46   P. Robinson

Dealing in property came to an end when, according to Herbert, he, 'became sick of the new laws that were brought in by the government favouring tenants too much'. His European connections paid off when he found work with an importing company in Carlton, an inner suburb of Melbourne. Travel still figured in his life with his Dutch partner: 'to America and places like that but always drawn back to Holland and Europe'. By this stage in his life, work had become mostly part-time and in credit control which was convenient because he was able, 'to go away for six months and come back and be assured of finding another job in the same field'. In 1987, Herbert retired to live on his investments and never worked again.

Arran was born in the English midlands in 1940 and after a lot of travel and many moves settled in Melbourne where he was interviewed in 2010. He had at least ten different jobs over the course of his working life. Born into a lower-middle-class family, his first job was as a photographer for an advertising agency which was then followed by work as a photographer on board ship for an international cruise company that operated in the Mediterranean. In the early 1960s, he was one of three photographers employed on a cruise ship that sailed to Australia, which was the setting for the start of his history of three decades of love travel:

> I met someone in Fremantle. When the ship arrived at Fremantle this young man wanted to come aboard and I thought, 'Well, why not?' so I got him a pass and he came on board and I took him around the ship and then he said, 'How 'bout you come with me and I'll take you for a drink?' I said, 'Fine' and we went off on a motorbike and went to the Cottlesloe pub [in Perth]. We went through Kings Park. It was a very nice introduction to Australia actually.

Arran's relationship with the stranger who took him to the Cottelsloe pub on his motorbike became a significant, turning point in his life, for the young man belonged to a wheat-farming family which owned a 40,000-acre property east of Perth. On being taken to see this, Arran recalled that he thought, 'this has to be the country to live in'. He returned to London and applied to emigrate to Australia: 'A ten-pound Pom I became and was on the first migrant flight from Heathrow to Sydney and that was

2 Working Lives of Men Aged 60 and Older   47

in October 1962'.[19] His first job in Australia was with a large photographic studio where he worked as a coordinator: 'these days they would call it a stylist. I designed sets and chose the clothes for the models'. After seven years, he was 'poached by a designer who ran a graphic design company' and worked as the company's account executive. The next stage of his working life was influenced again by love travel. Following his 'would-be lover', he left Australia and went to Cape Town where he worked as a salesman, after which they went to London where Arran got a job in a large department store in Kensington. Next, Arran and his partner returned to Australia via Canada and the USA. On settling in Melbourne, Arran decided to cut ties with his previous work connections and start a new career in gardening. His reasons related to a workplace culture he had no wish to embrace:

> This was a time of drugs, in the 1970s, and I thought, 'I cannot cope with advertising ... I don't want to know about it'. I needed to purify myself, so I got a job in a huge indoor plant nursery.

For more than five years he worked in nurseries until he returned to study, completed final years secondary school, got a place in a university and qualified to practise as a mental health worker, which was his occupation at the time of interview.

What do the life histories of Amery and Herbert, both born in 1927, have in common and how do they compare with the life history of Arran born 13 years later in the early years of World War II? Both Amery and Herbert would have been infants at the start of the Depression and teenagers at the start of World War II. Neither mentioned either major world event when retelling the story of his working life, possibly because in each case its beginning coincided with the end of the war and the outbreak of peace. Each man began his working life slightly before the beginning of what historians have called the 'long boom',[20] that period in Australian history, and in the history of other countries like Canada and the USA, that ran from 1947 to 1974 and was characterised by full or near-full male employment and rising standards of living. And this helps explain the continuous working lives of the men, something they shared with straight men of their generation.

The peripatetic nature of Arran's life was prefigured in his decision to take a job as a photographer on a cruise ship and I would argue that having neither wife nor partner in England, he was able to indulge his nascent wanderlust and take risks a paterfamilias could not but which other single men and women also enjoyed from the 1960s onward when cruise liners plied the Southampton–Perth route.

The men who had one job or at most a couple of jobs during their working lives were examples of a fairly standard model which existed for male workers during the long boom in the West and which came to an end after the right-wing economic 'reforms' of the 1980s.[21] Richard Sennett underlined the existential effect on workers of the loss of guaranteed long-term employment in the following:

> How can long-term purposes be pursued in a short-term society? How can durable social relations be sustained? How can a human being develop a narrative of identity and life history in a society composed of episodes and fragments? The conditions of the new economy feed instead on experience which drifts in time, from place to place, from job to job.[22]

Some evidence of the effect of these changes is in evidence in the next two chapters where the work histories are examined of those who lived through the period of neo-liberal 'reforms' (the middle cohort) and those who were born into the brave new world that they created (the young cohort).

Men from this cohort who had one job in their working life had to move location as their job demanded. This included, for example, a man who worked as a librarian in Melbourne for 45 years and moved six times from one suburban library to another; a man who was a bricklayer, also in Melbourne, and for 33 years moved from building site to building site for work; as well as a man who lived in New York and worked as an international trade representative for almost 40 years.[23]

Because of the small size of this subset of the old age-cohort, it is not clear if the following feature of these men's working histories can be generalised to a wider population of men, gay or straight from the same generation, but, by comparison with the other men whose

2 Working Lives of Men Aged 60 and Older 49

working histories were represented by the work-as-work narrative, most of the men who had had one job or a couple of jobs in their work life provided fairly cursory accounts of why they enjoyed work. In other words, men whose working lives were typical of the time and who had the opportunity to develop the 'narrative of identity' to which Sennett referred related mostly mundane accounts of what they enjoyed about work. The librarian from Melbourne (aged 77) said he enjoyed 'contact with people' and another man from Auckland (aged 75) who worked in office products and commercial stationery said he enjoyed the following about his work:

I did very well in sales and I was winning all their competitions and ... I just did what I loved doing and the outcome was that I made the [sales] figures so I enjoyed that part of it.[24]

The one exception to this was Parry (aged 63) from New York who had been an international trade representative for most of his working life. His account of what he enjoyed about work was similar to those that some of the men related who had had many jobs. The following is from his interview:

The easy part was travel. The second part was ... cultural learning. Coming from America as a young African-American man, I did not have a lot of understanding of the world in school ... [and] I lucked into these opportunities ... I spent almost 16 years going back and forth between China. I was one of the first Americans in China when Nixon signed the agreement. I was in Hong Kong waiting for the first train load of Americans to go in ... I found travelling expanded my knowledge of not only cultures but our abilities as human beings to get along with each other, understand each other, and of course the diversity of how we handle things differently. My biggest passion is always going into hardware stores in other countries and learning how people handle issues or have solutions to problems that seem so day to day but they have a different take on how a solution gets done.

Parry's account was as rich as those of the men who had many jobs and whose jobs, examined earlier, included travel. It was rich because

50   P. Robinson

it touched on the limitations of an African American's upbringing during and just after World War II. As well, there was his chance presence in China when in 1972 President Richard Nixon signed formal understandings with Chairman Mao Tse-tung, ending decades of China's diplomatic isolation. It was rich also for his stated understanding of how travel increased his acceptance of others, nicely illustrated with his metaphor of tools in foreign hardware stores.

Richard Sennett argues that guaranteed, long-term employment allowed generations of workers to develop narratives of self-identity. The contrast made just now between the relatively rich work narratives of men with many jobs or jobs that included travel when compared with those of the men who had one job only or perhaps two jobs in their life does not contradict Sennett's claim. It provides nuance and exception to the general rule that workers who had a job for life were able to make plans and shape a life more securely than can today's workers who must accept the new work-place norm which comprises short-term contracts and casualised employment.

Care or Creative Work

A group of ten men had careers in which care or creativity were central features. Three men worked in education, two worked in religious organisations, two were involved in crafts for children, as well as a composer, a poet, and a man who was a retail manager. Five of the men were from Melbourne, two were from Sydney, one was from Auckland, one from Manchester and another man was from New York. Four were in their 80s, two were in their 70s, and four in their 60s.[25]

Since second-wave feminism in the 1960s and feminist scholarship and research that followed in its wake, care work has generally been understood as something women do as a matter of course or because they have no choice and whether or not they are paid for it.[26] Given some of the stereotypes that exist about gay men, such as, for example, that they are more inclined to feminine interests or activities than heterosexual men, some readers will not be surprised that some of the men aged 60 and over had work histories that were shaped by a care

2 Working Lives of Men Aged 60 and Older 51

narrative. Their work in care occupations did not mean, however, that they were feminine or effeminate, for they were not.

Care was a central feature of the working histories of six men: three of these worked in education, two in religious organisations, and one man was a retail manager. It would be unwise to assume that everyone working in education or religious organisations is motivated by the impulse to care for others because these areas of employment include administrative and policy positions and each is hierarchical with opportunities for ambition and political manoeuvring. The work histories of these five men were characterised, however, by care for their students or congregations as was that of the man who was a manager in the retail sector. Excerpts from their interviews are included here.

The oldest man in the group, 87-year-old Randall, worked for a religious organisation and described what he liked about work as follows: 'I was always interested in people ... and I wanted to work with young people'. A desire to work with young people ran through the work histories of a number of men from this group. Another man from Melbourne, Clancy (aged 81) worked in retail stores all his life and said that when he was manager he, 'enjoyed the company of what I call the juvenile delinquents, the younger members of staff, men and women'. Basil was the other man who worked for a religious organisation. He was 75 and lived in Auckland. Work with a church took him to the Pacific islands, which he said was enjoyable because he, 'just loved being with the people. I had a very close affinity with them'. Two of the remaining men from this group worked in education and both said they enjoyed 'working with people': people of all ages in the case of 62-year-old Hugh and young people in the case of Anselm (aged 61), both of whom were from Melbourne. Hugh said he enjoyed private tuition because he felt too exposed in the classroom: 'I always got on quite well with the students but I found discipline not an easy thing to do. I had to do quite a lot of shouting'. Anselm worked at a university and said: 'the chief satisfaction of my working life was teaching, having the ... privilege to work with younger people'. These men, whose working lives were shaped by care narratives, had teaching or mentoring roles of one sort or another. For some, it was with students at school or university, for one it was as mentor to younger staff members, and for two men it was in the form of the pastoral care they provided their religious communities. Different settings connected by a similar interest in others and the educational, personal or possibly even spiritual development in those younger than them were the common threads running through their separate work histories.

One possible failing in my interview programme is that I did not ask the men to explain the reason(s) they took the jobs they did when they were telling me the story of their working life. In the case of the men whose work histories were identified as caring, I did not ask them if they purposely sought employment in care work or if care was an aspect that attracted them to the jobs that made up their work history. There are two possible reasons for this. First, the principal reason for the interview when it was held was to inquire as to how age or ageing affected the men's lives and relationships; it was not only to investigate their working life.[27] Secondly, the question about their working life was the first I asked them to answer, was an 'ice-breaker' for them and me, and I was not on the lookout for any themes in the work histories they recounted. That came later and underpins one of the main reasons for this book, that is, to examine relatively uncomplicated accounts of men's work histories in order to analyse how they understood their working life and whether it made sense to them and what they enjoyed about work. Now to return to evidence of creative narratives in the work histories in a small group of men aged 60 and over.

Creativity

Creative narratives were evident in the work histories of four men: two who were involved in children's crafts, a composer and a poet. What are 'creative narratives'? They would certainly include narratives of work in fields that are commonly understood to be 'creative', such as, in the case of the four men here, those working in children's crafts, the composer and the poet. There are also the so-called 'creative industries', such as architecture, advertising, music, painting, sculpture and writing, for example.

2 Working Lives of Men Aged 60 and Older   53

Excerpts from the work histories of two men in their 80s who worked in children's crafts are representative here of the creative narrative. The men were from Sydney and Melbourne respectively. Godfrey came from a lower-middle-class family and spent most of his working life teaching primary-aged children. As a teenager in post-World War II Sydney, he became involved in the school-of-arts movement, which was associated with the earlier mechanics-institutes movement that had spread from Glasgow to British colonies in the early nineteenth century, arriving in Sydney in the 1830s. One of its guiding principles was to provide education for working men and women and thus help develop an educated artisan class, which its founders believed would lead to a more egalitarian society.[28] Godfrey explained how his career began: 'I got terribly interested in working with children in the plastic arts … and I stayed with that work in community after-school care for 35 years'. Teaching children to work with clay or ceramics sustained him until well into his 50s when he accepted a redundancy payment. In the following, he explained what he enjoyed about his work and why he retired well before retirement age:

> I was working with kids from five to 25 … Some of the children are incredibly creative. They are very stimulating in their creativity, so much so that we kept a lot of their work. We wouldn't let them take it home because adults are often scathing or scoffing at the feeble efforts of children. And children's art work is a very serious matter for children, it's a means of communication. Children don't have language skills but they do have pictorial skill … Eventually, I got to an age where I felt I was just beginning to repeat myself and I opted for early retirement, redundancy actually was offered, and I took it.

Godfrey drew considerable satisfaction from the creativity he enabled in the children he taught. His protectiveness, which from his account was shared by other teachers, might today appear overbearing or intrusive. But it is an interesting account of the pastoral and emotional care-work some teachers provide and additionally so, because it is rare to hear it revealed in this way or views about parents' effect on children expressed so honestly.

The other man was Hector who was born in 1928 to upper-middle-class parents in Melbourne. His life and the route he took to craft work with children could not have been more different than Godfrey's. Hector's first job was in his father's accounting practice. After a relatively short time there, he moved to a larger, accounting firm in the CBD and, when his father died prematurely, was thrown into the world of international commerce, an enterprise his father had developed during World War II. Marriage followed and, when his father's business affairs were finally wound up, he had funds to satisfy his and his wife's long-time wish, which was to open a toy shop:

> Our ambition was to establish a stock of toys, a collection of toys that were of the best quality, that gave the best outcomes for children, that made the best contribution to their play and that were in general positive rather than negative.

Like Godfrey, Hector and his wife enjoyed facilitating children's play and creativity. Their toy shop was established in the 1960s and was still in business when Hector had his interview. Its longevity being explained partly by his enthusiasm for the toys he made and sold and the loyalty of their customers:

> I still am [a toy seller] and I still share the original criteria I [used to] apply to the toys that we sell ... Some of our customers are into the second and nearly the third generation. Those who were child customers in the 1960s are now the parents and grandparents of my customers today. We are much loved and admired by those who value us.

Hector and his wife had a daughter shortly after their shop opened and then about three decades later he began a relationship with his male partner, which was in its 25th year at the time of interview. When asked what he enjoyed about his work, Hector said: 'I'm not interested in money; it is the toys that keep me interested and the people and the kids. That's why I keep doing it'. And he had no plans of retiring: 'I don't like the idea of retirement if you're fit enough to work'.

Social or Political Change

A relatively small group of three men found work meaningful for the social or political change they believed it involved or the change they believed they could effect through it. Two of them were in their 70s and the third in this 60s. They were from London and Sydney and worked as journalist, judge, and HIV-AIDS activist.[29] The men worked in areas where they respectively believed they could advance social change, extend human rights, and improve services for men living with HIV-AIDS. Their work histories are examined in order.

The man who said the appeal of his work was that it helped him contribute to social change was Drake, a 77-year-old from Sydney. Formerly married with two children, he and his male partner had been together for more than 30 years. He worked in journalism all his life beginning in print journalism and moving on to radio and television journalism. The social issues that caught his attention when he was a young man and married included world poverty, refugees and mental health, which coincidentally are still major issues requiring international contributions. When asked whether he experienced resistance to his reforming work, he replied that he had and then added by way of personal context:

> My refugee work with the Australian Council of Churches [meant] I became more and more politically radicalized … At the age of 18, I was President of … [a rural] branch of the Young Liberals and my wife was the President of the women's branch of the National Party … [but] by the time both of us were in our early 30s, we were marching in the streets in favour of women's liberation and anti-Vietnam, the whole works. I had become radicalized and I had broadened my vision of what was wrong with the world and I had become involved in overseas development issues, in world poverty issues.

Like many young, university-educated Australians in the late 1960s, Drake came from a conservative background and was influenced by the powerful rhetoric and drama of social reform that was in the air at the time. His political shift and his wife's were significant, hers possibly more so than his because in the 1960s the National Party was a deeply conservative party representing farming and mining interests, its members not inclined to support women's liberation and certainly not gay liberation. In Australia, it was not until the early 2000s that politicians from that side of politics began to speak in favour of gay people's rights and that was mostly in the context of the marriage-equality programme.[30] Spokes-people from the conservative side of Australian politics, including conservative members of the Australian Labor Party, were eloquently silent during the years of the HIV-AIDS epidemic.

The second man from this group was Christian. He was 72, lived in Sydney, and had a partner of more than 40 years. A retired, eminent judge, he said that he had enjoyed working in the law because, 'it was an intellectual as well as an emotional challenge'. He explained in more detail what he meant by intellectual and emotional challenge:

> It is a life that presents you with countless puzzles and your responsibility is to try to solve the puzzles; not according to your own whims but according to some rules and principles about law and justice. Some people love to begin their day doing a cross-word puzzle. I had the great pleasure of spending my whole life doing puzzles.

Christian is known internationally and in Australia as a man of influence who frequently lends his support to helping reduce opprobrium or persecution that people living with HIV-AIDS experience in the developing world and other matters concerning the rights of LGBTI people. When asked whether concern for human rights had been an important feature of his working life, he replied:

> I hope human rights are important to all judges. They may not express it in terms of universal human rights but our legal system is based upon notions of basic rights and basic civic responsibilities, duties, and privileges. Of course, I was interested in human rights. Human rights permeate the law and my job, where possible, was to try to give effect to human rights in the legal decisions that I made.

2 Working Lives of Men Aged 60 and Older   57

For this man, retirement did not bring with it any lessening of his daily workload. 'I was banished into the nether-world of retirement in 2009. Since then, I have been involved in large numbers of international committees, twelve honorary professorships, lots of mediation, arbitration, speeches, conferences, book reviews, and so on.'

The third man from this group of three was 62-year-old Arthur who lived in London and spent part of each year in India. South Asian by birth, he had devoted most of his working life advocating in South Asia for people living with HIV-AIDS (PLWHA). [31] After finishing a university degree in science, he briefly worked in a science-related area and then became a meditation teacher. But it was the situation of South Asian men in the face of HIV AIDS that propelled his career. When asked why he moved into this area of advocacy and activism, he replied:

> I got angry. Some friends died [of AIDS] from lack of services, stupidity. I operate from a passionate anger ... I know quite a few friends in Australia ... We shared common discussions over the last 20 years ... We all operate from that anger that why should we be the ones who are denied services.

Arthur lobbied governments and international organisations to raise funds to pay for education and awareness campaigns for men who had sex with men (msm) in South Asian countries. The problem for these countries was according to Arthur not so much to accept the presence of HIV-AIDS but that msm existed:

> You look at all the AIDS countries in South Asia. India was becoming more aware that there were these population groups [msm] but they didn't signify them in any specific way, [which was] partly to do with the law, the invisibility of the issue, and partly to do with shame. 'We are such good countries. We should not have horrible people like these here.' For Bangladesh and Pakistan there were issues around religion and Nepal was focusing on injecting drug users. India was focusing on female sex workers. Afghanistan of course nothing was going on but fighting. And Sri Lanka, because the prevalence was so low ... didn't think it was an issue.

58   P. Robinson

Arthur devoted himself also to writing papers for international conferences and educational pamphlets for clinics on the ground where South Asian men with the disease or who were at risk could receive treatment and information about how the virus spread. The anger that sparked his involvement in helping to prevent the spread of HIV-AIDS in South Asia arose from a deep frustration with the shame that prevented people from accepting msm in their midst, the slowness of South Asian governments also to accept that HIV-AIDS was real, and the stupidity of cumbersome bureaucracies that frustrated the sort of change he believed necessary to save lives.

In the next major section, the focus turns to the experiences of three men who spoke in their interviews of the effect sexuality had on their working lives. The fact of being able to choose whether or not to come out at work is a relatively recent phenomenon, following as it does in the wake of the gradual, increasing acceptance of gay men and lesbians since the 1970s. What is worth remembering here, however, is that the working lives the men recounted occurred in the 1950s and 1960s when general social attitudes to gay people were still relatively oppressive.

Being 'Out' at Work

Together with other non-heterosexuals, gay men must decide whether they want to 'come out' to their work colleagues or fellow workers. This sets them apart from the rest of the population. And how their fellow workers treat them if they come out can affect their career. While gay men and lesbians are now more likely to have a relatively easier time coming out than previous generations,[32] the act of coming out is still not always straightforward. Gay people can spend their life coming out time and again, as circumstances require. In her work on sexual orientation and the self, Eve Kosofsky Sedgwick explained how she had to come out each semester to new classes of university students.[33] And Gilbert Herdt wrote the following about the effect coming out can have on an individual's career:

2 Working Lives of Men Aged 60 and Older 59

Gays who come out risk losing their jobs or their income—the result of the diminished social status of the employer or the family and the loss of face or privilege in the community that 'homosexuals' unwittingly transfer to their significant others in a homophobic society. Such losses of socioeconomic status and class standing pose a formidable barrier to coming out.[34]

Things have changed since Herdt wrote which was at about the time when the triple-therapy treatment was being trialled and HIV-AIDS was still an unmanageable disease. I would argue that since then (mid 1990s) the disease has receded as a major stigmatising factor in the lives of gay people. Also, while what Herdt wrote could still describe the effect of coming out on gay men living in small towns and provincial cities across Australia and North America and other masculinist societies, the lives of other gay men who worked, for example, in professions in major cities such as Hong Kong, London and Sydney were not being affected in this way.

As mentioned in Chap. 1, the primary data used for this book were almost entirely from the 'international sample' of 82 gay men who were aged 18–87 when interviewed in 2009–2011. A second data set was occasionally used, comprising interviews with 80 Australian gay men aged 20–79 who were interviewed 2001–2003 and known as the 'all-Australian sample'. This section draws on data from the all-Australian sample. Men from both data sets were not asked about being 'out' in the workplace but three men from the old cohort of the all-Australian sample did raise the matter and spoke about their sexuality and the extent to which it affected their working life.[35]

The fact that they referred to their homosexuality in relation to their work history suggested it had been an issue for them or for others in the workplace and their accounts included detailed, personal information about how they or their workmates handled it.[36] The three men whose accounts are discussed here are Oscar, aged 65, Geoffrey, aged 69, and Harold, aged 74.[37] Oscar was a factory manager, Geoffrey worked in entertainment, and Harold in education. After a brief sketch of some principal features of the socio-political context of the post-war decades in Australia, the men's accounts are discussed in order.

60   P. Robinson

Interviewed in 2002, the men would have come of age (turned 21) in 1952, 1954 and 1957 respectively. They grew up in post-war Australia and were young adults at the beginning of and throughout the Cold War, a period of acute homophobia and social repression.[38] The Australian novelist George Johnston described the effect that this period had on Australian social and political attitudes and beliefs:

> The waves of strikes and stoppages and the general restless tumult in the land were attributed by a great many Australians, seeking simplest solution to dilemmas altogether too baffling, to the evil threat of Communism. In Europe the Cold War was developing in bitterness and intensity ... In Australia, it was a time of prevalent suspicion, and almost any non conformity was suspect; these were a people disillusioned and disturbed and somebody had to be blamed for what was going wrong: it was a time of irresponsible accusations and superficial examinations on the part of some, and on the part of more a weary ostrich-wish just to bury the head in the sand.[39]

Canadian historian Angus McLaren noted these developments affecting gay men in North America during the Cold War: more than 4000 homosexuals were discharged from the US military in the last three years of the 1940s; following the beginnings of the McCarthy-inspired 'witch trials', the US military and public service began to purge from their ranks people regarded as 'security risks', which naturally included homosexuals; and in 1952 the American Psychiatric Association determined homosexuality to be a 'sociopathic personality disorder'.

McLaren argued that allies of the USA undertook similar surveillance and arrests of homosexuals also for reasons of 'national security'. In Canada, for example, the Royal Canadian Mounted Police began collecting information on suspected gay men such that by 1960 they had files on more than 9000. In West Germany, almost 40,000 men were found guilty of homosexual offences between the mid 1950s and mid 1960s,[40] while in the UK, homosexual offences rose by 500% in the 1950s.[41] Australia was no different and the Cold War saw increased surveillance and arrests of gay men for 'unnatural offences'.[42] 'In almost every Western country the 1950s and 1960s ... [were] a period in which gay subcultures were forced to become more rigorously clandestine than in the 1920s and 1930s. Repression became much more intense that it had been before the war.'[43] In his argument regarding 'deviant careers', US sociologist Howard Becker argued that if a person breaks an important rule, s/he will be seen as different from other people, as someone who, 'will not act as a moral human being and therefore might break other important rules'.[44] Just such a logic would help explain why homosexuals were subject to intense scrutiny of intelligence agencies during the Cold War.

The three men were interviewed in the early 2000s when the meaning of the act of 'coming out' was understood to make a public declaration of one's gayness, to declare that one was not heterosexual. While this section is headed 'Being "out" at work', in their answers the three men spoke about how being homosexual or camp affected their workplace relationships, often referring to whether or not they were out at work.

At 65 years of age, Oscar was the youngest of the three men whose stories are considered here. He had been married and waited until after his wife's death to come out and as the following except shows, he felt no compulsion to end the marriage and come out and believed that he would still be married if she had not died.

> I was married for 22 years and very happily married and I would still be married if my wife was still alive. But towards the end of those 22 years, I did realise that I was attracted to men. I had a few experiences with men here and there. All with married men I might add. And then when my wife died I 'came out'.

His coming out was neither easy or a pleasant experience for in declaring his homosexuality he lost many friends:

> I did lose quite a number of friends. Some of 20 years standing. Pretty difficult because we'd all been through a lot of things together. Because I was married for 22 years and they were friends of mine, of my wife and myself, and so it was pretty traumatic. They stopped sending Christmas

cards: no communication. Two of my best friends haven't spoken to me for 16 years.

Oscar's experience while not necessarily typical does say a great deal about the personal risks men from his age cohort took in coming out. The pain of his friends' rejection might have been the reason he remained closeted at work and came out to no one. In the following extract, Oscar explained his role and responsibilities:

> I ran at one stage eleven factories in Australia. I still work for the same company part time ... I was 24 when I joined the industry. I enjoy the challenge of getting the same final product ... to end up with the same product from year to year.

When I observed in our interview that the industry he worked for was traditional and conservative, Oscar replied:

> *Very*! It's a very conservative industry ... Basically nobody 'comes out' ... Because that's the end of their career or they find it very difficult to move up the ladder of achievements, despite the fact they might be absolutely brilliant. It is a very conservative industry. Most of them are typical 'poofta' bashers. I do not discuss my sex at work, but they have worked it out. They did not understand when there were three of us living together for seven years. None of my friends understood that.

Oscar's home life developed an unusual quality when a younger man he met when travelling asked to continue their intimate relationship and Oscar's long-term partner agreed to the three of them sharing their house. The younger man moved in and Oscar maintained separate relations with each partner under the same roof. Neither friends nor workmates understood his relationship when it comprised three men, which is not surprising given its uncommon nature. And his workmates knew he was gay without being told:

> Quite a lot of the guys I work with I have not officially 'come out' to, but *they know*. And they just take me for who I am. I do not try anything on

2 Working Lives of Men Aged 60 and Older 63

with any of them of course and ... I am friends with quite a few of them away from the office. It has made not a lot of difference to their acceptance of me. It was difficult for me to accept to 'come out' ... because I had led a very happy 22 years in the 'straight' world. However, we did know a lot of gay people because my wife was in theatre and she knew lots of gay men.

Oscar's life was a success by any measure. He earned and kept the respect of a work force he managed in an extremely conservative manufacturing industry. He had an 18-year gay relationship after a heterosexual marriage of 22 years and transformed that relationship so a third man could live with him and his long-term partner. And he survived some very painful rejection when he came out after the death of his wife.

At the same time, these extracts from Oscar's working history reveal a great deal about the issues involved in coming out at work for men from his generation. He came out to some friends and had heartache as a result but at work he relied on a lot of people 'just knowing', that is, on picking up some 'vibe' or feeling that he was not quite like them (the 'normals').

When Geoffrey (aged 69) was young, camp men like him had to be discreet about their private life if not completely closeted at work. As they and their sexual practices and relations were illegal, so much more was at risk if they were exposed. As mentioned in the introduction to this section, the late 1940s and 1950s (when Geoffrey was in his 20s) were a time of heightened surveillance of camp men's social/sexual activities and arrests and humiliation if caught were common. This is in contrast with the 2010s where gay men in most liberal western societies can rely on protection from legislation that forbids discrimination in the workplace on the basis of a person's sexual orientation.[45] It is not possible to know, however, how many gay men still live their lives as did Geoffrey and are closeted at work.

Same-sex attracted men who are or were married or in a heterosexual relationship might need to be discreet about their private life—until they break with their heterosexual past and come out. There would

64   P. Robinson

be other gay men who would be discreet about their homosexuality at work as a form of protection against bullying in the workplace—for example, in workplaces where the dominant *mores* are strongly heterosexual, it would be sensible for a gay man to keep secret his social/sexual life. Writing about the homophobia they observed in working-class masculinities in Australia in the 1980s, Connell, Davis and Dowsett wrote: 'An ideology of masculinity [existed] in which physical prowess and social power are fused with aggressive heterosexuality. "Poofters" are culturally supposed to be contemptibly inadequate, feminised men.'[46]

Writing at about the time Oscar was still married and Geoffrey was living in Sydney and coming of age, US sociologist Howard Becker argued that any person who was characterised as deviant in 1950s society was cut off from participation in more conventional groups. In relation to the marginalisation camp men experienced at the time: 'being homosexual may not affect one's ability to do office work, but to be known as a homosexual in an office may make it impossible to continue working there'.[47] And I would argue this was largely the case because of the repressive effect the Cold War had on the social/sexual *mores* of the USA and its allies that were described above. If the gay person's manner were not out of the ordinary, however, and he passed for a 'normal' male, there were other areas of life that drew attention to his difference and, according to Becker, could jeopardise his continued employment. Becker argued that certain workplaces 'pre-suppose a certain kind of family life'.

Same-sex attracted men therefore faced difficulties where 'the assumption of normal sexual interests and propensities for marriage is made without question'. Becker argued that while the expectation of marriage created problems for the heterosexual male—the single man stood out from the crowd of married men, in other words—it was more so for the homosexual male: 'The necessity of marrying often creates difficult enough problems for the normal male, and places the homosexual in an almost impossible situation'.[48] Becker was writing more than 40 years ago. Some of his claims still apply, especially in regard to the degree of intolerance gay men can experience in some workplaces, antidiscrimination laws notwithstanding.

In Australia, for example, dominant males in some workplaces, such as the building, forestry and manufacturing industries can continue to enforce fairly rigid, traditional views of maleness and masculinity, which do not accept homosexuality or alternative versions of masculinity.[49] In a recent case in Melbourne, a former police officer killed himself as a result of the homophobic bullying he received from other police officers. The circumstances of his death and the bullying he received from older men at work suggest that, despite equal opportunity legislation which makes it an offence to discriminate against a person on the basis of his/her sexuality, some workplaces are in the 2010s still unsafe for gay men.[50] That homophobia is still oppressive to some gay men supports an argument Dennis Altman made more than 30 years ago, which is that it 'mutates' to adapt to different expressions of homosexuality as more men come out and being gay becomes less of an issue. His argument was that homophobia never truly goes away but continues to shadow and diminish gay men. 'It is, however, an argument against the liberal belief that greater knowledge necessarily leads to greater acceptance.'[51]

One more recent case concerned a contestant on a British television programme, Celebrity Big Brother, who said, when asked, that he would stand with his back 'against a brick wall' if he had to share the Big Brother House with a gay contestant.[52] This occurred in early January 2016. For decades, gay men have had to listen to this sort of crude, low-level homophobia, which is annoying because it assumes we are sexually interested in straight men and only in non-consensual, anal sex. It speaks volumes also about the sexual insecurities of all males.[53] The controversy the contestant's opinion created was discussed in *The Guardian* and is an example of what Altman meant when he argued that homophobia shadows every move or advance gay men make. In the past, gay men overheard such comments in private, possibly at work, possibly in changing rooms of gymnasiums or sports clubs and were shamed by them or read equally base jokes on walls of toilets, train stations or buses. Now, a homophobic quip is nationally broadcast on British television and neither challenged on screen nor erased by editors from the pre-recorded programme.[54]

66   P. Robinson

When introducing his account of his working life, Geoffrey said that men from his generation who had long-term relationships spent most of their adult lives being 'illegal'. Geoffrey and his partner had been together for 40 years. I asked him if he were using the term 'illegal' literally. He explained that they had been illegal because their relationship covered a time when it was illegal to have sex with a man. When he described his workplace, he said how he was treated and why he believed he was respected:

> You went to work and if you behaved yourself, nobody worried about you. You probably had people there who thought, 'Oh, this old poof,' but, as long as you did your work, no one worried … I worked in maintenance and nobody ever said, 'You old poof' because I did my job and that was it. They respected me because I could do my job. People like us worked in the artistic side of things and, as long as everybody did their job, no one worried. It is like hairdressers. There's hardly a hairdresser that wasn't a queen and they had the confidence of their clients.

Geoffrey's workmates might have suspected that he was camp but according to his account no one called him an 'old poof' because he did his job well and the same disjunction that exists today could have existed then, which is that until and unless a gay person comes out and directly states he is camp or gay or same-sex attracted, many people will continue to believe he is straight. To what extent his behaviour was a form of 'passing' is debatable. His behaviour at work was unlikely to constitute 'passing' in its fullest sense for the reason that Geoffrey provided: there were people in the workplace who knew and probably saw him as, 'this old poof' but, and his qualification is important, 'as long as you did your work, no one worried'. In the world Geoffrey described, it makes sense that he and people like him were more likely to avoid negative attention if they 'went to work and behaved' themselves. This belief and account of workplace behaviour is similar—but for different reasons—to the practices that Richard Sennett and Jonathan Cobb found in the workplace that they observed in the 1970s in the USA where, for example, it was risky to stand out from the crowd comprising one's fellow workers. In *The Hidden Injuries of Class*, Sennett and Cobb wrote:

2 Working Lives of Men Aged 60 and Older   67

> If he [the factory worker] demonstrates his ability to the full, he stands out as an individual, not merely losing the affection of his comrades but, by becoming an example of the unusual person who is hard-working, putting them in the shade. His sensitivity to the prospect of shaming others leads him to hold himself back. But holding himself back, he makes himself feel weak. Holding himself back, in order that others not be shamed, he comes to feel he is doing something wrong. He is neither fraternal nor individualistic; he tries to be both, and feels that if only he were a more competent person, he could solve the dilemma.[55]

Because of their sexuality, gay men are less likely to be subject to the same tension between individualistic and fraternal drives that Sennett and Cobb identified as a source of weakness for the (heterosexual) factory worker. It is likely, however, that camp men like Geoffrey were aware of the dynamics, which in Australian and British contexts would have been understood as the requirements of mate-ship.

Their sexuality and what they represented meant that camp men could not share the fraternal bonds of heterosexual masculinity. And I would argue that in many workplaces in the 2010s an embargo of the sort still exists. It did not mean that Geoffrey and camp men like him were unaware of its rules or demands and that, because of their outsider status and intimate knowledge of men, it could be argued that as homosexual workers they had and men like them continue to have a very acute understanding of masculinities' practices, possibly more so than do straight men. Camp men in the 1960s were not affected by the same concerns and in the same way as were the factory workers that Sennett and Cobb observed but according to Becker they faced other difficulties in the workplace: 'in some male work groups where heterosexual prowess is required to retain esteem in the group, the homosexual has obvious difficulties'.[56] Geoffrey's effeminate mannerisms or campstyle—high voice, expressive lips and eye brows, hand on hip when speaking—most likely prevented him from passing as a heterosexual man but they gave him the advantage of fitting a common stereotype of what a camp man in Australia (and England and New Zealand) was then meant to be. He might have been mocked but as he said, 'they respected me because I could do my job'.

Historians and anthropologists have argued that effeminacy is and has often been seen as the principal revealing sign of sexual deviance in men. Charges of effeminacy are used by heterosexual men as a means of regulating the expression of masculinity: 'Some responsibility is also borne by the further (incorrect) assumption that any male involved in a homosexual relationship is effeminate and that effeminacy entails timidity'.[57] Geoffrey believed that, for as long as he did his job well and competently, he would not attract any negative attention from the straight men with whom he worked. And this approach, he said, applied to the other camp men who worked where he worked. Revealingly, he said: 'You went to work and you behaved yourself'. His meaning is not clear but it is reasonable to assume that by 'behave yourself' Geoffrey meant that he and his workmates who were camp made sure that they were good employees, if not ideal workers, that they were not disruptive, that they did not cut corners, that they were regarded by their employers as 'good boys' for a lot was at risk. US historian, George Chauncey described the level of persecution homosexual men experienced in the 1950s as follows:

> Fifty years ago … homosexuals were not just ridiculed and scorned. They were systematically denied their civil rights: their right to free assembly, to patronize public accommodations, to free speech, to a free press, to a form of intimacy of their own choosing. And they confronted a degree of policing and harassment that is almost unimaginable to us today.

The oldest men from this group of three, Harold (aged 74) was single and living in a country town in New South Wales when I interviewed him. His experience of being a camp man in the workplace was varied and complicated. As a boy and young man, his role in his extended family was as primary carer for his aunts, uncles, mother and brother. He boasted that he had worked hard all his life and that his father worked throughout the Depression—relatively uncommon when so many men were out of work for periods then—and that his mother took in work at home:

2 Working Lives of Men Aged 60 and Older 69

Dad had a labourer's job. He worked 16 hours each day. But in addition we grew every vegetable …We never saw that we did without. We had a car when nobody else did.

Like many from his generation and class, his attitude to work formed as a young boy during the 1930s Depression and in some ways is an Antipodean's echo of Thatcher-ite domestic principles: 'I learned the lessons that you don't buy anything until you can afford it, you live under your income, you put a bit away for a rainy day, and you work hard'. Again, like many people from his generation, he grew up with a strong belief in the importance of financial independence, which guided later decisions. He had a sense of needing to be secure and, in his own words, to 'own a roof over my head and be financial enough to take care of myself for as long as I possibly can. I have enjoyed the achievement', and that the quest for financial independence motivated him in his career: 'It was always the satisfaction of achieving something that made work enjoyable for me.'

The strong work ethic he gained from his family and growing up in the Depression Harold applied to his first job after university: 'I did a science degree, followed by an education degree, and I went secondary teaching in 1952. I loved my teaching experience and I was posted to the country'. He was careful to keep his sexuality a secret and became a popular, respected teacher. He had a promising career as the principal of a small country primary school until on a trip to the state capital two police officers arrested him at a gay beat. He recalled that, 'one of the policemen was very sympathetic and one was very aggressive. I was terribly concerned … I had to come to [capital city] for the court case the day before speech night at my last week in the school'. Harold's friends hired an expensive barrister for him and the magistrate found him guilty of loitering with intent and put him on a good behaviour bond for 12 months. He then moved to the capital city with his partner and they bought a house. It seemed his career had been saved until one of the arresting policemen appeared at his front door.

Two years later, one of the policemen knocked on my door and told me that he had had 'to pull a few strings' to make sure that nothing was reported to the education department. He said that I would have to be very careful in future. At that stage I decided to get out of teaching. It forced my hand. I was sorry about that because I did enjoy my teaching.

Harold immediately resigned from the education department because he feared the policeman intended to blackmail him and then moved interstate with his mother to live in two units that he bought for them. He was 34. He successfully applied for a position in the public service and stayed in the same job until he retired at 65. When at work in the public service, Harold adopted an extremely strict approach to camp colleagues and refused to allow any talk of sexual identity:

I had gay people working for me and they did not get any favours from me and they knew that. We did not even talk about it ... We were there as people working. And I would not have tolerated that.

It is not clear whether Harold's court experience caused him to adopt this severe attitude towards other camp men who worked for him. It would be understandable if it did but, on the other hand, his approach when teaching had been 'totally professional', in his view, and he had never been or wanted to be 'out' at work, so it might have been a continuation of his own very strict self-regulation, which he relaxed at a beat to considerable cost.

The saddest aspect of Harold's story is that police blackmail of gay men was not unusual at the time and resulted in the blighting of many promising careers like his.[58] In the USA, for example, police were permitted until 1980 to use wire taps to collect evidence against people suspected of engaging in sodomy.[59] Blackmailing gay men mostly came to an end in most liberal democracies when homosexuality was decriminalised between the 1970s and 2000s.[60]

Conclusion

Sexuality and its effect on the working lives of an age cohort of gay men aged 60 and older was the focus of this chapter. Discussion of the men's working lives drew on interviews from the international sample and the discussion concerning being out at work from the all-Australian sample. At the start of the chapter I stated my intention of searching for evidence that the socially repressive era (1940s, 1950s) had on the men's working lives or the effect on them of the period of relative tolerance that began in the late 1950s. On the whole, there was relatively little evidence in the men's stories that the repressive period affected their working lives or that the period of greater tolerance did so either. The exceptions to this general finding were found in the work histories of the three men who specifically spoke about sexuality and work.

All three men were aware of the masculine requirements of their time and the assumptions that other men held about manliness and the male in the workplace. Two were keenly aware and remained closeted. The third man was less concerned because he worked in entertainment, a field where gays and lesbians have long found employment and been accepted. He was not out as it would be understood in the 2010s and, while he did not hide his sexuality, he was quietly proud that, even though they might have thought it, none of his workmates called him an 'old poof'. There were also three other examples of the effects of socially repressive views or values on men's working lives. The first concerned the story one man told of visiting the docks each day in the hope of being able to find passage out of Australia. He eventually did go overseas where he found a boyfriend. From his interview, it was difficult to establish if his desire to escape Australia in the 1950s was a case of sexual oppression, class oppression or both. A second man recounted the story of a relatively happy heterosexual marriage he had before exploring relationships with other camp men. He never divorced and at the time of interview still shared a social life with his wife, his partner and his daughter. Many gay men and women from his generation married in order to pass as straight and, while this was a distinctive possibility in his case, he said nothing definitively in his interview to confirm it. The third man worked most of his adult life to improve the life of people living with HIV-AIDS in South Asia and to counter the administrative and political apathy there that he believed prevented people being properly educated about the risk of HIV-AIDS. South Asian by birth and a resident of London, his working life was less affected by the changing levels of social tolerance in the West than by the long-standing repression of sexual difference in countries such as Afghanistan, Bangladesh, India and Sri Lanka.

In the work-as-work narrative the men's jobs included working-class and middle-class jobs such as bricklayer, electrician, psychologist and store-man. Principal features of their careers included first, those who had many different jobs, changing often, and second, others who had one job only or at most a couple across the course of their working lives. In other words, there was evidence of some men being able to move around, try different jobs and other men conforming to the dominant work narrative of the long boom, which for men was having a job for life.[61] It could be argued then that, on the whole, their working lives were no different from those that straight men had from the same generation.

The care-or-creative narrative comprised jobs men had that were in teaching, religion, and arts and crafts, all of which, according to Pierre Bourdieu, were where women were most often to be found at work, were occupations where, because of men's domination of 'public space and field of power', women concentrated: 'those quasi-extensions of the domestic space, the welfare services ... and education ... [and] domains of symbolic production (the literary, artistic or journalistic fields)'.[62] And, as Donald Johnson's research showed, gay men in Washington were attracted to feminised occupations in the post-war decades, roughly about the time men from this cohort also were employed. In other words, there is evidence of men from this cohort finding work in occupations that attracted large numbers of women, that is, feminised rather than feminine occupations. One of the primary reasons for this being, as mentioned, their desire to avoid workplaces affected by homophobia or sexism.

The social-or-political-change narrative represented jobs a small number of men had in journalism, law and AIDS activism. It is possible that their choices were influenced by their experience of personal discrimination because of their sexuality but, because none made a clear statement to the effect, it can only be inferred that they like others who are outsiders have a stronger appreciation of the need for social change or justice and tend to congregate in jobs with reformist agendas or contribute however possible through their everyday jobs. Finally, there was evidence of the care and the social and political change narratives intersecting in two ways. First, because education assists social change, the men who taught, here included in the caring narrative, were also working in a job that assisted social or political change. Second, the man who devoted his life to raising awareness in South Asia of HIV-AIDS and lobbying governments to educate people at risk was involved in both a caring occupation and in promotion of social or political change. Because of gay men's involvement in caring for their own in the HIV-AIDS epidemic and because their sexual identity was conflated with the illness, care work of gay men became political in the 1980s and 1990s. The work they did promoted marked social and political change, the effects of which are still being felt. There is increasing evidence in the work narratives of the men from younger cohorts—discussed in the next two chapters—of the care narrative intersecting with the social and political change narrative and chiefly because any care work in the HIV-AIDS field had a socio-political effect.

Notes

1. See Chap. 1 for 21 as marker for adulthood.
2. See Australian Bureau of Statistics (2006) 'From Generation to generation' in *A Picture of the Nation* (Canberra: Australian Bureau of Statistics): http://www.ausstats.abs.gov.au/Ausstats/subscriber.nsf/0/FCB1A3CF0893DAE4CA25754C0013D844/$F

74 P. Robinson

ile/20700_generation.pdf. Accessed 4 January 2017 (Australian Bureau of Statistics 2006).

3. For more on the long boom in the context of twentieth-century Australia, see S. Macintyre (2003) *A Concise History of Australia* (Port Melbourne: Cambridge University Press), pp. 196–235. In Australia, this was the second 'long boom'. The term was first used to describe the period 1860–1890 when the Australian colonies experienced sustained economic growth as a result of the gold rushes of the 1850s; see R. McGhee (1967) 'The Long Boom, 1860–1890' in J. Griffin (ed.) *Essays in Economic History of Australia 1788–1939* (Brisbane: Jacaranda Press), pp. 135–185. For more on state benefits provided to married couples in Australia, see J. Murphy (2000) *Imagining the Fifties: Private Sentiment and Political Culture in Menzies' Australia* (Sydney: University of New South Wales Press Ltd), pp. 84–89 (Macintyre 2003; McGhee 1967; Murphy 2000).

4. A. McLaren (2002) *Sexual Blackmail: A Modern History* (Cambridge Mass.: Harvard University Press), pp. 250–254 (McLaren 2002).

5. See P. Robinson (2008) *The Changing World of Gay Men* (Basingstoke and New York: Palgrave Macmillan), pp. 8–11, 18–28 (Robinson 2008b).

6. Before their interview, each man was asked to provide an approximate value of his income expressed in US dollars. I provided them with a rough scale beginning at US$10,000, then US$30,000, US$50,000, US$70,000, US$100,000, US$130,000. In November 2016, these income steps were worth US$11,193 (US$10,000); US$33,581 (US$30,000); US$55,969 (US$55,000); US$78,356 (US$70,000); US$111,938 (US$100,000); US$145,519 (US$130,000); source: Historical Currency Conversions, https://futureboy.us/fsp/dollar.fsp. Accessed 22 November 2016.

7. David Johnson shows that in Washington in the 1950s certain types of jobs were understood to be the sort that 'fairies' would take or were only for fairies and argues that gay men sought feminised jobs such as clerical or stenographical ones: D.K. Johnson (2004) *The Lavender Scare: The Cold War Persecution of Gays and Lesbians in the Federal Government* (Chicago & London: University of Chicago Press), pp. 43–46 (Johnson 2004).

8. See Appendix A.

9. R. Sennett (1998) *The Corrosion of Character: The Personal Consequences of Work in the New Capitalism* (New York: W.W. Norton & Company), pp. 98–99 (Sennett 1998).

10. Note on terminology: 'camp' was the term that many pre-liberation men who were same-sex attracted used for each other. Over time and in the wake of the gay liberation movement, it was replaced by the word, 'gay', after which other formulations were created that reflected changing understandings of sex, love, intimacy between men, such as 'same-sex attracted', 'men who have sex with men' (msm). For more on terminologies for gay men and same-sex attracted males, see E. White (1980) 'The political vocabulary of homosexuality' in B.R.S. Fone (ed.) (1998) *The Columbia Anthology of Gay Literature: Readings from Western Antiquity to the Present Day* (New York: Columbia University Press), pp. 777–785 and P. Robinson (2013) *Gay Men's Relationships Across the Life Course* (Basingstoke and New York: Palgrave Macmillan), pp. 3–34 (White 1980; Robinson 2013).

11. Macintyre *A Concise History*, p. 196.

12. Amery (82) Sydney; Herbert (82) Melbourne; Lucas (75) Auckland; Jeffrey (72) Auckland; Arran (70) Melbourne; Sean (67) Auckland.

13. A man from the all-Australian sample.

14. More in the next chapter.

15. Until the late 1960s, Matriculation was the name in Victoria and other Australian states of the certificate awarded to students who successfully completed their final year of secondary school. The term originally referred to examinations that students were required to pass in order to qualify for a place at university. At Oxford University, for example, students are still required to matriculate in order to mark their admission to the university, see: http://www.ox.ac.uk/students/new/matriculation. Accessed 8 December 2015.

16. A starting-price bookmaker or 'SP bookie' provided illegal bets on horse races. The odds offered were those published at the start of the day and did not shorten if the number of bets rose before the horse race or greyhound race. The service SP bookies offered greatly increased with the advent of radio and private telephones. The following definition was used in an investigation of the Criminal Justice Commission, Queensland: 'The acceptance of *unlawful* wagers by a person on his own behalf or on the behalf of another, at an agreed rate, on any

sporting event or other event or contingency' (emphasis in the original), see Criminal Justice Commission, Queensland (1990) 'SP Bookmaking and other Aspects of Criminal Activity in the Racing Industry: An Issues Paper' (Toowong, Qld: Research & Coordination Division, Criminal Justice Commission), p. 8 (Criminal Justice Commission, Queensland 1990).

17. N. Brown (2015) 'Government, Law and Citizenship' in A. Bashford and S. Macintyre (eds) *The Cambridge History of Australia Vol 2: The Commonwealth of Australia* (Port Melbourne: Cambridge University Press), p. 418 (Brown 2015).

18. GPO is the acronym for the General Post Office or the principal sorting office and offices of the postal service in Australia, which was originally located in the state capital. In Herbert's case, the Melbourne GPO was located on the corner of Bourke Street and Elizabeth Street, Melbourne. The building still stands but is now a shopping emporium and offices. TAA was the acronym for Trans Australian Airways, a government-owned aircraft company that operated domestic air services in Australia from 1946 to 1994, see: http://aviationcollection.org/TAA/taa.htm. Accessed 5 May 2016.

19. 'Pom' is the abbreviated form of 'pommy', a term given to newly arrived settlers in the Australian colonies and which carried over after Federation as a term for English or British people in general. It is still used today. There are a number of explanations for its derivation including as an abbreviation of pomegranate, signifying the red-cheeked face of the newly arrived English in Australia and as rhyming slang for immigrant. Regarding pommy's derivation from pomegranate and pomegranate as rhyming slang for immigrant, see B. Moore (ed.) (1997) *Australian Concise Oxford Dictionary of Current English* (South Melbourne: Oxford University Press), p. 1041 (Moore 1997).

20. As mentioned, this was the second long boom in Australia.

21. U. Beck (1992) *Risk Society: Towards a New Modernity*, trans. M. Ritter (London: Sage Publications), p. 142 (Beck 1992).

22. Sennett *The Corrosion of Character*, pp. 26–27.

23. Ambrose (77) Melbourne; Baden (65) Melbourne; Parry (63) New York.

24. Basil (75) Auckland.

25. Randall (87) Melbourne; Clancy (81) Melbourne; Godfrey (81) Sydney; Hector (81) Melbourne; Basil (75) Auckland; Colin (72)

New York; Fergus (63) Manchester; Alec (62) Sydney; Hugh (62) Melbourne; Anselm (61) Melbourne.

26. A. Hochschild (2003, 1983) *The Managed Heart: Commercialization of Human Feeling* (Berkeley: University of California Press) (Hochschild 2003, 1983).

27. See Chap. 1 for background.

28. For more on school-of-arts movement in Sydney, see http://diction-aryofsydney.org/entry/the_school_of_arts_movement. Accessed 11 December 2015.

29. Drake (77) Sydney; Christian (72) Sydney; Arthur (62) London.

30. Conservative MP from Queensland, Warren Entsch has a history of supporting gay people and marriage equality; see, for example, M. Knott (2015) 'Meet Warren Entsch, Queensland's unlikely but vocal LGBTI champion', *The Age* (Melbourne: Fairfax Media Ltd) (Knott 2015).

31. The acronym, PLWHA (people living with HIV-AIDS) is used in this book even though in some contexts it has been superceded by PLHIV (people living with HIV).

32. For discussion of changing meaning of coming out, see Robinson *Changing World*, pp. 26–28, 43–46, 62–66.

33. E.K. Sedgwick (1990) *Epistemology of the Closet* (Berkeley: University of California Press) (Sedgwick 1990).

34. G. Herdt (1997) *Same Sex, Different Cultures: Exploring Gay and Lesbian Lives* (Boulder, Colorado: Westview Press), p. 159 (Herdt 1997).

35. See, for example, report showing prejudice in Russia against working with gay people: A. Day (2013) 'Russia: 51% of population would not want a gay neighbour or work colleague', *Pink News*, 11 Sep 2013: http://www.pinknews.co.uk/2013/09/11/russia-51-of-population-would-not-under-any-circumstances-want-a-gay-neighbour-or-work-colleague/. Accessed 11 January 2016 (Day 2013).

36. Another small group of men referred to the effect their sexuality had on their working lives and they were New Zealanders from the middle cohort of the international sample. Their stories are discussed in Chap. 3.

37. Excerpts from interviews with Geoffrey and Harold were used in a previous publication on their experiences of homophobia: P. Robinson

(2008) 'Older gay men's recollections of anti-homosexual prejudice in Australia' in S. Robinson (ed.) *Homophobia: an Australian History* (Sydney: Federation Press), pp. 218–235 (Robinson 2008a).

38. For more on this period and its effects on camp men in Australia, England and other US allies, see Robinson *The Changing World*, pp. 21–25 (Robinson 2008b).

39. G. Johnston (1969) *Clean Straw for Nothing* (London: Collins), pp. 87–88 (Johnston 1969).

40. While the situation in West Germany in the 1950s was oppressive for gay men, it was considerably better than what it had been under the Nazis where men convicted of homosexuality were sent to concentration camps and members of the SS found guilty of homosexual activity were executed. See R. Lautmann (1981) 'The Pink Triangle: The Persecution of Homosexual Males in Concentration Camps in Nazi Germany' in S. J. Licata and R. P. Petersen (eds) *Historical Perspectives on Homosexuality* (New York: The Haworth Press and Stein and Day), p. 141 (Lautmann 1981).

41. A. McLaren (1999) *Twentieth Century Sexuality: A History* (Oxford: Blackwell Publishers Ltd), pp. 162–163 (McLaren 1999).

42. F. Bongiorno (2012) *The Sex Lives of Australians: A History* (Melbourne: Black Inc.), pp. 232–233; K. Holmes and S. Pinto (2015) 'Gender and Sexuality' in Bashford and Macintyre *The Cambridge History of Australia Vol 2*, p. 323 (Bongiorno 2012; Holmes and Pinto 2015).

43. D. Eribon (2004) *Insult and the Making of the Gay Self*, trans. M. Lucey (Durham, NC: Duke University Press), pp. 22–23 (Eribon 2004).

44. H.S. Becker (1963) *Outsiders: Studies in the Sociology of Deviance* (New York: The Free Press), p. 34 (Becker 1963).

45. Regarding legal protections provided in Australian jurisdictions, see Australian Human Rights Commission (2015) *Resilient Individuals: Sexual Orientation, Gender Identity & Intersex Rights: National Consultation Report 2015* (Sydney: Australian Human Rights Commission), pp. 71–77 (Australian Human Rights Commission 2015).

46. R.W. Connell, M.H. Davis and G.W. Dowsett (1993) 'A Bastard of a Life: Homosexual Desire and Practice among Men in Working-class Milieux' in *The Australian and New Zealand Journal of Sociology*, vol. 29, no. 1, pp. 118–119 (Connell et al. 1993).

47. Becker *Outsiders*, p. 34.

48. Becker *Outsiders*, pp. 35–36.
49. In an article published by *The Age* in 2010, a journalist retold a mother's story of how her two children took their own lives because of male bullies in the work-place: H. Westerman (2010) 'In Harm's Way', *The Age* (Melbourne: Fairfax Media Ltd.) (Westerman 2010).
50. 'He'd still be alive if he'd never joined the police', *The Age*, 10 December 2015 (*The Age* 2015).
51. D. Altman (1982) *The Homosexualization of America, the Americanization of the Homosexual* (New York: St Martin's Press), p. 22 (Altman 1982).
52. For link between fear of anal sex, poor sex education for teenagers, and risk of HIV-AIDS, see P. Robinson (2016) 'Marriage equality', *Nexus* (Melbourne: The Australian Sociological Association): http://hdl.handle.net/1959.3/431298. Accessed 31 December 2016 (Robinson 2016).
53. *The Wire* (Home Box Office, 2005) is a US television series set in Baltimore in the early 2000s where most of the action concerns the activities of police officers recording telephone conversations between members of gangs dealing illicit drugs on housing projects and occasionally apprehending them. Members of the drug gangs are mostly in their late teens, early 20s and unemployed. Police officers refer to anyone who is a nuisance as an 'arse-hole'. Anal sex is frequently implied or referred to by the police officers, rarely by members of the drug gangs. An example of its use included the following exchange between two heterosexual police officers: Younger, black, police officer to middle-aged, white, police officer: 'You look fresh today'. Middle-aged, white, police officer: 'I got laid last night'. Younger, black, police officer, laughing: 'Oh yeah? Your arse hole still hurting?' (First season, 2004, episode 6, 26.20–26.25). This is contemporary police drama where masculinity is represented by dominant, traditional, heterosexual values. The fear of anal sex by its repeated reference is noteworthy. Whether it is related to increased visibility and acceptance gay men is moot. See: http://www.hbo.com/the-wire. Accessed 16 January 2017.
54. C. Foufas (2016) 'Homophobia is not entertainment. Channel 5 should be ashamed', *The Guardian*: http://www.theguardian.com/commentisfree/2016/jan/08/homophobia-winston-mckenzie-celebrity-big-brother-channel-5-tyson-fury. Accessed 9 January 2016 (Foufas 2016).

80 P. Robinson

55. R. Sennett and J. Cobb (1973) *The Hidden Injuries of Class* (New York: Alfred Knopf), p. 104 (Sennett and Cobb 1973).
56. Becker *Outsiders*, p. 36.
57. K.J. Dover (1978) *Greek Homosexuality* (London: Gerald Duckworth & Co. Ltd). See also J. Boswell (1990) 'Sexual and Ethical Categories in Premodern Europe' in D.P. McWhirter, S.A. Sanders and J.M. Reinisch (eds.) *Homosexuality/Heterosexuality: Concepts of Sexual Orientation* (New York: Oxford University Press), pp. 15–31; McLaren *Twentieth Century Sexuality*, p. 187; A. Bérubé (1991) *Coming Out Under Fire: The History of Gay Men and Women in World War Two* (New York: Penguin Books), p. 156 (Dover 1978; Boswell 1990; Bérubé 1991).
58. For examination of post-war blackmail in England and the USA, see McLaren *Sexual Blackmail*, pp. 220–238.
59. McLaren *Sexual Blackmail*, p. 245.
60. For more on blackmail and entrapment by police forces in the United States, see, for example, J. Rechy (1977) *The Sexual Outlaw: A Documentary* (New York: Grove Press Inc), pp. 98–103 (Rechy 1977). There is no reason to believe police behaviours that Rechy documented were different in other countries (Rechy 1977).
61. P. Bourdieu (2003) *Firing Back: Against the Tyranny of the Market 2*, trans. L. Wacquant (New York: The New Press), p. 29 (Bourdieu 2003); Macintyre *Concise History*, p. 196 (Bourdieu 2003).
62. P. Bourdieu (2001) *Masculine Domination*, trans. R. Nice (Cambridge: Polity), pp. 93–94 (Bourdieu 2001).

References

Altman, D. 1982. *The Homosexualization of America, The Americanization of the Homosexual*. New York: St Martin's Press.
Australian Bureau of Statistics. 2006. From Generation to generation. In *A Picture of the Nation*. Canberra: Australian Bureau of Statistics. http://www. ausstats.abs.gov.au/Ausstats/subscriber.nsf/0/FCB1A3CF0893DAE4CA257 54C0013D844/$File/20700_generation.pdf. Accessed 4 Jan 2017.
Australian Human Rights Commission. 2015. *Resilient Individuals: Sexual Orientation, Gender Identity and Intersex Rights: National Consultation Report 2015*. Sydney: Australian Human Rights Commission.

2 Working Lives of Men Aged 60 and Older 81

Beck, U. 1992. *Risk Society: Towards a New Modernity*, trans. M. Ritter. London: Sage Publications.

Becker, H.S. 1963. *Outsiders: Studies in the Sociology of Deviance*. New York: The Free Press.

Bérubé, A. 1991. *Coming Out Under Fire: The History of Gay Men and Women in World War Two*. New York: Penguin Books.

Bongiorno, F. 2012. *The Sex Lives of Australians: A History*. Melbourne: Black Inc.

Boswell, J. 1990. Sexual and Ethical Categories in Premodern Europe. In *Homosexuality/Heterosexuality: Concepts of Sexual Orientation*, ed. D.P. McWhirter, S.A. Sanders, and J.M. Reinisch, 15–31. New York: Oxford University Press.

Bourdieu, P. 2001. *Masculine Domination*, trans. R. Nice. Cambridge: Polity.

Bourdieu, P. 2003. *Firing Back: Against the Tyranny of the Market 2*, trans. L. Wacquant. New York: The New Press.

Brown, N. 2015. Government, Law and Citizenship. In *The Cambridge History of Australia Vol 2: The Commonwealth of Australia*, ed. A. Bashford, and S. Macintyre, 403–428. Port Melbourne: Cambridge University Press.

Connell, R.W., M.H. Davis, and G.W. Dowsett. 1993. A Bastard of a Life: Homosexual Desire and Practice among Men in Working-class Milieux. *The Australian and New Zealand Journal of Sociology* 29 (1): 118–119.

Criminal Justice Commission, Queensland. 1990. SP Bookmaking and other Aspects of Criminal Activity in the Racing Industry: An Issues Paper. Toowong, Qld: Research & Coordination Division, Criminal Justice Commission.

Day, A. 2013. Russia: 51% of Population Would Not Want a Gay Neighbour or Work Colleague. In *Pink News*. 11 Sep 2013. http://www.pinknews.co.uk/2013/09/11/russia-51-of-population-would-not-under-any-circumstances-want-a-gay-neighbour-or-work-colleague/. Accessed 11 Jan 2016.

Dover, K.J. 1978. *Greek Homosexuality*. London: Gerald Duckworth & Co., Ltd.

Eribon, D. 2004. *Insult and the Making of the Gay Self*, trans. M. Lucey. Durham, NC: Duke University Press.

Foufas, C. 2016. Homophobia is Not Entertainment. Channel 5 Should be Ashamed. In *The Guardian*. http://www.theguardian.com/commentis-free/2016/jan/08/homophobia-winston-mckenzie-celebrity-big-brother-channel-5-tyson-fury. Accessed 9 Jan 2016.

Herdt, G. 1997. *Same Sex, Different Cultures: Exploring Gay and Lesbian Lives.* Boulder, Colorado: Westview Press.

Hochschild, A. 2003, 1983. *The Managed Heart: Commercialization of Human Feeling.* Berkeley: University of California Press.

Holmes, K., and S. Pinto. 2015. Gender and Sexuality. In *The Cambridge History of Australia Vol 2: The Commonwealth of Australia*, vol. 2, ed. A. Bashford, and S. Macintyre, 308–331. Port Melbourne: Cambridge University Press.

Johnson, D.K. 2004. *The Lavender Scare: The Cold War Persecution of Gays and Lesbians in the Federal Government.* Chicago & London: University of Chicago Press.

Johnston, G. 1969. *Clean Straw for Nothing.* London: Collins.

Knott, M. 2015. Meet Warren Entsch, Queensland's unlikely but vocal LGBTI champion. In *The Age.* Melbourne: Fairfax Media Ltd.

Lautmann, R. 1981. The Pink Triangle: The Persecution of Homosexual Males in Concentration Camps in Nazi Germany. In *Historical Perspectives on Homosexuality*, eds. S.J. Licata, and R.P. Petersen. New York: The Haworth Press and Stein and Day.

Macintyre, S. 2003. *A Concise History of Australia.* Port Melbourne: Cambridge University Press.

McGhee, R. 1967. The Long Boom, 1860–1890. In *Essays in Economic History of Australia 1788–1939*, ed. J. Griffin, 135–185. Brisbane: Jacaranda Press.

McLaren, A. 1999. *Twentieth Century Sexuality: A History.* Oxford: Blackwell Publishers Ltd.

McLaren, A. 2002. *Sexual Blackmail: A Modern History.* Cambridge, Mass: Harvard University Press.

Mondimore, F.M. 1996. *A Natural History of Homosexuality.* Baltimore: Johns Hopkins University Press.

Moore, B. (ed.). 1997. *Australian Concise Oxford Dictionary of Current English.* South Melbourne: Oxford University Press.

Murphy, J. 2000. *Imagining the Fifties: Private Sentiment and Political Culture in Menzies' Australia.* Sydney: University of New South Wales Press Ltd.

Rechy, J. 1977. *The Sexual Outlaw: A Documentary.* New York: Grove Press Inc.

Robinson, P. 2008a. Older Gay Men's Recollections of Anti-Homosexual Prejudice in Australia. In *Homophobia: An Australian History*, ed. S. Robinson, 218–235. Sydney: Federation Press.

Robinson, P. 2008b. *The Changing World of Gay Men*. Basingstoke and New York: Palgrave Macmillan, 8–11, 18–28.

Robinson, P. 2013. *Gay Men's Relationships Across the Life Course*. Basingstoke: Palgrave Macmillan.

Robinson, P. 2016. Marriage Equality Gay Marriage. In *Nexus*. Melbourne: The Australian Sociological Association. http://hdl.handle. net/1959.3/431298. Accessed 31 Dec 2016.

School-of-Arts Movement, Sydney. http://dictionaryofsydney.org/entry/the_ school_of_arts_movement. Accessed 11 Dec 2015.

Sedgwick, E.K. 1990. *Epistemology of the Closet*. Berkeley: University of California Press.

Sennett, R. 1998. *The Corrosion of Character: The Personal Consequences of Work in the New Capitalism*. New York: W.W. Norton & Company.

Sennett, R., and J. Cobb. 1973. *The Hidden Injuries of Class*. New York: Alfred Knopf.

Simon, D. 2002. *The Wire*. New York: Home Box Office. http://www.hbo. com/the-wire. Accessed 16 Jan 2017.

The Age. 2015. *He'd Still be Alive if He'd Never Joined the Police*. Melbourne: Fairfax Media Ltd.

Westerman, H. 2010. In Harm's Way. In *The Age*. Melbourne: Fairfax Media Ltd.

White, E. 1980. The Political Vocabulary of Homosexuality. In The Columbia Anthology of Gay Literature: Readings from Western Antiquity to the Present Day, 1998. ed. B.R.S. Fone, 777–785. New York: Columbia University Press.

3

Working Lives of Men Aged 45–60

I am a school counsellor at a school which runs from pre-kindergarten, three-and four-year-olds, up through high school graduation which is 18-year-olds. One of the things I enjoy very much is the great variety, working with kids of all ... different ages, boys and girls. I have always enjoyed working with children: for most of my career that is what I have done and I find it very energising and enriching.
(Timothy, aged 46, New York)

Introduction

Like the preceding chapter, the focus of this chapter is on the working lives of a cohort from the international sample, in this case the 'middle cohort' that comprised 28 men from the baby boomer generation aged 45–60.[1] Their work histories are examined for what they revealed about the meaning of work what joy, if any, they found in work. Also, like the previous chapter, there is a section on whether the men could be 'out' at work and if so what it meant to be so. The 28 men were born between 1950 and the early 1960s and so reached social/sexual maturity between

© The Author(s) 2017
P. Robinson, *Gay Men's Working Lives, Retirement and Old Age,*
Genders and Sexualities in the Social Sciences,
DOI 10.1057/978-1-137-43532-3_3

the early 1970s and early 1980s. Because of the changes that occurred to the world of work, their careers and work histories are quite different from those of the men from the older cohort.

The youngest men turned 21 just as liberal democracies began to undertake the most radical economic readjustment since the introduction of the welfare state, that is, when, in the 1980s and influenced by the theories of economic rationalists, governments began to sell off publicly owned assets and utilities in order to privilege financial markets and owners of capital.[2] The effect of this economic revolution on everyday workers was, over the next 30 years, to remove security and certainty of employment that they and the generation before them had assumed to be a right.[3] This age cohort included such workers, but also men who had successful careers in multi-national corporations and who did not find the introduction of short-term work contracts and casualisation an impediment to high-paid, white-collar jobs.

The work histories of the men from this age cohort were distinctive also because many of them began paid employment and careers in the context of greater acceptance of gay men but also on the cusp of the outbreak of the HIV-AIDS epidemic in the West. In the previous chapter there was evidence from some of the stories the men from the old cohort recounted of having to hide their sexuality from work colleagues and workmates. In this chapter too there are stories from men who were not confident or willing to be 'out' in the workplace but on the whole fewer of the sample were afraid of the consequences of people at work finding out about their sexuality.

The first section examines the men's work histories and how different groups from the age cohort were connected by four principal work narratives. In this chapter these are work-as-work, care work, travel as work's central organising feature, and social or political change. Three of the narratives, work-as-work, care, and social or political change, are continuations of those used to understand men's working lives in the previous chapter. Travel is a special feature of this age cohort because the men's early adulthood—which in western liberal democracies is the optimum time for people to embark on care-free, adventurous travel—coincided with a time of affluence and advances in mass, long-haul, air transport. The second and shorter section in this chapter considers the stories three men told about the effect their sexuality had on their job, career, or sense of self.

Almost all the men from this age cohort were middle class. There were two exceptions: a working-class man (self-declared) and a man from the upper classes.[4] Because of the 1970s expansion of higher education in liberal democracies, it is less surprising that 24 men, that is, the majority of these interviewees, had university qualifications and a very small minority of four men had trade or secondary school qualifications.[5] Ten were in their 40s and eighteen in their 50s. None was retired and two were university students. In 2009–2010, their incomes were between the equivalent of US$10,000 and US$200,000 per annum.[6] Ten had incomes ranging from US$10,000 to US$50,000; eight from US$50,000 to US$70,000; and ten from US$70,000 to US$200,000 per annum.[7] In other words, their incomes were almost evenly spread between low income, middle income and relatively high income. Two men were each living on poverty incomes of approximately US$10,000 per annum. One of them was single and living on benefits in Los Angeles, the other in Hong Kong had the support of a long-standing partner.[8]

Work Narratives

The men from the middle cohort had jobs in three principal areas: professions or public service; what I call international corporate-professions; and education. A group of eight were employed in a profession or public service and they were from Hong Kong, London, Melbourne, New York and Sydney; they included men who worked in counselling, engineering and social work.[9] Another eight were employed in international corporate-professions. Until the start of cheaper international air travel and the expansion in multi-national corporations in the 1970s, members of the corporate-professional international elite were mostly diplomats and their families or senior executives and their families with corporations that had long association with former European colonies, such as the British shipping firm P&O had with India and Australiaand New Zealand,[10] that Australian trading and manufacturing firms such as Burns Philp and the Colonial Sugar Refinery Company had with former British colonies and dependencies in the Pacific.[11]

In the 1980s, the corporate-professional international elite expanded to include employees of internationally focused firms working in accounting, advertising, agriculture, food, law, manufacturing, mining, public relations, to name a few. The eight men who belonged to this group were from Hong Kong, London, Melbourne and New York.[12] The third employment area, education, was where six worked in universities and schools and included two who were tertiary students.[13] The remaining six were employed in clerical positions, small business, and one was living on welfare payments.[14]

Just as in the previous chapter, the work histories of these men aged 45–60 were examined for narratives common to their working lives, analysis being guided by a desire to understand how they regarded work, its purpose, and what they enjoyed about it. In the case of this cohort, four principal work narratives were identified. And, just as for the older cohort, two of the principal narratives were work-as-work and social or political change. A care narrative was also identified but, unlike in Chap. 2, there was no evidence of a creative narrative.

The intersection in two narratives identified in Chap. 2 was present also in the work histories of the middle cohort. The narratives where it was most obvious were care and social-or-political-change. The intersection occurred for men engaged in HIV-AIDS work and because of how HIV-AIDS was understood in the 1980s. At the beginning of the decade, news of the disease created panic and hysteria in cities where its presence was detected—mostly in gay men or intravenous drug users. The panic and hysteria quickly transformed into judgements about 'lifestyles' where monogamous couples were seen as virtuous whereas sexually adventurous, or to use the language of the time, promiscuous gay men and intravenous drug users were demonised.[15] Intense stigma attached to the disease and to people most at risk. Homophobia intensified and gay men became the target of sexual conservatives and fundamentalist Christians.[16] To work in HIV-AIDS-related fields, which were strongly care-oriented, was also to take part in a political act because in doing so people risked being marginalised and stigmatised and they challenged powerful narratives about disease,

3 Working Lives of Men Aged 45–60 89

sexuality and individual responsibility. The social or political change that this sort of care work brought about concerned how gay men individually and communally responded to the threat AIDS posed to them and others like them and how outsiders came to see gay men and the gay and lesbian communities as a result of the communal health effort.

A new narrative 'travel' emerged, which included not only the work some men found in the airline industry, for example, and as expatriates for international corporations but also what in the previous chapter was designated 'love travel', that is, work got while travelling with a partner or lover or in pursuit of one or associated with a love interest found while travelling. More about these below and the greater opportunities for work while travelling that the expansion of mass tourism the age of the 'jumbo jet' made possible.

In summary, then, the four principal narratives used to explain the work histories of the men from the middle cohort were as follows: care ($n = 14$); travel ($n = 11$); work-as-work ($n = 6$); and social or political change ($n = 5$). They are presented in order.

Care Work

Fourteen men (or half this cohort) worked in care occupations or professions. These included school or university teaching, counselling, nursing, librarianship or health activism in, for example, not-for-profit organisations working in the area of HIV-AIDS or disabilities. School or university teaching were included in the care narrative for the same reason as was explained in the previous chapter: because of the element of pastoral care involved in the occupation and which the men from this section referred to in their work histories. The relatively large number of men connected by a similar narrative can be accounted for by the fact that during the course of their lives care occupations and professions experienced not only considerable growth and expansion—for example, nursing and similar occupations were professionalised requiring university qualifications—but also greater social acceptance as career paths for men as well as for women.

90   P. Robinson

Ten of the men were in their 50s and 4 in their 40s and came from all the capital cities in the international sample, with the exception of Mumbai.[17] Their work experiences and histories are represented here by those of two men, one of whom was from Los Angeles, the other from Manchester. Both had worked in organisations involved in HIV-AIDS education or prevention campaigns. Given the age cohort to which these men belonged—as mentioned, they came of age in the 1970s and 1980s—it is not surprising that among them were men who had devoted energy and time to HIV-AIDS. And the stories they recounted illustrate a generational change between how men from the oldest cohort understood care—more as generally understood and practised—and how the men from this cohort understood it—which is more strongly directed toward care for their own kind.

Marvin and Ben had quite different stories to recount of their experiences in HIV-AIDS activism and working with gay men and activists. At the time of interview, 59-year-old Marvin was working for a not-for-profit organisation in Los Angeles and 52-year-old Ben was completing further studies in Manchester.

Marvin's work history was varied. As a young man, he found work in show business and was doing very well prior to the outbreak of HIV-AIDS in the USA. But, in the early 1980s, when men began dying of mysterious illnesses later understood as AIDS-related, he joined an AIDS project in California and began an extended period of community activity that personally affected him:

> You established relationships with these men and it was amazing and they were all shapes and colours and we all spoke the same language. It was such an amazing time in that there was this sense of community.

He continued working for the project until a former partner died of AIDS. This loss affected his involvement in the community, his work and mental health:

> I still grieve every day … I experience the worst kind of survivor guilt … When I got my test results and they told me I was negative, I was devastated. I know that sounds ridiculous. You are supposed to be happy,

3 Working Lives of Men Aged 45–60   91

joyous and free but I just never ever arrived at that point of view because
... I had been a member of something so special and now I'm no longer a
member of that.

As I have discussed elsewhere, this age cohort of gay men had to wait up
to five years after AIDS was identified to learn what caused it and what
sexual acts put an individual at risk of contracting the disease.[18] All of
this changed when the link was discovered between HIV and AIDS,
an HIV blood-test was developed, and governments in countries like
Australia, England and New Zealand made the test freely available. For
many gay men, routine testing became common from the early 1990s.[19]

Marvin was speaking, however, about the time when HIV tests were
not routine and about the USA where for years the Reagan administration refused to discuss or acknowledge HIV-AIDS.[20] People like
Marvin—working closely with friends and acquaintances from clubs,
bars, parties and other gay community activities—were often extremely
traumatised by what they witnessed:

What do you say when everybody that you have ever loved, ever cared
about, everybody you ever really respected, all of a sudden they are taken
away from you and you are left to your own devices? ... I went to work
for AIDS Project before we were even an AIDS Project so everybody in the
early days that walked in those doors pretty much died within the first year.

His response to the test result might surprise many readers. I would
argue that a number of factors help explain why some gay community
workers who were deeply involved in working with men who were living with the disease and who saw so many die in the early years would
develop the survivor guilt he spoke of and want to 'be like them'. At the
time and in the early years of the 1980s, the public discourse around
AIDS was largely judgemental and condemnatory. Intravenous drug
users, sex workers and gay men were blamed for 'spreading' the disease.[21] Historians argue that homosexuality, gay identity and AIDS were
conflated in the public mind and in some cases also in the minds of gay
men directly affected by the progress of the disease and others less vis-
cerally affected who looked on agog and aghast.[22]

Marvin said that he experienced 'survivor guilt'. By the mid 1990s, commentators were referring to the emotional toll on gay men who had been to too many funerals and witnessed too many friends dying. It is possible to understand that some carers and others personally involved in the 'front-line' fight against AIDS could develop feelings of guilt for not contracting the disease as a result of the heavy weight of grief and trauma they had to carry—and, like Marvin believe they 'deserved' to be HIV-positive—especially in the USA where, while Ronald Reagan was president, the government did not seem to care, seemed positively indifferent to the plight of thousands of young gay men who were dying or very ill.

The other man whose working life included time in an organisation with an HIV-AIDS focus was Ben from Manchester. He dropped out of university because at that time in his life coming out and understanding the gay world were more important to him than university studies: 'It was more important to me to find refuge among gay others than continue with my degree in the late 1970s. It was a more hostile climate as well'. By late 1970s the experimentation of the 1960s had begun to lose its appeal. Costly social reform was less practicable as western economies struggled with increased wages and resources costs—the latter as a result of the oil crises in the Middle East—and falling revenues or the fiscal paradox known as stagflation. Simultaneously, governments committed to social reform were replaced by conservative ones. For sexually adventurous people, Herpes curtailed the allure of lots of anonymous sex and for gay men and women gay liberation transformed from relatively effortless participation in public demonstrations to hard work in courts and lobbying politicians to effect real change to their legal rights. Unbeknown to gay men and intravenous drug users in the West, they were living on the cusp of the AIDS epidemic.

Ben followed the advice of a gay friend and moved to London where he found a job in the civil service. By the mid 1980s, his interest revived in university and he enrolled in a social sciences degree. On graduation, he found work as a research assistant in the HIV-AIDS area, after which he worked as a disability rights campaigner and then as a special needs advocate for deaf people. When he returned to northern England with his boyfriend, he began postgraduate studies.

3 Working Lives of Men Aged 45–60   93

Both Marvin and Ben had stories of negative or frustrating experiences in some of the jobs they had over the course of their working lives. Neither related to homophobia. Marvin said he found it difficult working with younger people because he could not understand their work culture and Ben vowed never again to work in an organisation staffed by gay men. Their reservations are discussed in order.

When Marvin was asked whether his workmates affected his enjoyment of work, he replied with a very definite, 'No'. I asked him to elaborate:

> Most of the kids I work with are in their 20s, the administrators and big bosses are certainly my age but I work with a bunch of young kids and it is difficult sometimes because I don't share their mind-set, the same values they have and there is a tendency for me to go okay been there, done that and I don't say I grow very impatient but I sometimes surrender my power because of my frustration at working in a playpen.

People under the age of 30 might be disappointed to hear someone in Marvin's position describe them as 'kids' or that working with them was like 'working in a playpen'. But a difference of almost 30 years in age might help explain why the 59-year-old Marvin regarded people in their 20s paternally, as if they were his children. As a generation, baby boomers were critical of the old when they were in their 20s. Many of them who are now in their late 50s and early 60s are as old if not older than the older generation they sought to unseat in the 1960s and 1970s. And perhaps understandably, their children—or in the case of gay men the generation of the children they could have raised—resent being patronised because of their youthfulness. These and other generational differences between the age cohort of the baby boomers and the one comprising men their children's age are examined in more depth in the next chapter.

I am not sure what Marvin meant when he said that he sometimes surrendered 'power because of my frustration at working in a playpen' and I did not ask him to explain. It could mean that he joined the younger people 'at their level' instead of taking charge or using his authority and experience to help or lead them. When I asked Marvin to

94   P. Robinson

explain what he meant by the difference in values that he experienced in relation to his younger workmates, he replied:

> Most of these kids for example are right out of school. They are research assistants and they are there not because they have a vested interest in [disability] but because it is a job. It is a means to getting ahead in what will probably be a different career field. When I was at AIDS Project, one of the glorious things about being there was everybody was there because they had some kind of a personal experience that brought them to the workplace. And ... the people I most relate to in my job are people who either have kids with [the disability] or have experienced it in a very personal way ... When you apply public-health dogma to an epidemic, the compassion, the human factor sometimes goes out the window ... It is a job for those people as opposed to, not on a mission or anything like that, but if I'm going to take this vow of poverty I certainly want to believe in what I'm doing. I don't think there's that mission [for the other workers].

Marvin's experience with the AIDS Project in the 1980s had had a profound effect on him. It was also when his former boyfriend died of AIDS and when gay men everywhere were alarmed and anxious about their own sexual pasts, the means of infection and the disease's course.[23] How he and fellow workers had worked together deeply affected his later life and work. I suspect that because of the intense, emotional, labour involved in working for the AIDS Project Marvin's experience there became a template against which he measured jobs he later had in the not-for-profit sector. And when he compared his memory of the dedication of the people he worked with in the AIDS Project, he was disappointed with the approach or attitude of his current workmates. Community-based organisations and others working in a support capacity with ill or disabled people would understand the dichotomy which Marvin referred to and I suspect both types of workers would be useful, those who worked with a mission and those who were more matter-of-fact.

The workplace reservations about which Ben spoke concerned frustrations he had experienced when he worked in an organisation staffed by gay men. It could have been galling for him because the organisation was working in the HIV-AIDS field and in the 1980s gay men working for such organisations often drew on all their energies and more and adopted the mission-like approach about which Marvin spoke. Ben experienced bullying in this workplace as he explained in this extract from his interview:

> It was a crushing experience and the project director was quite a bully and felt free to make very personal comments about my looks and what he saw as my professional inadequacies. Very little support or training was offered to help me improve. He and his in-group practically ostracised me because I didn't fit in with them and was under-confident and perhaps a little awkward among them.

Ben's experience was directly opposite to what Marvin remembered from his time in the AIDS Project. The only explanation Ben could provide for the bullying and negative attention he received from his boss and co-workers was that he was different from them. I did not ask Ben to elaborate and he did not explain. It might have been because of the clothes he wore, his accent, his class background, or the version of gay man he represented that his boss and co-workers decided to pick on him. Most likely it was because he was last person to join the team for, as Norbert Elias and John Scotson found in their study of insiders and outsiders in a new town in England in the 1970s, the most recently arrived are regarded as different by those who arrived before them simply because they were the latecomers.[24]

For gay men and people who belong to minorities, it can be dispiriting to find that bullying or discriminatory behaviour occur in organisations staffed by gay people or who belong to the same minority group. It can be more upsetting when the gay person is only recently 'out' as seemed to be the case for Ben from the work history he provided. As I have discussed elsewhere, coming out is a process that takes time and takes place over time.[25] A great many expectations hang on the act of coming out and the reality it will bring when a gay person believes s/he is ready to come out. For many, there is the expectation that all the pain of living in the closet—of living—will come to an end and that socialising and having social/sexual relationships with other same-sex attracted

96   P. Robinson

people will be relatively easy or care free. This is not always the case as studies of the gay scene have shown.[26]

What do the extracts from the life histories of these two men say about care work? First, that it can mean that a lot of time has to be spent at the shop front, that is, dealing directly with the people seeking assistance, which was the sort of work Marvin did for the AIDS Project in Los Angeles. Secondly, that it can include work behind the scenes such as that which Ben did when he was a disability activist in London. Thirdly, that fine motives and committed workers do not always that work is any easier than other type of work or that the internal culture of organisations devoted to care is less political than in other workplaces. And fourthly, that the type of care work that men from this age cohort took up was directed at helping people like themselves. This preference for caring for their own was writ large during the 20 years of the HIV-AIDS crisis in the West. Caring for people like themselves distinguished them from the men from the old cohort whose care work was more general, did not have the same focus because their lives were lived more secretly, gay community organisations did not exist, and they never faced the health emergency of HIV-AIDS. And it distinguished their care work also from the men from the young cohort for reasons examined in the following chapter.

Travel

Two separate groups comprised this narrative representing the working histories of eleven men. The first group consisted of six men who found work in the travel industry—working for airline companies, for example—and the work that others found in the corporate-professional international sector. The second group comprised five men who were involved in 'love travel', which as explained in Chap. 2 was the sort of work interviewees got while travelling with a partner or lover or in pursuit of one or associated with a love interest that developed while travelling.

The fact that travel shaped the working lives of more men from this cohort than the previous one was a consequence of increasing affluence, the expansion of mass-transit tourism made possible with the introduction of the 'jumbo jet' in the 1970s and long-haul planes that followed with their very large passenger capacities. Together with this was the baby boomers' belief in overseas travel as a means of self-discovery, a form of secular pilgrimage, which in the 1970s and 1980s was the case for many hundreds of thousands of young adults from Australia, England, New Zealand and the USA. A well-beaten path led generations of Australians to London, which for many was the jumping off point for exploring Europe.

Establish yourself in London and then approach the crossing of the English Channel to deal with Europeans who do not speak English was the conventional wisdom for Australians of a certain age and class for most of the twentieth century and before. Our relative geographical isolation is often used to explain the strong attraction overseas travel has exerted on generations of Australians. Precursors of the backpacker established the hippie route in the 1960s and 1970s that included extended stop-offs in South-East Asia, India and Afghanistan (before the Soviet invasion) as a prelude to exploring the youth hostels of Europe.[27] In the last quarter of the twentieth century, Australian tourists became more familiar with holiday destinations in Asian countries to the north of the continent, such as Bali and Thailand and more recently Vietnam.[28]

Travel Work

Six men had working histories with a travel narrative. Some worked in the travel industry, others travelled for work and career advancement. Four of the men were in their 50s and two in their 40s. They came from Auckland, Hong Kong, London, Melbourne and New York.[29] Their stories are represented here by excerpts from the interviews of Logan (aged 56) and Nathan (aged 50) both from Auckland.

Logan was born in London and raised in a small country town in New Zealand. When in his early 20s he returned to London, he found work in the travel industry and spent the next two decades of his life working for airlines: always on the ground and, despite the commonly held image of airline stewards and gay men, was never a steward. There was an element of chance about the start of his career in travel, as he explained in the following extract of interview:

> I used to walk past the British Airways office. It was in Regent Street, a huge office, and I used to walk past that thinking that's where I want to be. At the time, I was working ... [in a] toy shop as a demonstrator and I thought, 'How do I get there?' I did a correspondence course in travel, first time anybody outside of the travel industry had actually done it and I was almost completed ...[when] British Airways ... were looking at new staff, new people, a younger vision and I applied for a job and remarkably I got it based on the training I did. That is where my real career started ... in the travel industry when I was about 21.

Logan worked in London for about a decade and then returned to New Zealand to work as a trainer with the national carrier until he was moved overseas to work in Europe, Egypt and Hong Kong. When he needed a change of career direction, he taught travel and tourism courses in higher education before retraining as a counsellor until finally deciding to work as a drag queen. In Logan's case, returning to London in his early 20s could have been the means of escaping small-town New Zealand, the limitations of which are discussed in more depth in the section below on being out at work. Whatever his reasons, Logan spent a large part of his adult life working overseas and away from New Zealand before returning to transform into a fairly well-known drag queen:

> I could not imagine a different life. Would I be a drag queen? Probably not. Or would I have the [drag] persona I have in New Zealand now? Probably not. Would I do advertisements on TV? Probably not. I could not imagine ... [being straight] no. I think I would probably still be in ... [small country town] with seven kids working on a dairy farm.

I did not ask, and Logan did not volunteer any connection between travel and his personal development between his early 20s and early 50s. The movement backwards and forwards between Britain and Europe and New Zealand might have been related to self-discovery or to retracing his family's migration or to following the demands of work in the travel industry.

3 Working Lives of Men Aged 45–60   99

Nathan is a 50-year-old restaurateur and bar owner from Auckland, notable for being the man from this age cohort who had had the greatest number of jobs. At the time of interview, he had had more than 15 different jobs ranging from sales and hospitality to commercial property management. Like other men from New Zealand, he had worked overseas for part of his working life. His work travels took him to Europe and Australia. He did not explain why he left New Zealand except to say that he and his partner at the time left to travel around the world. When they arrived in Australia on the way home, his partner met someone else and returned to Europe. Nathan remained in Australia and experimented with different forms of catering and hospitality:

> I set up a catering company with two lesbian friends of mine and we did catering and what is called riders which is looking after special guests or movie stars or whatever, looking after all the little things they needed done, which is really entertaining and a lot of fun, terribly long nights and days [*laughs*] but yeah it was quite rewarding.

Willing to try anything, he then moved into work in the public service before returning to New Zealand where he took a job in corporate sales. To please a new partner, he moved into marketing for a film company before starting work in commercial property management. When later he was made redundant, he and his partner bought one of the gay bars in Auckland, which brought to an end a life of fairly constant movement and change. The bar, said Nathan, allowed him to merge his social life and work life:

> The reasons we got the bar [are] one, we didn't want to lose it because it was going up for sale and it was our local and it was what we enjoyed going to and two … I think it was at drinks at our place on a Sunday [and someone said] 'Why don't you just buy … [the bar]? You won't have to clean up the mess here afterwards!' … We still entertain quite a lot … We have two lots of friends that have completely merged together … friends who have got beautiful properties with pools and things and we take off to theirs, so it's all just an extension of owning the bar as well.

100   P. Robinson

Like other men whose working histories were included in the travel narrative, Logan and Nathan took partners with them on their travels or met partners overseas. Their working lives, however, did not have strong 'love travel' elements in them. The travel they undertook was mainly shaped by work, sometime wanderlust. In the next section, there is evidence from men's work histories of love travel—here understood as travel undertaken for the purpose of maintaining or securing a love relationship—as the principal motivation for the travel.

Love Travel

Five men had love travel stories to relate, some more affecting than others.[30] They are represented here by excerpts from the work histories of two men, 53-year-old Ryan from London and 47-year-old Duncan from Hong Kong.

Ryan did not work in or write journalism about travel or tourism. He worked in the arts in London and travel affected his working life when he accompanied his partner whose job involved overseas travel. Together they spent time in South East Asia and Ryan began writing on indigenous culture and heritage. His work was picked up and syndicated by news agencies in the USA and Europe. And so developed his life as a freelance journalist, which he said was far from secure:

> Freelance is pretty much the bottom of the food chain in terms of journalists … More stuff is going online and work is done in-house and so journalists are really struggling. Newspapers in England are becoming increasingly provincial in the way they're thinking. It seems like the other side of the world is no longer exotic anymore and there's not such a need to write about it if we can find out about it through the internet. Freelancers are not having a good time.

His initial relocation to South-East Asia with his partner was not upset when they broke up. Ryan continued to work from a base there, returning annually to Europe. In this sense, therefore, I would argue love travel played an important role in his life and work. The second man

3 Working Lives of Men Aged 45–60   101

whose life was shaped by love travel was Duncan and a brief account of his working history follows.

In the late 1980s, Duncan left Australia where he had grown up and gone to university and travelled through Europe, stopping in London. It was there that he met his life partner. In the following extract from his interview, he explained the circumstances of their meeting:

> I was living in [London] with some German lesbians … [The people] in my household flat as well as the flat below were all good friends. They were connected households and we had this massive party. I met [my partner] … through a friend at the party and we spent a torturous six weeks courting each other. Actually, I was courting … and he finally capitulated and the relationship began.

While his partner had a passport which allowed him to remain in Britain, Duncan was travelling on an Australian passport which meant they could not remain in London indefinitely. This legal impediment caused their first move as a couple, which was to Holland:

> A couple of years later we ended up in Amsterdam when my visa ran out because … at the time Amsterdam and Denmark allowed gay partners, non-European gay partners to stay so that was the reason for our moving.

When the recession began in the late 1980s, early 1990s, they found Europe a less promising place for Duncan's work—which was in the corporate professional world—and they moved to Hong Kong. After five years there, he returned to London in order to study and they were apart for two years, a more difficult separation than either imagined it would be:

> We spent two years apart whilst he ran a business here … and … while I [studied] and I suppose … I assumed after seven or eight years of being together that two years apart would not be difficult. I underestimated how difficult that would be. We survived it and … then the last … twelve years or thirteen years … we spent in Britain together but now we're back in Hong Kong.

102 P. Robinson

I imagine those two years were hard because you were so much younger then.

Yes. It was quite traumatic I think for both of us and quite difficult too because [my partner] had no desire to live in Australia which at the time allowed for de facto relationships. I was quite happy to live in Europe at the time but, you know, oddly enough the confluence of our immigration issues combined with the [1990] recession meant that Hong Kong provided the best mutual solution. It's midway between Australia and Europe.

No other man from the sample had a working life so strongly shaped by love travel. The impetus for the early moves Duncan and his partner had to take were influenced by visa restrictions and more importantly by non-recognition of the legal status of their relationship. Duncan referred to de facto recognition of same-sex relationships that had existed in Australia since the 1990s when ministers of immigration were willing and able to issue visas to partners of Australian residents in same-sex relationships of two years or more duration and to legal rights that the governments of Holland and Denmark accorded partners in same-sex relationships. Migratory moves in the later years of their relationship were driven by the demands of their separate working lives but there was evidence also that the need to look after their relationship was a high consideration in plans they made, at least from the testimony that Duncan provided in his interview.

Love travel is not an exclusively gay activity. It does not happen to everyone and for those on the move sexual adventure need not transform into a relationship. When it does, however, it can affect the course of the working lives of one or both parties. Here the discussion related to how two men, representatives of a larger group, travelled with their partners and how this affected their working lives. For gay people, the presence or absence of legal recognition afforded to same-sex relationships affects whether they can settle in the country where they met and began their relationship or return to the home country of one or other partner and live there. This was a formative factor in the love travel that Duncan and his partner undertook for more than 20 years. Legal recognition of same-sex relationships is slowly becoming more common in advanced economies as well as in some developing ones and as it does so

3 Working Lives of Men Aged 45–60   103

the difference will diminish and most likely disappear. In the next section, the focus turns to the narrative introduced in the previous chapter, which was found to be relevant also for men from this age cohort, work-as-work.

Work-as-Work

This narrative refers to work understood as something one does when one finishes school or university to support self or partner and/or family. When in the 1970s Sennett and Cobb examined what motivated automobile factory-workers in the USA, they found that the men worked in order to provide the means for their children to enjoy better lives than had been available to them.[31] When grown up, their children, some of whom Sennett interviewed in the 1990s, were not working in factories like their fathers but in white-collar jobs. Unlike their fathers, however, they were consumed by anxiety and apprehensions about the future.[32] Media reports of 'burn-out' or workplace stress would suggest that emotional or intellectual fulfilment is not a common feature of the lives of the average worker in the 2010s.[33] And perhaps the idea that work can bring either is something that only a very small minority of workers expect to enjoy, such as those working in the arts or in intellectual disciplines.

The six men whose work histories were connected by the pragmatic, 'no-nonsense' approach to work, were employed in a range of organisations including multi-national corporations, media, property and the professions. Four of the men were in their 50s and two in their 40s and they came from Auckland, Hong Kong, London, Melbourne and New York.[34] All but one were interested in making money rather than in the intrinsic satisfaction of their jobs. The interviewee who was not saw work as a means to being able to afford to live, pay his mortgage. Their work histories are represented here by accounts from the working lives of two men who were living in London, Tate (aged 51) and Ethan (aged 49).

Tate was one of the richest men interviewed for this book and lived in London. Born and educated in the USA, he had spent a large part

104   P. Robinson

of his adult life living and working in Europe. By virtue of his working history and income, he would be described as a member of the corporate-professional, international elite. When he finished his university studies, Tate resolved to leave the USA. His reasons were neither common nor mundane as the following extract testifies:

> The most important thing I realised was that I did not want to be in America because everyone I knew had gone to an Ivy League school, had read the same books, and thought the same things. They were not thinking about them in a particularly original or interesting way and ... there was sort of a cloud coming down over America, political correctness and intellectual terrorism, and I wanted to be different so I had to leave America.

It was the end of the 1970s and he was able to take advantage of the change to work practices that the advent of personal computers brought about, found convenient, well-paid, casual work in New York that enabled him to spend long working holidays in Paris where he said he wrote a novel each year he was there. After his 'American in Paris' experience, he began work as a fashion photographer and remained in Paris until his mid 30s when he moved to eastern Europe to begin a new phase of his career in magazines. Tate said the following about his time as a fashion photographer:

> I worked for seven years in Paris as a fashion photographer just long enough to sort of claim success and run away because it really was not something I was all that interested in. I love taking pictures but I did not like fashion and I just wanted to do it long enough so that I could claim that I had been successful and stop. I realised that I did not like doing it before I realised that I could quit with my head held high.

What made this somewhat gilded career an example of the work-as-work narrative? Partly that he had up to ten different jobs including university jobs between the ages of 20 and 35, but mainly that Tate's attitude to work was matter of fact, even cynical. Because he expressed no illusions, held no expectations about work, his working history was

3 Working Lives of Men Aged 45–60   105

an exemplar of the work-as-work narrative. He was pragmatic in his approach to work, able, possibly because of his privilege, to choose work that suited him and regard it as nothing. An attitude understandable in a worker in a factory or sweat shop who has little influence over the pace or nature of his/her working day but strange in a person born to privilege and able to work abroad in a city like Paris and exercise choice in terms of location and occupation. He explained also in his interview that at one point in his early adult life he travelled to Africa to live in relatively impoverished circumstances:

> I rented a hut on a beach in a sort of hotel, not really a luxury hotel. It was [Africa] … it is still quite Third World, not luxury travel or anything, anyway … an air-conditioned hut on the beach and lived there for a month all by myself … I wanted to do this because I wanted to see if I was a failure. If I would not find love, if I would not find a career, if I would not be successful in my career and successful in love, successful in all of the things that society would be judging me on, would I still be happy with myself? And at the end of the month the answer was yes. I mean I do not think I would have gone and done it if I had not known the answer was yes in the first place.

Only people with means of escape can risk testing their self-reliance as Tate said he did in Africa as a young man. What he described reminded me of popular television programmes where young westerners test their emotional and physical strength in Third World locations 'off the beaten track'. In the end, though, they get up and leave and the deprivations they endured become a distant memory of how they tested themselves and whether or not they were made of the 'right stuff'.

The second interviewee whose working history exemplified the work-as-work narrative came also from a privileged background and was living in London also as an expatriate when interviewed.

Ethan was brought up in a relatively privileged, extended, family in South Asia. When young, his parents and siblings migrated to New Zealand. After university and for almost 20 years, he worked as a waiter until his late 30s:

I did as a means to an end … to live rather than the other way round. That came to an end for a number of reasons including problems with … osteoarthritis which is also known as 'waiter's knee' but largely because when as I approached 40 I just thought it was starting to get a bit boring, even though I enjoyed the time and the freedom and all of that sort of thing.

As previously mentioned, Ethan was one of the few interviewees from the sample who saw work as the means to living a life. His interest in classical music and opera suggested that in his case work was the means to living a 'good' life in the sense the ancient Greeks understood it. When he broke from the catering industry, he did not work for six years, managing to keep his head above water and live in London. After his period of 'time out', he found work as an office manager, which enabled him to secure his life in London:

It's maddening and exhausting and I am paid a little bit more than I am worth. It is very tiring and I like the people I work with but I don't really enjoy it, so it is something I do so that I can afford to live and go to concerts and do the things I like doing. Having a permanent job made a big difference in getting a mortgage and things like that, so yes that is my work life; nothing to write about.

Ethan's material circumstances were straightened by comparison with Tate who never really experienced privation or had to worry about funding a mortgage.

Social or Political Change

The work histories of five men were notable for a social or political change narrative running through them.[35] This was understood to be work that contributed to social change or greater equality either explicitly or implicitly. Men with such jobs worked in the HIV-AIDS field as activists or as employees in programmes designed to improve the lot of people living with HIV-AIDS (PLWHA), others who worked on projects for governments at any level that increased social equality or

3 Working Lives of Men Aged 45–60 107

reduced inequalities in income or wealth and men who worked at the shop front to assist homeless people in urban centres. In the previous chapter, an intersection was noted between men's jobs characterised by care and also by social or political change. This was especially the case for men who worked in the HIV-AIDS field: the reason being that, because the identity of gay men and PLWHA was in the 1980s and 1990s conflated with the virus, any care work had a political dimension. And the work that gay men did then to care for their own promoted social and political change that gave rise to a stronger GLB community and the means to negotiate better, more equitable relations with the mainstream—evidence for which can be seen in the success in many liberal societies of marriage equality (Australia being the notable exception).

A brief account follows of the connection between the personal experience of each man and the work he did to contribute to social or political change. As mentioned in the earlier section on care, Marvin (aged 52) began working on the AIDS project in California at the outbreak of the AIDS epidemic in the USA in the early 1980s. Once this work finished, he moved on to other non-profit fields which became his life's work. One negative aspect to work in non-profit organisations was, according to Marvin, the relatively low pay, which he called a 'vow of poverty'.

Fifty-three-year-old Hilton had experience also with non-profit organisations working to support gay men. When interviewed, he was working for an organisation that assisted homeless men in New York, some of whom were HIV-positive or reformed drug addicts. He came to the job via his own experiences in prison after being convicted of drug trafficking and where he contracted HIV.

> I re-joined society and became a social worker ... because that was really the first opportunity available to me and ... today I work for a minority, not for profit, as a case manager and I have 30 clients who are all struggling to get their life on track.

His understanding of the route by which he came to his new career was notable for being largely positive, acknowledging the benefits he gained from rehabilitation in prison.

108 P. Robinson

Two men from Manchester complete the group of four whose personal experience led them to work for social and/or political justice. The first Mancunian was Ben whose working history included a spell with an HIV-AIDS-focused organisation staffed by gay men was discussed in depth in the section above on care. The second man from Manchester was Eddie (aged 45) who was working also in higher education when interviewed. His early career was in occupations including as a chef and then a delivery man. He too enrolled in postgraduate studies in Manchester and a special focus of his doctoral and postdoctoral studies was the living conditions and capacities of small working-class communities. His postgraduate studies reflected his own background in rural Lancashire.

The man whose working history included evidence of strong commitment to social and/or political justice which was not based on personal experience was 52-year-old Mike from Melbourne. His working life is here discussed in more detail. Mike is a high-flyer. He started work immediately on finishing an undergraduate degree and worked in New York and Washington for an international firm of consultants. When he returned to Australia, a socially progressive Labor Government had been elected, led by Bob Hawke, and Mike found work in one of the major policy departments of the federal public service in Canberra and then moved into the not-for-profit sector. When a reformist government was elected in the state of Victoria, he resumed work as a bureaucrat, this time in the Victorian public service. This was followed by another period with the not-for-profit sector.

In some ways, Mike's career path is a model one for a progressive member of the baby-boomer generation, engaging in public policy when reformist governments were elected to office and between time working in the not-for-profit sector. When I asked him what he liked about work, he said the following:

> I think the variety … In some respects, I was fortunate to be in organisations at times of very great change. The Hawke [federal] government … [had] the wages and incomes accord and all of that … And even with the election of the Bracks [Labor] government [in Victoria] and their focus on industry and community consultation and engagement and a more outward-looking public service.

3 Working Lives of Men Aged 45–60   109

I too had lived through these signal times of change in Australia and Victoria and asked Mike whether a commitment to social change drove his choice of work. His answer mostly confirmed my suspicion that he was a social reformer at heart:

> I think so … When I did my Honours degree in Economics my thesis was on … the developing world and … that was a focus which pushed me into areas where … [the focus was on] service to the community before oneself. And so … trying to … [be] involved in organisations and raising their profile in terms of how they inter-related with the rest of the world not just the community was an interesting challenge.

Men with personal experience of discrimination or disadvantage formed the majority of those from this group. Three men had found jobs in HIV-AIDS focused organisations at some point during the first 15 years of the epidemic in the West. One man who had been a crystal methamphetamine addict and dealer worked in a not-for-profit organisation supporting homeless men and former drug addicts. And one man with experience of material disadvantage had worked with impoverished communities in a former coal-mining district.

There was evidence in the narratives just discussed of similarities and differences with those examined in the previous chapter, some of which suggesting generational change in the type of work gay men took and how they understood it. The care narrative explained the work of more men from this cohort than the older cohort. And the type of care work they did differed: this cohort demonstrated a stronger inclination to help men like themselves, which in part was explained by their being at the centre of the HIV-AIDS crisis. Travel was a new narrative to explain some of this age cohort's working histories. Its most novel aspect was that love can inspire work for travel and while travelling. Classics' scholars would most likely baulk at this claim and cite the Trojan Wars as an early example of love as a catalyst for work and travel and medieval scholars the Crusades.

My claim is a smaller one and relates to the relatively recent evolution of international relationships and relationships developed while travelling in the age of mass transit: something that was either not available

110   P. Robinson

to the men from the old cohort or not represented in the working lives from the sample used for this book. The work-as-work narrative was present for this cohort but slightly less significant than it had been in the previous chapter. Social or political change was present also and likewise explained the working lives of a relatively small number of men. What was slightly different this time was that the intersection between the care narrative and the social-or-political-change narrative was clearer, more apparent; the reason being that more men from this cohort worked in HIV-AIDS-related fields where care work was political work because of how the disease was then understood.

Being 'Out' at Work

As mentioned several times, coming out is not something that occurs only once or is resolved the moment the gay person declares his or her sexuality. It is a process that can take time and takes place over time. There are people who never come out or never have to come out but these are mostly a relatively small minority.[36] The majority of gay people live with the assumption that almost everyone lives with from infancy, which is that they are straight children of straight parents, an assumption with which children of gay parents might have to live as well. In an earlier work on three generations of Australian gay men, I argued that each of the generations or age cohorts experienced coming out differently.[37] The men from the first age cohort, who were born between 1920s and 1940s, belonged to what the Australian Bureau of Statistics called the 'Lucky' generation. Many of these men spent their lives closeted, married or alone. When they did come out, it was privately and mostly to close friends or into the world of clandestine gay clubs and other meeting places.[38]

The second age cohort comprised men born between 1940s and 1960s, the baby boomers, who are the subject of this chapter. They were the first generation of gay men to try coming out publicly. Not all tried and not all succeeded and some found encouragement from the injunctions of gay liberationists, to be 'out and proud'.[39] In the previous chapter, I argued that only a small number of men aged 60 and over related

3 Working Lives of Men Aged 45–60   111

stories about their sexuality and its effect on their job or career because most kept their sexuality a secret. None of the men aged 60 and over from the international Anglophone sample had spoken of sexuality in relation to their jobs or careers. As mentioned, in order to discuss being out in the workplace in that chapter, I drew on examples of three men from the all-Australian sample. For this chapter, there were three men from the international Anglophone sample who raised the matter when relating their work history.

All three who spoke of sexuality in relation to work were in their 50s; two were from Auckland and one was an expatriate living in Hong Kong.[40] One man related a horrific story while the other men's stories were of relative acceptance and tolerance. Their accounts are discussed in order.

When relating his work history, 57-year-old Austin included an account of the humiliation he experienced when 'outed' at work. Homophobic murders and bashings are worse, of course, but Austin experienced a particularly nasty form of regular, public, intimidation and humiliation. Without exception, it was the worst account of homophobia related by any man from the combined all-Australian sample ($n = 80$) and international Anglophone sample ($n = 82$) that are used in this book.

Born and brought up in a small, rural township in New Zealand, Austin married, as many men did in the 1970s, as soon as he was out of school. He found a job locally where the only available work was agriculturally based. By the time he was in his 30s, Austin had a responsible position as an inspector in livestock processing plants where knives were standard work issue for employees cutting animal carcases. Married with children but discovered at a beat looking for male-to-male sex, the word quickly spread.

> I would get to work ... and the knives would start tapping. They would tap to the tune 'da da da da da da da, doo da, doo da' but when it got to the whole 40 people in one area they would be [singing] 'Austin takes it up the arse, doo da, doo da'.

He received zero support from owners of plants he had to visit for inspection. His wife disowned him and forbade him access to their

112   P. Robinson

children, all of which combined to push him over the edge and seriously affect his mental health:

> None of the bosses would react in a … [supportive] manner. They just thought it was a joke. It became very dangerous situation, especially with knives. And that is why I left … I was a mess. Just a mess.

Elsewhere, I have written about Austin's fatherhood experience and how when they came of age his children sought him out, re-established kinship bonds, and became his staunchest supporters.[41] His experience of homophobic bullying did not end when he left small-town New Zealand. Twenty years later and after a complete change of career, Austin again found himself the target of homophobia in the workplace. On this occasion it was a large school in a suburban setting.

> I had to go through all that again as a principal of a school where my employers would say, 'Get out of our school you fucking fag' or 'You AIDS-ridden bastard' nearly every day for nearly a year. And in 2008, I tried to commit suicide.

I was unable to verify Austin's account of the abuse he experienced in either workplace and accepted his versions as given. In relation to the second account, he said that the matter was before the Human Rights Commission and would soon be heard. The employers he referred to were members of the school council. At the time of interview, he was working for a not-for-profit, GLBT, support group in Auckland. His manager confirmed his version of events.

The two occasions of homophobic abuse that Austin said he experienced were separated by at least 20 years. The first occurred in the 1980s and was more physically threatening because of the real threat the tapping knives represented. It was also a symbolic expulsion from two groups of males: those who were his neighbours and those with whom he shared workplaces. His wife's rejection pronounced him unfit as a heterosexual male. As he said, he was left 'a mess'. The second occasion was during the time when New Zealanders were publicly debating same-sex marriage and prior to the New Zealand Parliament's passing a

3 Working Lives of Men Aged 45–60   113

Bill in favour of marriage equality. It did not occur in small-town New Zealand but symbolically represented expulsion again, this time by colleagues in the school where he was principal.[42] During the interview, Austin did not mention if the colleagues were male or female and I did not ask for details. On both occasions of homophobic abuse, his authority was defied and he was publicly humiliated. I would argue that this occurred because he challenged notions of acceptable masculinity, which, as Raewyn Connell has long argued, cannot include gay men, especially in leadership positions.[43]

The other accounts of being out at work were markedly different from Austin's. One man worked in a creative profession and lived with his long-term partner in Hong Kong. He said the following about being out in the workplace:

> I am an architect and I have been practising for over 30 years … Work-wise, as a profession, it is a sort of artistic profession where it is okay to be gay so there are not a lot of negative pressure or problems. I have never had any problems that way and I find it very interesting work.

The second man, Nathan from Auckland, had a career comprising different jobs in New Zealand and overseas. Like many gay men, he was a serial monogamist who had had a number of partners by age 50, the time of his interview. On being out in the workplace, he said of his early experience: 'My first partner was a waiter … He was also a customs officer, so he was a little bit more closeted than I was. I had never actually really hidden it myself'. One of his very first jobs was in a food factory. He recalled that then, which was the late 1970s, the gay and lesbian workers were in a majority: 'when I started … there were three gay boys working in the laboratories and one lesbian and there was a staff of twelve so we outnumbered the straights'. Nathan was aware that his experience did not mirror everyone's and that he had experienced only extremely mild forms of homophobia.

> You would get the odd wolf whistle or something like that to be silly but most people seemed to be more inquisitive than anything … We played on the company's soccer team and basketball team … so it confused them

114   P. Robinson

at first … I have never had a problem in that sense, unlike so many other people I know … And even … when I was travelling I think I was in the job about three days and the boss who was a notoriously well-known womanizer just came straight out and said, 'You're gay aren't you?' And I said, 'Yeah.' And he said, 'Oh that's cool. I thought you might've been.' [*Laughs*] Because he was so busy looking at women [*Laughs*].

The fact that Nathan and fellow gay workmates played in the factory sports team and that he and his womanising boss could talk about his homosexuality suggests sexual power can flow in different directions and that heterosexual males' dominance can be challenged or ignored.

The accounts from these three men are evidence of both social opposition to sexual difference and a degree of social acceptance in the lives of men born between 1950 and the early 1960s and who were in a position to come out during the time of gay liberation. The examples of opposition in the men's stories ranged from extreme to mild. If indicative of gay men's experience more generally, they reinforce the argument of Norbert Elias that social change does not occur uniformly nor at once and at the same time but sporadically and by small increments and that new fashions, ideas, practices first begin in the upper classes and then make their way through the rest of society.[44] The persistence of severe homophobia in some rural districts and country towns has been the focus of previous research and is generally accepted to be a feature of relative social isolation and lack of education.[45] It generally accompanies also 'red-neck' attitudes toward gender roles and marriage.

Conclusion

This chapter examined four principal work narratives that shaped the working lives of the men from the middle cohort, aged 45–60 when interviewed. The narratives were 'care', 'travel', 'work-as-work' and 'social or political change'. They mirrored three of the principal narratives identified in the work histories for the men aged 60 and over and included an additional one. The additional narrative concerned travel and work which I argued became a feature of this age cohort's working

3 Working Lives of Men Aged 45–60   115

lives because they came of age at a time of relative affluence when major advances were occurring in mass, long-haul, air transport.

The care narrative was visible in the working histories of the men from the 60-and-over age cohort discussed in the previous chapter as well as those of the men from this chapter's cohort. There was a difference, however, which was that it is more common in the 45–60 cohort. There are a number of reasons for this including the growth in the number of caring occupations that occurred in the 1970s as state-funded or in the case of the USA private-funded health care expanded and assumed a more central role in the lives of the citizens of developed economies. Corresponding with this was an increased acceptance of such jobs as being appropriate for male workers, where previously because of traditional understandings of gender roles it was assumed only female workers would be interested in or willing to undertake care work. For some of the men from the 45–60 age cohort, the HIV-AIDS epidemic affected their coming out or adulthood and was also a reason for taking on a career in health care.

Travel was the new narrative. It was mentioned in passing in the previous chapter when the working history of one man included elements of 'love travel'. In this chapter, it was more significant for reasons relating to affluence, the availability of relatively inexpensive plane tickets, the baby boomers' belief in the spiritual or self-realisation potential of travel and, in the case of gay men in Australia and New Zealand, the chance to escape the limitations of small towns or the suburbs and being able to 'find themselves' or come out or get lots of sex in foreign places where they were not known.

The work-as-work narrative represented the working histories of less than a quarter of the men from the baby-boomer cohort. In the previous chapter, where this narrative was also present, matter-of-fact jobs that people do 'to pay the bills' were in offices, factories, hospitals, schools, small businesses or warehouses. The men from the 45–60 age cohort whose working histories were shaped by the work-as-work narrative were employed in media, multi-national corporations, property, and the professions, so entirely white collar occupations. When asked what they enjoyed about work, they said that making money or making ends meet made it enjoyable, so they had no illusions about what

116   P. Robinson

it offered. The two men whose accounts were representative of the group came from relatively privileged backgrounds, one more so than the other. Despite their privilege, neither appeared to resent having to work, accepted its inevitability, outlining the steps in their careers without embellishment.

In this chapter as in the previous one, the work histories of only a small group of men were shaped around the impulse to effect social or political change. The working histories of five men from the 45–60 age cohort were in this category and four of these got involved in work contributing to social change or greater equality as a result of personal experience of disadvantage. Three worked in HIV-AIDS-related fields and the fourth on improving social and material capacity of working-class communities. The men who committed time and labour to helping with the HIV-AIDS epidemic responded to a once-in-a-century crisis that chiefly affected gay men in the West and as I explained elsewhere was seen at the time as a remarkable response to a health emergency by communities of men. The fifth man devoted a large part of his life to effecting social or political change from a personal belief in equality and social reform.

Gay men knew decades before the rest of the population that the stereotypes about their working lives being limited to jobs as hair dressers, waiters or airline stewards were as far from the truth as other stereotypes about our being sex obsessed or destined to live lonely lives of quiet desperation. But it was and is a powerful stereotype which I would argue underpins the reason why not one professional player of Australian Rules football has ever been prepared to come out. In Australia, the game has a mythic status, is strongly associated with heroic versions of masculinity and glories in strong homo-social ties between present and past players and club officials.[46] Gay men know and have friends who work in factories, laboratories, automobile dealerships and repair shops, who wash windows hanging from platforms on office towers and have served in the armed forces in times of war and peace. This chapter has shown men working in education at all levels, health care, not-for-profit organisations, and earning very large incomes in international corporate professions. None from this age cohort worked in effeminate occupations, which might say something about the sample and who answered my call for interview and perhaps also the men from this generation who were schooled in the no-nonsense masculinity of the 1950s and 1960s and either conformed or learned how to pass.

In the second section of the chapter, the stories of three men were examined for the effect their sexuality had on their job, career or sense of self. The material was sobering. Excerpts from the life stories of two men in their 50s showed that social change had brought benefits for some gay men. The story of the third man who was from small-town New Zealand was evidence to support the central argument that Norbert Elias made in *Civilizing Processes*, which was that social improvement is neither uniform nor universal. The man's story presented a paradox about how it is possible in a country that led the world in legalising same-sex marriage has space also for citizens who have no fear in using Old Testament views of homosexuality to berate and denounce a gay man in authority, a paradox that is in no way peculiar to New Zealand and could occur in any liberal democracy.

Notes

1. They belong to what the Australian Bureau of Statistics defined as the 'Baby Boomer' generation (born 1946–1966), see Australian Bureau of Statistics (2006) 'From Generation to generation' in *A Picture of the Nation* (Canberra: Australian Bureau of Statistics): http://www.ausstats. abs.gov.au/Ausstats/subscriber.nsf/0/FCB1A3CF0893DAE4CA2575 4C0013D844/$File/20700_generation.pdf accessed 4 January 2017 (Australian Bureau of Statistics 2006).
2. For the economic revolution Friedman's theories unleashed when used to steer monetary policy in UK and USA, see, for example, P. Krugman (2007) 'Who was Milton Friedman?' *New York Review of Books* http:// www.nybooks.com/articles/2007/02/15/who-was-milton-friedman/ accessed 20 March 2016 (Krugman 2007).
3. A 2016 scandal in England underlining the effect on workers of the gradual erosion of work rights and entitlements and security of employment was played out in the pages of *The Guardian*. See this account of the case of Sports Direct and their treatment of employees: S. Goodley and G. Ruddick (2016) 'Sports Direct's Mike Ashley admits

paying staff less than minimum wage', *The Guardian*: https://www.theguardian.com/business/2016/jun/07/sports-direct-agrees-back-pay-deal-with-hmrc-minimum-wage accessed 8 June 2016 (Goodley and Ruddick 2016).

4. Eddie (aged 45); Tate (aged 51) London.

5. See Appendix 2.

6. In US dollars as for 2010.

7. US$200,000 in 2009 would be worth approximately US$223,876 in 2016; source: Historical Currency Conversions, https://futureboy.us/fsp/dollar.fsp accessed 24 November 2016. See Chap. 2 for a fuller account of change in value of interviewees' approximate incomes 2009–2016.

8. See Appendices 2 and 4.

9. Raymond (aged 58) Hong Kong; Issac (aged 56) Sydney; Hilton (aged 53) New York; Mike (aged 52) Melbourne; Everett (aged 49) New York; Fred (aged 47) London; Alvin (aged 47) New York; Timothy (aged 46) New York.

10. http://www.poheritage.com/our-history/company-guides/peninsular-and-oriental-steam-navigation-company accessed 13 January 2016.

11. http://archivescollection.anu.edu.au/index.php/burns-philp-and-company-limited accessed 13 January 2016; http://archivescollection.anu.edu.au/index.php/dbumc accessed 13 January 2016.

12. Ryan (aged 53) London; Zachary (aged 52) Hong Kong; Tate (aged 51) London; Earl (aged 51) New York; Calvin (aged 51) Melbourne; Buck (aged 51) Hong Kong; Danny (aged 48) Hong Kong; Duncan (aged 47) Hong Kong.

13. Ward (aged 59) New York; Austin (aged 57) Auckland; Ben (aged 52) Manchester; Carl (aged 49) Auckland; Jude (aged 46) Los Angeles; Eddie (aged 45) Manchester.

14. Bernard (aged 59) Hong Kong; Marvin (aged 59) Los Angeles; Cam (aged 56) Los Angeles; Logan (aged 56) Auckland; Nathan (aged 50) Auckland; Ethan (aged 49) London.

15. F. Bongiorno (2012) *The Sex Lives of Australians: A History* (Melbourne: Black Inc.), pp. 293–295 (Bongiorno 2012).

16. For details of reaction to AIDS in early 1980s, see P. Robinson (2008b) *The Changing World of Gay Men* (Basingstoke and New York: Palgrave Macmillan), pp. 55–62 (Robinson 2008b).

17. Bernard (aged 59) Hong Kong; Marvin (aged 59) Los Angeles; Raymond (aged 59) Hong Kong; Ward (aged 59) New York; Austin

(aged 57) Auckland; Isaac (aged 56) Sydney; Hilton (aged 53) New York; Ben (aged 52) Manchester; Mike (52) Melbourne; Buck (aged 51) Hong Kong; Alvin (aged 47) New York; Fred (aged 47) London; Timothy (aged 46) New York; Eddie (aged 45) Manchester.

18. P. Robinson (2013) *Gay Men's Relationships Across the Life Course* (Basingstoke and New York: Palgrave Macmillan), pp. 145–164 (Robinson 2013).

19. The long-standing, gay community response to the threat gay men faced from the sexual transmission of HIV-AIDS was to recommend they use condoms when having anonymous sex or when the HIV status of the other man was not known. This continued well into the 2000s. In the late 1990s, a drug was available to men who had had unsafe sex and suspected they were at risk of contracting the virus. The treatment was known as post-exposure prophylaxis or PEP. In 2010s, some gay activists and drug companies began lobbying governments to introduce trials of a drug that could be taken before men engaged in risky sex. This costly treatment is known as pre-exposure prophylaxis or PrEP. In 2016, the Victorian state government agreed to fund an extended trial of PrEP for 2500 people at risk of HIV infection. As this article explains, for some time now gay men have been buying the drug on line (B. Priess, 'Thousands to get access to new HIV drug', *The Age*, 30 January 2016: http://www.theage.com.au/victoria/thousands-to-get-access-to-new-hiv-drug-20160129-gmgwda.html accessed 31 January 2016). In May 2016, the British National Health Service announced that it would not fund PrEP, see N. Khomani (2016) *The Guardian* 'NHS refusal to find HIV prevention is shameful, say charities': http://www.theguardian.com/society/2016/may/31/nhs-refusal-fund-hiv-aids-prevention-treatment-shameful-say-charities accessed 1 June 2016 (Priess 2016; Khomani 2016).

20. E. Fee and D. M. Fox (eds) (1988) *AIDS: The Burdens of History* (Berkeley: University of California Press); E. Fee and D. M. Fox (eds) (1992) *AIDS: The Making of a Chronic Disease* (Berkeley: University of California Press) (Fee and Fox 1988, 1992).

21. A. McLaren (1999) *Twentieth Century Sexuality: A History* (Oxford: Blackwell Publishers Ltd), pp. 194ff (McLaren 1999).

22. Robinson *The Changing World*, pp. 57–62.

23. P. Robinson and P. Geldens (2014) 'Stories of Two Generations of Australian Gay Men Living in the Presence of HIV-AIDS' in *Journal of*

Australian Studies, vol. 38, no. 2, pp. 233–245 (Robinson and Geldens 2014).

24. N. Elias and J. L. Scotson (1994, 1977) *The Established and The Outsiders: A Sociological Enquiry into Community Problems*, 2nd edn (London: Sage Publications Ltd.) (Elias and Scotson 1994, 1977).

25. Robinson *The Changing World*, pp. 43–46.

26. See, for example, Robinson *The Changing World*, pp. 72–94; P. Simpson (2013) 'Alienation, Ambivalence, Agency: Middle-aged Gay Men and Ageism in Manchester's Gay Village', *Sexualities* 16: 283–299 (Robinson 2008b; Simpson 2013).

27. European backpackers are now a common feature in inner suburbs of Australian cities and on farms and in rural towns, at tourist resorts, and in Australian rain forests and wilderness reserves. This has not always been the case and the Australian Bureau of Tourism Research began counting their numbers only in the mid to late 1980s. The reverse process, of young Australians travelling overseas with a back pack, peaked in the 1960s and 1970s when Australian backpackers were a common feature in European cities and islands of the Mediterranean.

28. A. Sobocinska and R. White (2015) 'Travel and Connections' in A. Bashford and S. Macintyre (eds) *The Cambridge History of Australia Vol 2: The Commonwealth of Australia* (Port Melbourne: Cambridge University Press), pp. 488–491 (Sobocinska and White 2015).

29. Logan (aged 56) Auckland; Ryan (aged 53) London; Calvin (aged 51) Melbourne; Nathan (aged 50) Auckland; Everett (aged 49) New York; Duncan (aged 47) Hong Kong.

30. Ryan (aged 53) London; Calvin (aged 51) Melbourne; Nathan (aged 50) Auckland; Everett (aged 49) New York; Duncan (aged 47) Hong Kong.

31. R. Sennett and J. Cobb (1993, 1972) *The Hidden Injuries of Class* (New York: Alfred Knopf) (Sennett and Cobb 1993, 1972).

32. R. Sennett (1998) *The Corrosion of Character: The Personal Consequences of Work in the New Capitalism* (New York: W.W. Norton & Company) (Sennett 1998).

33. See, for example, D. Andalo (2012) 'Time to talk about workplace stress', *The Guardian*: https://www.theguardian.com/careers/careersblog/workplace-stress accessed 5 January 2017; Campbell (2015) 'NHS workplace stress could push 80% of senior doctors to early retirement', *The Guardian*: https://www.theguardian.com/society/2015/sep/10/

nhs-lose-80-per-cent-senior-doctors-workplace-stress accessed 5 January 2017 (Andalo 2012; Campbell 2015).

34. Calvin (aged 51) Melbourne; Earl (aged 51) New York; Tate (aged 51) London; Nathan (aged 50) Auckland; Ethan (aged 49) London; Danny (aged 48) Hong Kong.
35. Marvin (aged 59) Los Angeles; Hilton (aged 53) New York; Ben (aged 52) Manchester; Mike (aged 52) Melbourne; Eddie (aged 45) Manchester.
36. For discussion of older gay men who never came out or never had to come out, see P. Robinson (2008a) 'Older Gay Men's Recollections of Anti-homosexual Prejudice in Australia' in S. Robinson (ed.) *Homophobia: an Australian History* (Sydney: Federation Press), pp. 218–235 and Robinson *The Changing World*, pp. 29–30, 47–48 (Robinson 2008a, b).
37. Robinson *The Changing World*.
38. Robinson *The Changing World*, pp. 26–34.
39. Robinson *The Changing World*, pp. 43–52.
40. Austin (aged 57) Auckland; Zachary (aged 52) Hong Kong; Nathan (aged 50) Auckland.
41. Robinson *Gay Men's Relationships*, pp. 94–95.
42. D. Schwartz (2013) 'NZ legalises same-sex marriage', Australian Broadcasting Corporation, http://www.abc.net.au/news/2013-04-17/nz-legalises-same-sex-marriage/4635086 accessed 18 March 2016 (Schwartz 2013).
43. See, for example, R. W. Connell (1997) 'Gender Politics for Men' in *International Journal of Sociology and Social Policy*, 17, 1/2, pp. 62–77 and R. W. Connell (2003) 'Introduction: Australian masculinities' in S. Tomsen and M. Donaldson (eds) *Male Trouble: looking at Australian Masculinities* (Melbourne: Pluto Press), pp. 9–21 (Connell 1997, 2003).
44. E. Norbert (2000, 1939) *The Civilizing Process: sociogenetic and psychogenetic investigations*, trans. E. Jephcott with some notes and corrections by the author, ed. E. Dunning, J. Goudsblom and S. Mennell, rev. edn, Oxford: Blackwell Publishers Ltd., *passim* (Norbert 2000, 1939).
45. S. Tomsen (2002) *Hatred, murder and male honour: anti-homosexual homicides in NSW*, 1980–2000 (Canberra: Australian Institute of Criminology), pp. 32–42 (Tomsen 2002).

46. The major football code in Victoria, Tasmania, Western Australia and South Australia, Australian Rules originally began as a contest in Melbourne between suburban teams when it was known as the Victorian Football League. Teams from the other states were included in the competition in the 1980s and 1990s as the League sought a stronger national orientation. It is like neither soccer nor rugby but a fast moving game during which players may run with the ball, bounce it, and kick it to other players. For more on mythic status of Australian Rules football, see D. Williamson (1978) *The Club* (Sydney: Currency Press Pty. Ltd.) (Williamson 1978).

References

Andalo, D. 2012. Time to Talk About Workplace Stress. *The Guardian*. https://www.theguardian.com/careers/careers-blog/workplace-stress. Accessed 5 Jan 2017.

Australian Bureau of Statistics. 2006. From Generation to Generation. In *A Picture of the Nation*. Canberra: Australian Bureau of Statistics. http://www.ausstats.abs.gov.au/Ausstats/subscriber.nsf/0/FCB1A3CF0893DAE4CA257 54C0013D844/$File/20700_generation.pdf. Accessed 4 Jan 2017.

Bongiorno, F. 2012. *The Sex Lives of Australians: A History*. Melbourne: Black Inc.

Campbell, D. 2015. NHS Workplace Stress Could Push 80% of Senior Doctors to Early Retirement. *The Guardian*. https://www.theguardian.com/society/2015/sep/10/nhs-lose-80-per-cent-senior-doctors-workplace-stress. Accessed 5 Jan 2017.

Connell, R.W. 1997. Gender Politics for Men. *International Journal of Sociology and Social Policy* 17 (1/2): 62–77.

Connell, R.W. 2003. Introduction: Australian masculinities. In *Male Trouble: Looking at Australian Masculinities*, ed. S. Tomsen, and M. Donaldson, 9–21. Melbourne: Pluto Press.

Elias, N. 2000, 1939. *The Civilizing Process: Sociogenetic and Psychogenetic Investigations*, trans. ed. E. Jephcott with some notes and corrections by the author, eds. E. Dunning, J. Goudsblom, and S. Mennell, rev. (eds.). Oxford: Blackwell Publishers Ltd.

Elias, N., and J.L. Scotson. 1994, 1977. *The Established and the Outsiders: A Sociological Enquiry into Community Problems*, 2nd ed. London: Sage.

Fee, E., and D.M. Fox (eds.). 1988. *AIDS: The Burdens of History.* Berkeley: University of California Press.

Fee, E., and D.M. Fox (eds.). 1992. *AIDS: The Making of a Chronic Disease.* Berkeley: University of California Press.

Goodley, S., and Ruddick, G. 2016. Sports Direct's Mike Ashley Admits Paying Staff Less Than Minimum Wage. *The Guardian.* https://www.theguardian.com/business/2016/jun/07/sports-direct-agrees-back-pay-deal-with-hmrc-minimum-wage. Accessed 8 June 2016.

Khomani, N. 2016. NHS Refusal to Find HIV Prevention Is Shameful, Say Charities. *The Guardian.*http://www.theguardian.com/society/2016/may/31/nhs-refusal-fund-hiv-aids-prevention-treatment-shameful-say-charities. *Accessed 1 June 2016.*

Krugman, P. 2007. Who Was Milton Friedman? *New York Review of Books.* http://www.nybooks.com/articles/2007/02/15/who-was-milton-friedman/. Accessed 20 Mar 2016.

McLaren, A. 1999. *Twentieth Century Sexuality: A History.* Oxford: Blackwell Publishers Ltd.

Priess, B. 2016. Thousands to Get Access to New HIV Drug. *The Age*, Jan 30. http://www.theage.com.au/victoria/thousands-to-get-access-to-new-hiv-drug-20160129-gmgwda.html. Accessed 31 Jan 2016.

Robinson, P. 2008a. Older Gay Men's Recollections of Anti-Homosexual Prejudice in Australia. In *Homophobia: An Australian History*, ed. S. Robinson, 218–235. Sydney: Federation Press.

Robinson, P. 2008b. *The Changing World of Gay Men.* Basingstoke: Palgrave Macmillan.

Robinson, P. 2013. *Gay Men's Relationships Across the Life Course.* Basingstoke: Palgrave Macmillan.

Robinson, P., and P. Geldens. 2014. Stories of Two Generations of Australian Gay Men Living in the Presence of HIV-AIDS. *Journal of Australian Studies* 38 (2): 233–245.

Schwartz, D. 2013. NZ Legalises Same-Sex Marriage. *Australian Broadcasting Corporation*.http://www.abc.net.au/news/2013-04-17/nz-legalises-same-sex-marriage/4635086. Accessed 18 Mar 2016.

Sennett, R. 1998. *The Corrosion of Character: The Personal Consequences of Work in the New Capitalism.* New York: W.W. Norton & Company.

Sennett, R., and Cobb, J. 1993, 1972. *The Hidden Injuries of Class.* New York: Alfred Knopf.

Simpson, P. 2013. Alienation, Ambivalence, Agency: Middle-Aged Gay Men and Ageism in Manchester's Gay Village. *Sexualities* 16: 283–299.

Sobocinska, A., and R. White. 2015. Travel and Connections. In *The Cambridge History of Australia Vol 2: The Commonwealth of Australia*, ed. A. Bashford, and S. Macintyre, 472–493. Port Melbourne: Cambridge University Press.

Tomsen, S. 2002. *Hatred, Murder and Male Honour: Anti-Homosexual Homicides in NSW, 1980–2000*. Canberra: Australian Institute of Criminology.

Williamson, D. 1978. *The Club*. Sydney: Currency Press Pty. Ltd.

4

Working Lives of Men Aged 45 and Younger

I had a fairly circuitous route to where I am now. When I was a child, I always knew that I wanted to be a car designer so my education from the age of about six was directed towards doing that. I started working as a product designer after I finished my Masters in automotive design ... but I was not really satisfied with just designing products, so I moved into design strategy specifically in the automotive industry.
(Eamon, aged 28, London)

Introduction

The men whose work histories are examined in this chapter were born between 1965 and 1993 and so belong to either 'Generation X and Y' or 'i-Generation'.[1] Their working lives are examined in much the same way as were the working lives of the other cohorts. They came of age (turned 21) between 1986 and 2000,[2] an important period in gay social history for two reasons. The first was the waning of the HIV-AIDS epidemic in the West—a result of the discovery of the triple therapy— and secondly, the slow growth of the marriage-equality movement in

© The Author(s) 2017
P. Robinson, *Gay Men's Working Lives, Retirement and Old Age*,
Genders and Sexualities in the Social Sciences,
DOI 10.1057/978-1-137-43532-3_4

125

liberal democracies. The period saw a consolidation of the monetarist reforms of the 1980s with increased casualisation of jobs throughout the economy and growth in wealth for the top 1%.[3] Two financial crashes occurred also in the final decades of the twentieth century, which could be seen as precursors to the 2008–2009 global financial crisis: the stock market crashes in the four 'tiger' economies of South-East Asia (1997) and in major western economies the burst of the dot.com bubble (1997–2000).[4]

At first glance, this cohort might appear less well educated than the middle cohort where more than 80% of interviewees had universitydegrees. In the case of this cohort, slightly less than 60% had them. But the cohort included seven who were university students when interviewed. If their number were added to those with university qualifications, the number with university qualifications would be equivalent to that of the middle cohort. The large proportion of men with university qualifications in the two younger cohorts distinguishes them from the old cohort where slightly less than half the men had university degrees.[5]

Incomes for this cohort were divided into four levels: those earning more than US$100,000 per annum; US$50,000–100,000 per annum; US$25,000–50,000 per annum; and US$25,000 or less per annum.[6] The cohort included no high-income earners but a significant minority living below the poverty line—all but one of whom were university students. The students' poverty was relative and resulted from low-paying, part-time jobs which they held in addition to their studies. The practice of combining part-time work with full-time university studies has a long history and was especially beneficial for baby boomers when they were university students and the prevailing economic conditions meant part-time work was plentiful in the holidays.

The situation facing i-Generation university students was similar but different. Similar in that many now had part-time jobs but different because they had them while studying whereas for the previous generation they were able to pick up casual work over the long vacation and that in Australia, for example, many were eligible for teaching scholarships or Commonwealth scholarships that offset university fees. Similar in that a university degree is still seen as likely to ensure more secure employment in the long run but different because it no longer

4 Working Lives of Men Aged 45 and Younger 127

guarantees rapid transition to full-time employment or employment in the sector(s) for which they trained. Anecdotal evidence from former students of mine who graduated in social science suggests that, for many, the part-time job they had while at university is the only employment they can rely on in the year or years following completion of their studies.[7]

The majority earned between US\$25,000 and US\$50,000, which meant that in 2010 terms their incomes were equivalent to average or below-average household incomes in the USA.[8] Three of the five earning the highest incomes were in their 30s, one in his 40s and one in his 20s. These worked in finance, law, business and information technology.

Work Narratives

Education was the largest single occupational category for this cohort, comprising as it did nine who were undergraduate or postgraduate students in tertiary education and two who were academic staff. Business was the next category, then retail and clerical, each of which had small numbers. More than half of these men came of age between 1995 and 2010,[9] and so, as young adults just starting, witnessed the two financial crashes of the 1990s—the tiger economies and the dot.com entrepreneurs—as well as the 2008–2009 global crash.

Approximately one-third of the men from this cohort, who were in their late 20s or early 30s, were in the early stages of their career, and about the same number were established in theirs. The remaining were tertiary students. Those in the early stages of a career worked in fields as varied as clerical, finance, law, psychology and sales, while those established in their career worked in business, education, human resources and information technology.

As with the older cohorts, these men's work stories were examined for narratives that were common to or explained their working lives. Five principal ones were identified, (the same as for the middle cohort): creativity ($n = 8$); care ($n = 5$); social or political change ($n = 5$); work-as-work ($n = 4$); and travel ($n = 1$). In the same way as in the other chapters, an individual's life story might contain several

128   P. Robinson

narratives—Gavin and Hayden (below), for example. Surprisingly, only one man had a narrative featuring travel: the theme that was so important to the baby boomers of the previous chapter.

Creativity

The eight men whose working lives were best explained by a common creativity narrative represented slightly more than a quarter of the young cohort. All but one were in their 20s. Six had been educated at non-government schools and four were still at universitywhen interviewed. Five were from Melbourne, two from London and one from New York.[10] As explained in Chap. 2, the 'creative narrative' covers work in 'creative' industries, such as architecture, advertising, design, fashion, music, painting, sculpture and writing. For some in this group the narrative expressed their creative work intentions or career expectations. The latter was especially the case for some of the young men from non-government schools who were working in menial jobs after or while at university.

Among the areas of creative work in which the men were employed or intended to seek employment were interior design or decoration, fashion, and mechanical design, the first two being areas where for decades gay men have found employment. Two exceptions to these creative areas were a man in his mid 30s from New York and another from London in his late 20s. I classified their work histories as influenced by the creative narrative even though they were not working in creative industries. There is more about their working life after the next section which deals with the working lives of those from upper-middle-class families.

The creativity narrative best represented the working lives of the six who had been to non-government schools and whose background was upper-middle-class. Their working lives or work aspirations are considered as a single sub group and begin this section. All were in their 20s, came from Melbourne or London, and were universityeducated or enrolled in university courses when interviewed.[11] They were working or planned to work in car design, interior decoration, interior design,

4 Working Lives of Men Aged 45 and Younger 129

fashion design, or scriptwriting. Two were working in other fields but aspired to work in creative industries: Denis (aged 27) and Jamie (aged 21) both from Melbourne. Their working histories are considered first, followed by the three men still at university, also from Melbourne.

When interviewed, 27-year-old Denis was working as a 'door bitch' for a gay nightclub in Melbourne and shared a house with other gay men in an inner-city suburb that was popular with 'hipsters' and students. An extremely confident, self-assured man, he wanted to work in film as a writer and director, which had been his aspiration for at least 20 years:

> When I was super young, even as early as five and six … I would have thought my grown-up job would be either being an animator or an actor or a creative writer. And I think for me, directing seems to combine those two things. You are sort of pulling together all of the performance stuff of acting because you are really relating that back with actors and helping them grow their performance. And then you are also involving the visual story telling … or painting a picture with the things you put into the scene. And then you are also combining the story-telling aspect … especially for me because I write the scripts myself. But a director's total job is to tell a story using the elements, the screen elements. So to me it combines my three favourite things.

He grew up in a family where artistic endeavour was valued. Both his parents as well as other relatives worked in creative fields and Denis believed this inheritance fed what he called, the 'creative passion' in him:

> My father was an actor and stage director and my mother was an interior designer and her father was a fine arts painter … and my dad's uncle was a famous stage actor and theatre restaurant owner … I believe everyone has creative passion, a creative fire inside them which then captures whatever they are exposed to.

His class privilege could provide Denis with the opportunity to explore his creative passions or at least allow him to explore them while eking out an artist's life on a 'door bitch's' wages, a not unusual path for the children of the upper-middle classes in cities like Melbourne. And as he said, there were strong precedents in his family for doing so.

Jamie was enrolled in a business course when we spoke and unhappy about being there. At a cross-road in his life, he had just decided not to complete the business course which he had taken to please his father and instead to enrol in an interior-design course like other school friends. He had enrolled in business after a disappointing work-experience internship:

> I had a bad experience at an architect's office where I went for work experience in Year 10. I was malleable and so like I decided that it was not for me after only a week working there ... and after that we had to choose our subjects so I went to Commerce side.

In Melbourne, where Jamie went to school, secondary schools ask students at the end of Year 10—when they are approximately 15—to choose a group of science, humanities/social science subjects or a blend of both as the focus of their studies in Years 11 and 12, the results for which are then used for entrance to institutions of higher-education or vocational-education. Either a desire to please his father or a belief he had inherited his father's aptitudes lay behind his vocational choice: 'I find that I have got a commerce brain and that's probably from my father who works in commerce, he's a stockbroker':

> Interior design would be much more fun and more ... like it will suit my personality a bit more because I like being creative, being a bit innovative with designs and, yeah, I think it will suit me a lot better. Yeah it is terrible that I have come to that conclusion three years into the degree but, yeah.

After three years of being relatively miserable, Jamie was in a position, largely, I would argue, because of class privilege, to change university courses.[12] An interesting observation arising from analysing these men's transcripts concerned their belief that they had inherited interests or in their terms, 'passions' from parents or other family members. I am not sure how widespread is such thinking in the i-Generation but if it is it

4 Working Lives of Men Aged 45 and Younger   131

would either suggest the triumph of scientific or medical understanding over social understanding of the self or the increasing tendency of middle-class families to understand themselves according to the precepts of the dominant class, that is, that 'it's all in the breeding'.

The three still at university who planned careers in creative fields were from Melbourne: two wanted to find work in fashion, the other in interior design.[13] One of the men, Todd (aged 21) had the advantage of being the child of parents who had made a lot of money from fashion, mostly manufacture of casual wear offshore (China) for mid-range department stores in Melbourne and Sydney. Enrolled in a fashion course at university, his parents met his every wish: provided design and cutting space for him in one of their warehouses and ensured he was well nourished, emotionally, materially and socially. A design career in fashion was virtually guaranteed:

> We are going to Sydney for Australia Fashion Week in May ... and I am really looking forward to ... not networking in the sense of social climbing but meeting people and listening to their ideas ... so it is exciting.

The two others came from similarly privileged backgrounds but their parents were not in the rag-trade. The one who wanted to work in interior design was Zane who was completing a degree in Arts (languages and politics) when interviewed. He had part-time jobs with a successful interior designer in an upper-middle-class suburb and with a society caterer. The experience he gained working with the interior designer had whetted his appetite and he said that it interested him and that he wanted to make a lot of money from doing it: 'I want to get into importing ... furnishings from different countries and ... work as an interior designer in Melbourne and have a store and that kind of stuff'. The other man was Garth, aged 23. He was studying fashion and it obsessed him:

> I did work for a Melbourne label last year for a while but that was unpaid but I did really enjoy that ... I like every aspect of fashion: designing clothes, making them, producing them. Whether it is doing promotional-based work or theoretical research and stuff, I like all of it. So, whatever I end up doing I will probably be happy with.

The class privilege mentioned in relation to these men was apparent in the relative ease with which they spoke about finding paid and unpaid work in fields or close to those where they intended to work. I would argue the confidence with which they described finding work that suited them and the success they had in getting it were a result of their parent's or family's social capital, that is, the friends or business associates of their parents, or friends of their parents—especially connections made at their non-government school or later at university or fashion college—enabled them to find part-time jobs or internships in areas of interest to them, a facility not available to all young people looking for an introduction to their chosen occupation.

Findlay, a 33-year-old from New York, was not working in a creative industry and had a job that at first did not appear to have much connection with creativity. An African American who had spent a short spell in prison for drug possession, Findlay was outgoing and optimistic and in a relationship with a slightly older white man. He was working as a filing clerk in an architects' office when we had our interview, during his lunchtime, in a noisy, fast-food restaurant three streets south of Columbus Circle, New York.

When relating his work history, he said that he initially had trouble adjusting to the nine-to-five routine after years being 'on the scene'. Like many young, gay men, he was attracted to gay bars and clubs and for most of his 20s, organised his life around 'clubbing', so much so that, 'what ... [went] on in the morning I was never concerned with; it was the night time that was happening for me; I liked it, it was interesting'. His prison experience was not a hardship and his family had taken care of his affairs while he was there.

> Right now, coming home from prison you have to start from the very bottom. I started at a job that paid me $40 a day. Coming from prison you get 12 cents a day so that was a big come up but that was in the world so I had to pay for Metro, food, haircuts, just travelling, just everyday living. Have you thought about the money you spend every day? Just on necessities of life. Luckily when I came home, my family was there for me. They took care of my apartment while I was away.

4 Working Lives of Men Aged 45 and Younger   133

Either prison discipline or getting off drugs seemed to teach him the importance of getting a good job to pay the bills and might have convinced him also that his days as a clubber were at an end, which is not uncommon for gay men in their 30s and 40s: 'I don't go out as much as I used to because ... money is a factor these days. I have no desire to be a part of that crowd anymore'. His practical approach to work suggests a 'work-as-work' mentality, which by necessity it was, but his real working interest, as yet unrealised, was in music and recording.

Findlay had studied music and audio research in Florida and said when relating his work history that while he liked the filing job in the architects' office, it was not 'his field', that he had spent years working in hip-hop and rhythm and blues (R&B) but only in a non-paid capacity and intended one day to earn his income working with and representing hip-hop and R&B artists. For this reason, his working life was included with these men from the young cohort.

Bailey's working history was very different from Findlay's, starting after university graduation in a bank, progressing to a job in statistical research, and then to one in a university. What their two working lives had in common was a latent or eventual expression of creativity. As mentioned, Findlay's was latent at the time of interview, although a feature of his after-hours life. Bailey's, by contrast, found expression in the sort of work available to him in academia:

> I really enjoy the daily challenge of my role as well as the interaction with both staff and students. I find it highly rewarding seeing the outcomes of my work both in terms of experimental findings and the understanding and successes of students. I also like the freedom and flexibility given to me to explore my own avenues of research within the centre to allow national and international collaboration ... interaction with the undergraduates has been rewarding and seeing them take an idea and run with it to generate some truly unique projects and perspectives.

Bailey was employed to teach undergraduates while completing his Ph.D. and appeared to be blossoming in the university setting. His other workplace experiences had varied from hum-drum to abusive.

134　　P. Robinson

Work in the bank had been satisfactory: the chief benefit, he said, being the friends he made working there. His next job, which was in statistical research in a government department, affected him both personally and professionally.

> Within a short period of time there, I started having issues with my direct line manager who was a bully, not only in professional terms but also with regards to my sexuality. Having taken this up with the union formal grievance procedures were set in place (which the union dropped when I left). I have very few positive experiences from the [experience] except I have learnt how not to manage staff, treat people or generally conduct oneself. I did enjoy the opportunity to speak with professionals and hone my interviewing technique.

As discussed in previous chapters, notably in sections on being out in the workplace, experience of being bullied because of their sexuality is not uncommon for gay men. Bailey's account suggests a strong awareness of his rights and willingness to speak up and enlist the support of his union. The fact the union dropped grievance procedures, possibly for workplace bullying because of sexuality, might suggest a closeted homophobia in the union or its leadership.[14] It is worth noting that Bailey left with a positive sense of skills acquired at the same workplace where he had been bullied. For earlier generations of gay men, a similar experience might have been more scaring either because the subject could not be aired or because homophobia was more prevalent.

Care

Caring for people like themselves was the most distinctive feature of the care work undertaken by the middle cohort as discussed in the previous chapter. In caring for people like themselves, they distinguished themselves from the old cohort where care work was of a more general nature. There are two reasons for this. First, because the middle cohort comprised men from the gay-liberation era, they could be more public about their sexuality than the older men and take on care work for people like themselves. Secondly, unlike those before them and those

4 Working Lives of Men Aged 45 and Younger   135

after them, the middle cohort had to cope with the AIDS epidemic and any involvement in this field meant caring for men like themselves. The older men, by contrast, were mostly closeted, could not be 'out' about themselves, and so could not care for people like them publicly. And, because of their age and when they reached adulthood, they were mostly spared the ordeal of AIDS.

The care work of the young cohort was similar to that of the old generation: directed toward the general public rather than people like themselves. There are two historically contingent reasons for this—again related to gay men's identity and the AIDS crisis. The first reason is that the generation comprising the young cohort have experienced a far greater level of acceptance than those before them and a greater sense of normality about their sexuality: managing 'outsider' status or identity has been less traumatic for them. The second reason is that once AIDS ceased being a death sentence and became more of a manageable disease, which began in 1996 with the discovery of an effective antiretroviral therapy, gay men's social involvement in the caring of people with the disease or at risk of contracting it declined. As scientific advances allowed for greater individualised treatment of the disease, the need declined for the level of communal presence which had been such a major feature of gay men's lives since the early 1980s.

Despite the fact that there were fewer opportunities for those from the young cohort to work in AIDS-related fields, the type of care work they chose to do—working-class education reform or aged-care advocacy, for example—was likely to contribute to social or political change. There were five whose working histories were shaped by the care narrative. Three were in their 30s and two in their 40s and they were from Auckland, Melbourne, and Sydney.[15] The working histories of two of them are examined in depth as representative of the whole group. They are Callum, a 43-year-old from Melbourne and Gavin, a 31-year-old from Auckland.

Callum worked in higher education and was researching working-class education when interviewed. His partner of six years was 46 and worked in an elite profession. They owned property together in Melbourne and in the country. When he left school, his first job was as a teaching assistant in a centre for intellectually disabled people.

He described how, when he visited the centre to apply for the job, he recalled childhood memories of its 'blue buses':

> I saw these blue buses and it ... freaked me out because blue buses in my childhood were these symbols ... they indicated retarded, mental people so it was scary. But I went for the job and I had the interview and I remember being very nervous.

The regular salary he earned meant he was able to move out of home and establish himself in an inner-city suburb popular with gay men and close to the beach. He remained in the job for 12 months and enjoyed the sociability of the other workers. His resignation coincided with another decision, to enrol in a universitycourse. Soon after, he found other work in the residential disability sector, which continued during the six years he spent studying for his degree. When asked what he liked about the work, he explained that it was the other workers and the residents:

> The thing I liked about the work ... [was] the other workers were quite kooky. I think it attracts people who are a bit crazy. But because of their craziness, there is a capacity to deal with difference in their personalities that I liked. Some of them were just nuts though. And the people that I worked with, the people with disabilities, were always fascinating. Their life stories were always interesting to me.

He found the domestic side of the job boring: 'because I really was not built to be a housekeeper or maid or whatever' and, once he graduated from university, found work in a TAFE college teaching people who wanted to work as disability care workers.[16] The pragmatism and agility that he showed in moving with work experience from carer to teacher of future carers was typical of Callum's working history in care-related occupations. Some years later, he returned to university and enrolled in postgraduate courses, finally enrolling in a Ph.D. which he completed in the early 2010s. When asked what he liked about his work now, he said the following:

> There are two things I love about my work. I like research and reading and thinking and I like then sharing that with other people to see how

4 Working Lives of Men Aged 45 and Younger 137

they react with it … I am not an elitist when it comes to knowledge so I love working with people like plumbers and electricians as much as I love working with people who have high-level degrees.

Teaching is one of the caring professions. It attracts women and is one where women have been welcome and succeeded. Callum's working life was defined by his engagement with caring occupations, either as a carer himself or as a teacher of carers. He rebelled against what he regarded as 'women's work' or the domestic element and requirements of residential care for disabled people. Before beginning his Ph.D., he worked for a year at a TAFE observing how working-class students acquired knowledge but also how men taught and learnt:

> I spent a year and a half at [a college of] TAFE learning what carpentry teachers do, what plumbing teachers do, what electrician teachers do. I spent a lot of time doing that and … it was really a breath of fresh air that worked for me because a lot of my work life had been tied up with women and so-called women's work. Doing this stuff in trades, I learnt a lot about men, men who would say that they are straight, butch men but they are just men. So that was what was really good about it.

His interest in working-class education and the extent to which it provides working-class students with what they need was a form of care as well I would argue. Callum came from a Catholic family, had seven siblings, and defined his parents as working class. In one sense, therefore, his interest in working-class education was an expression of care for children like himself and it could be said sprang from his own lived experience of it.

Gavin's occupation was both different from Callum's and an unusual version of care work. He worked in shipping and on first reading my response to his transcript was to classify his job as shaped by the work-as-work narrative until toward the end when he explained what he enjoyed about work. In answer to a prompt to answer the second half of the question—'What do you enjoy/have you enjoyed about work?'—Gavin focused on his present job, saying that he enjoyed helping people solve their problems, to 'make their move into another part of their life'. When I read this a second and third time, the astuteness of Gavin's observation became clear. To an outsider it might seem that a shipping clerk's work is concerned with organising the transfer of inanimate objects like boxes and crates and containers whereas in truth when cartage contractors and shipping merchants arrange personal and family uplifts they are involved in and assisting a significant life transition for their client. Gavin's astuteness was in being aware of this dimension of his work and, as explained below, in valuing it.

His job when interviewed was in sales with a shipping company: moving people and goods across the Tasman Sea between Australia and New Zealand. A Maori by birth, his working life had begun at 16 when he left school and got a job picking fruit on the east coast of New Zealand. This was followed by a stint in hospitality which he first found promising until he realised at 24 what was required to succeed:

> I was looking around and thought: 'If I really want to make any money, hospitality is not the place to be unless you own the restaurant and in order to be able to get the money to own a restaurant I am going to need a better job', so ... I went and put myself through the Maritime College and I did my Diploma in shipping and freight logistics.

He completed his apprenticeship in Melbourne, returned to New Zealand, and found work in a very large Scandinavian shipping company. Disheartened by what he found, Gavin moved to another position within the company:

> It disillusioned me with the industry ... because basically you were just a number in a huge company and I really did not enjoy it. So what I did though is I took a promotion in-house and went across to ... a separate company but owned by the same company in the same building. But that was even more disheartening really because it was just a big mess and no one knew what they were doing there and I was only in my second year in the shipping industry.

His career was interrupted at this point when his mother and grandmother died and a few months later he became quite ill and was unable to work for two years:

My nerve has been squashed ... between my vertebrae and they cannot operate on it ... All the pain has been diverted to my chest so ... at times it feels like I am having a heart attack.

Despite his physical disability and the pain it caused, Gavin returned to work in sales and, as mentioned, his account of what he enjoyed about it strongly suggested a form of care work:

I guess you are helping people make their move into another part of their life ... From my growing up ... I didn't really get that. My parents were not that strict on us ... and so everything I did I did by myself. I guess I have ... got a maternal nature ... towards other people. I just like to see things get done I suppose, I like to see people happy ... And basically doing what I do now in sales it is nice to see people getting a good deal because ... in my industry there are a lot of rip-off merchants.

In this short extract, Gavin revealed a lot about himself and how he developed his caring attitude to customers and clients. In some ways, it is reminiscent of Arlie Hochschild's notion of emotion work which she argues is often expected of women and they find themselves providing no matter what their job.[17] As mentioned, I am not sure every working person associated with domestic removals would understand their job description to include 'helping people ... move into another part of their life', although this is precisely what they do. To put it another way, Gavin showed an acute awareness of the personal dimension of his job that might escape many others, a degree of empathy possibly neither required by employers nor expected by customers. And in saying what he did in his interview, he underlined what I would argue is a vital care aspect of customer assistance.

Social or Political Change

Intersections between work narratives were most pronounced where they concerned care or social/political change. In the case of the middle cohort, the chief reason for this was that in the 1980s and 1990s, the sort of AIDS-related care work that they gravitated toward was political

140 P. Robinson

by nature because of fairly widespread homophobia and the ease with which homosexuality and AIDS were conflated in the media and public discourse.[18] For those from the young cohort, an intersection occurred because the sort of work they did to assist social or political change—supporting homeless people or fostering indigenous culture, for example—was also a form of caring for others who were not like them either in terms of their sexuality or socio-economic circumstances.

Five men had working lives that contributed to social or political change. One was in his 40s, three were in their 30s, and one in his 20s. They were from Auckland, London, Melbourne, and Sydney and were university educated.[19] Four of their work histories are considered here, beginning with that of Noah (aged 42) from Auckland. Maori by birth, Noah, who had a relatively trouble-free coming out when he was 24, said the only homophobia he had experienced was from a member of the public:

> There have been moments when I have had confrontations with members of the public. I remember one incident. I was in Wellington with the gay rugby team and ... we ended up at a pub afterwards and I got into a scuffle with a supposedly straight guy at the pub who was homophobic. And that is really the only incident I have come across. Otherwise it has been quite accepting.

When I asked him if other staff at the school where he worked knew he was gay, he said his boss knew and a few other staff members, that he did not 'announce' it, but was open about his sexuality if the subject came up. In the gay parlance of the baby-boomer generation, he was 'straight-acting'. After leaving school, Noah worked as a labourer on building sites and continued doing this until, in his early 30s, he enrolled in university. On graduating with a degree in education, he became a secondary school teacher.

Until this point, his career had been fairly matter-of-fact with no strong suggestion of a commitment to social or political change. Evidence of it came, however, in the subjects Maori language, history and culture that he taught his primary-school students. Efforts to preserve indigenous language and culture can been interpreted as

4 Working Lives of Men Aged 45 and Younger 141

protecting unenlightened values such as child marriage or preserving and defending valuable cultural heritage against erosion or extinction. I interpreted Noah's teaching of Maori language, history and culture as a social good with political benefits for Maori in his part of New Zealand.

One of the richest men from this cohort was Guy (aged 38) who lived in London. Like Noah, he had begun work in a rather matter-of-fact way after completing his education, with the exception that in his case he had considerable family wealth behind him. He took off a gap year between finishing school and starting work as a trainee accountant. Finding this unappealing he took off another year before becoming a private investor, after which he, 'took charge of my family property ... and have been doing that for five years'. To this point, Guy's career narrative showed little sign of involvement in social or political change until in his interview he added that, at the same time as running his family property, he was involved in a charity for homeless people in London.

The two remaining men lived in Australia. Leo (aged 31) was from Sydney and Hayden (aged 21) from Melbourne. Leo's work history had a strong social-change narrative and Hayden, who was still at university hoped to find overseas work involving social and political change when he completed his studies.

A sensitive, intelligent man, Leo's postgraduate qualifications were in psychology and he worked for a large business as an organisational psychologist. Like most university-educated people of his generation, he had worked part-time while studying and travelled overseas before graduating. His part-time jobs included bar-tending and hospitality work, shop sales, and telephone-marketing. When he began full-time work, his first jobs were unrewarding ones in market research. Then he found a new job in occupational rehabilitation which focused on helping people who had been injured or were unwell return to work and which suggested evidence of the care narrative. When he explained his motivation and understanding of the work he was doing, there was evidence of a stronger social/political change narrative:

> There was a scheme called Pathways to Work in the UK ... [where I worked] which aimed at assisting people on disability benefits pensions

back into employment and enabling them to better manage their condition ... Here, I am working at one of the workers compensation insurers ... seeing things from the other side this time and trying to improve their injury management practices, and obviously they want to reduce their liability. My motivation is probably more about helping people restore their quality of life.

Since they were established in fourteenth-century Genoa, the business model for insurance companies has been to receive more in premiums than they pay out in compensation. In such a setting, Leo seemed to position himself as an independent professional with powers to influence how the company treated claimants. A more cynical interpretation would be that Leo felt morally compromised working for the employers' side in workers compensation and was justifying doing so. When I asked him to elaborate, he explained his moral position, which focused on achieving social benefits for workers and their employers:

Part of the role was to educate employers that [if] you want a sustainable return to work ... there's no point pushing someone back before they're ready. But also I guess making employers aware that offering some form of suitable duties or modified duties that are within that person's capacity is often quite important to keep the person involved with the workplace and feel that the workplace actually is trying to accommodate and care for their needs as they recover, and so they do not lose that social support that they get at work, that sense of identity that they get from work.

His approach was less adversarial than can occur in negotiations between employers and employees. And showed considerable insight into how transition from sick role to productive worker could be achieved and the importance of work as identity.

Twenty-one-year-old Hayden was studying law at a university in Melbourne when I interviewed him. When I asked him about his working life, he focused on the part-time jobs he had while a student:

I have had a lot of menial jobs over the last few years and was working in a bar and then before that in an ice-cream shop and things like that and I made the transition to an office job, I did that last year as well. I was in

4 Working Lives of Men Aged 45 and Younger 143

an advertising firm. [*Pause*] ... I guess it is interesting finally seeing where I have always thought I will end up in an office. That is sort of nice to see, also kind of overwhelmingly scary but it is all right. It is also nice to be doing a bit more challenging work.

This young man, educated at one of Melbourne's elite schools for boys, had had experience in standard, part-time jobs that university students find and then more recently in an architect's office, less standard and possibly as a result of connections of parents or family. I asked Hayden what he expected to enjoy about the sort of work he could expect with a law degree. It was here that he revealed a mild interest in social/political change, an inclination to avoid a conventional career:

> I am sort of veering away from the corporate world a little bit. I can imagine not liking working in a suit and working in an office building every single day of my life. In my arts degree, I do Spanish and development studies. Those are my areas of study so once I get my Articles the plan is to work with an NGO or something like that. I love travel and I love languages and ... it seems to fit my lifestyle. Most of the people I've met who work for NGOs are working overseas and helping people seems to be a good sort of corollary of that.

It was not clear how much of Hayden's future career projections was likely to be realised and how much was a third-year university student's wishful thinking. The appeal of travel seemed as important to him as 'helping people' which he explained as a 'good sort of corollary', suggesting an overlap between the tentative social/political narrative and the travel narrative.

Work-as-Work

The work histories of four men were shaped by this narrative: a relatively small number when compared to the work histories of men from the older cohorts. In the old cohort, work-as-work described the work history of twelve men and in the middle cohort, six men. This narrative was much less significant in the stories of the young cohort than the older two. Work-as-work was the most important work narrative for the old cohort, the second most important for the middle cohort and for the young cohort third in importance.

This decline in number and significance over time could suggest an increase in unwillingness to accept work with which the men cannot or do not identify, in other words, an increasing tendency among young, gay men to look for work that is personally or professionally meaningful, not simply something done to pay the bills. If this is so, as I suspect it is, it would be a consequence of increasing affluence and individualisation. The smaller number could be a feature also of there being fewer men with working-class backgrounds or jobs in this cohort than in the older ones and an increasing proportion of men with university qualifications.[20]

The four men whose narrative featured work as work were from Auckland, Los Angeles, Melbourne and New York. Two were in their 30s, one in his 40s, and the fourth was 18.[21] The oldest of the four was Kyle who began when he was 12: 'I was kiwi fruit picking and working in a pack house'. He later went to university and, like many in his family before him, qualified as a school teacher. After teaching for four years in his early 20s, he left and was working in sales for a large company when interviewed. When I asked him why he left teaching, he said that, even though he had enjoyed it, he found it 'thankless': 'I was born and bred in it. I know what happens. It is not nine to three or eight to three, it is a lifetime'. As well, he boasted, his annual income rose by almost ten thousand dollars when he changed jobs.

Evan, the man from Los Angeles, was 35 and worked in information technology.

> I work as a computer professional. I have not liked my work for a while but … I have grown to like my work more. I guess people think that computer engineering is not the sort of work gay men do but there are people who are gay and also do that kind of computer engineering work.

> *What sort of computer work do you do?*

> It is mainly computer programming. It requires a lot of patience and sometimes I am not patient … And sometimes it is busy and things are

4 Working Lives of Men Aged 45 and Younger   145

not on time. Also computer technology is always being updated so you have to learn to update your knowledge.

While not complaining of homophobia, Evan observed that people did not expect gay men to work in his field and that his work was not a source of much joy or interest. Because of the difficulties of the interview conditions—held in a noisy restaurant attached to a hotel and English as his second language—I do not have an accurate transcription of all Evan's spoken words but he did stress the pressures of his work and that might explain why for him it was 'just a job'.

Findlay's work history was examined in the section on creative narrative where I argued his story had a strong 'work-as-work' element until he revealed his previous education in music and continuing enthusiasm for it, especially rap and hip-hop. His work history contained intersecting narratives, and evidence for work-as-work was found in the pragmatic approach to finding work after a short period of time in prison and determination to have a successful life with his partner, which meant having to resume taking responsibility for his expenses, including his flat, which his family had looked after when he was in prison.

The final work history for this section belongs to Dougal, an 18-year-old from Melbourne. When I interviewed him, he was working in a garden supply shop while deciding if he wanted to go to TAFE and study to become an electrician or work with his father. His knowledge of the gay world was limited to what he had discovered on the internet and through a government-funded support group for teenage gays and lesbians. When asked what he expected to enjoy about work as an electrician, his answer suggested a matter-of-fact approach—'electricians are in short supply'—with barely a glimmer of interest in the work itself:

It is in high demand at the moment; electricians are in short supply so there is always money to made in it. And it was one of the only things that aroused my interest in Year 12 at high school.

What interests you about being an electrician?

I can understand it, I find it easy. It is very practical work rather than theoretical.

146   P. Robinson

It is expecting a lot for the average 18-year-old to have a clear sense of her/his work path. Even many who enrol in vocational courses change their mind during studies or after graduation. In Dougal's case, he had no real sense of why he was interested in being an electrician, except that it made sense to enrol because they were in short supply, knowledge no doubt gleaned from his father who was a builder or older brothers who were in trades. And its appeal? He found studying it easy and it was not too theoretical, which as mentioned is probably about as much as most parents of teenagers get in response to any question about what they want to do.

Travel

This narrative showed the most radical generational shift of all the work narratives. From being unnecessary in relation to the working lives of the old cohort—occasional hints at love travel only—it became one of the central narratives to capture the work histories of the men from the middle cohort, returning to relative insignificance in relation to those from this cohort: where it explained the working life of only one man. If this trend were applied to the general population, it would suggest the baby-boomer generation went out of their way to make travel a part of their working lives or incorporated it in work whenever possible and did not relegate it to holidays only.

The man who shaped his working life around its travel opportunities was Jacob, a 42-year-old Aboriginal from Melbourne. His working life began as a school boy when he worked in a large grocery store in rural Victoria and then in hospitality before going to university. The first indication of his inclination to incorporate travel in his working life came when Jacob sketched the years immediately following graduation:

> I left university and moved interstate and started ... a semi-professional job for a large accounting firm and then went from there into market research ... [where] I have been employed most of the time since ... I would describe myself as in and out of employment in terms of doing professional jobs for two or three years, having a break, maybe doing

4 Working Lives of Men Aged 45 and Younger   147

some research consultancies in between, travelling overseas ... [For example] I lived in London for eight years and [was] self-employed in London on and off.

Living without a fixed base did not seem to concern Jacob or the partner he met in Darwin 11 years before. As the following account of their first years together shows, they seemed very capable of organising their life as a couple in the face of the travel demands of Jacob's work:

> We spent the first six months apart because I moved back to London and then he packed up and moved to London with me ... We lived predominantly in London but may have come back for three to six months and lived in Australia ... And we ... [can use] a property in London that a friend of ours owns so it was very easy and flexible to come and go.

When I asked Jacob what he enjoyed about his work as a researcher—he completed a doctorate shortly before our interview—he reiterated the appeal for him of flexibility and being able to move for work, of combining travel with his work: 'being able to undertake research contracts, short term research contracts, going off to wonderful locations, travelling around either Australia or overseas'. Unlike other researchers who try to make a life out of short-term contracts, Jacob was unconcerned about its precariousness, saying instead that good work and a good reputation can be their own reward, which for him was another aspect of his work he enjoyed:

> My research is mainly qualitative research, going out and doing interviews with people. And being able to build up a reputation so that when contracts do come along ... people will approach you to apply. And the nature of that means that you can get paid good money to do it.

According to Jacob, there were two disadvantages to his way of life. The first was that he was not contributing to his own superannuation or pension scheme, which since the late 1980s has been the central feature of old age planning in Australia. And secondly, neither he nor his partner had seriously thought about buying property, a consequence, he said, 'with myself not necessarily settling down in the one spot'. When weighed in the balance, he was still pleased with what his life enabled him to do:

> Being gay and in a relationship we … have the flexibility to move around and do what … [we] like … You can travel on next to nothing, you do not have to drag the kids around looking for airfares. You can be flexible and have enough disposable income to be a little bit more flexible.

Jacob explained later in his interview that he did not support the public campaign for gay marriage, arguing that all that was required was equality in terms of property and employment rights so that, in his case, he would be entitled to his partner's superannuation or pension. Issues such as this arose for many gay men during the HIV-AIDS epidemic when they found themselves shut out from property arrangements or agreements which would not have been the case if they had been in a heterosexual relationship.[22] In the extract above from his interview, Jacob explained the benefits of flexibility he enjoyed as flowing from not being tied down in the same way as are heterosexual couples. At the same time, as mentioned, he was aware as a man in his early 40s that he was not sensibly attending to his long-term ageing needs.

Being 'Out' at Work

Since the 1970s when coming out became both more public and more political, its meaning and import have continued to change. There is at least one reason for this. Because so many more heterosexuals now know 'out' gay people than before, the gay person has ceased to be the shadowy, troubling figure he once was and so, in the 2010s, is less likely to be a source of shame for himself or his family or friends. In more affluent cities, the change has been so marked that, according to US scholar Ritch Savin-Williams, some young, gay, New Yorkers had no idea what it meant to come out and had no experience of doing so.[23]

This change is partly borne out in the accounts of four men from this cohort who made mention of sexuality—and whether or not it was an

4 Working Lives of Men Aged 45 and Younger 149

issue—in the context of telling the story of their working life. Two of the men were in their 40s, one in his 30s and one in his 20s. They were from London, Melbourne, New York and Sydney.[24]

Kendall, a 44-year-old New Yorker raised the notion of 'gay' occupations, that is, that there are some occupations more suited to gay men, which was referred to also by Evan (above in work-as-work). In his work history, Kendall said the following about his fears of the homophobia he thought he might find in the workplace and his experiences:

> I remember in college being terribly afraid about how ... [to] be in the business world as a gay man. Long story short, it worked out okay. I ended up working for a gay CPA firm for the first 12 years of my life. Then I went in the closet for about a year and a half when I went to work for a union. Now, I work for a music publishing company and my immediate boss is gay and it is a pretty progressive company and nobody seems to care.

Born in 1965, Kendall would have been in his final year at college in the mid to late 1980s when homophobia was intense because of public narratives that conflated homosexuality and AIDS—which could help to explain the fears he held as a tertiary student who was about to graduate and planning his future. His account is of interest for another reason: that he had to return to the closet when he worked for a union. Not all unions are male-dominated or homophobic or both but it would seem Kendall found himself working for one where he felt unsafe to be open about his sexuality even though this would have been toward the end of the 1990s or at the beginning of the new century when the period of acute homophobia associated with AIDS had passed and there were signs of greater social tolerance.

In London, a man born in the same year as Kendall, discussed accommodating sexual identity and a career from the perspective of someone who had achieved considerable success in elite workplaces. After graduating from the oldest university in England, Jonathan (aged 44) got a job in one of the British Government's foremost policy departments and worked there for a decade. After that, he reckoned private enterprise was a more attractive career option:

I left and I went to do an MBA for two years full-time, wanted to be an investment banker because I knew that they earned money and so I spent the middle bit of my MBA working for [a prestigious investment bank], hated it and so decided I had to do something else and got introduced to the firm I now work in which is ... a big international head-hunting firm and realised that I quite liked what they did so I joined them in 2001 and I have been there ever since.

Jonathan met his partner of ten years when he was studying for his MBA and changing jobs. Neither man was obviously a high achiever and both held very responsible, highly paid jobs. When asked what he liked about his work, Jonathan replied:

It is a really nice firm, nice people. I am quite a sociable person so I enjoy working with people, very bright colleagues lots of them, I enjoy all that side of things ... Not all the people I meet are interesting but I meet a lot of people some of whom are very interesting.

While his job satisfied a strong sociable need in Jonathan—and the opportunity to mix with intelligent and interesting colleagues and clients—he was aware also of the pitfalls of work in the corporate-professional elite and it was at this point in the story of his working life that he referred to what he saw as the 'advantages' of his sexuality.

His account resonated with that of Jacob (discussed above under travel work) who said that in his view one of the chief benefits of being gay was the flexibility in their work and relationships that it allowed. In the following extract, Jonathan explained how being gay could save him from becoming a slave to the corporate machine or culture:

Any kind of corporate type job is necessarily quite constrained in ... that your whole week is mapped out. You do not have very much autonomy. You are very much at the beck and call of your clients and this is fine and it is part of life. I realise that ... One of the things that I know is a consistent theme in me is that being gay I can have this sort of slightly Peter Pan sense that life does not need to be like that and that you ... want to break free of it in a way that I just do not notice in my straight colleagues ... They might have it in the back of their minds but ... because

4 Working Lives of Men Aged 45 and Younger   151

most of them have children and it is … what they must have known from an early age was going to be the pattern of their lives, they just accept it more than I do. Whereas I just sort of think, 'I do not have to be like this … Life could be different'.

In the work histories of the previous age cohorts, interviewees hinted at the opportunities that being gay brought them or described the affective gains they achieved travelling for love. But often included with these were accounts of lives diminished by shame or the fear of exposure. Greater tolerance of sexual difference has without doubt improved the lot of gay men and lesbians. As evidence of this is, for example, Jonathan's belief that in the 2010s he has greater life choices than his straight colleagues—a view that gay men in similar elite occupations might also share. Against the advantages that he claims to enjoy is the reality of entrenched homophobia, which gay men in different occupations can experience as their standing improves. In October 2016, for example, four police officers alleged in New South Wales that they had been singled out to take drug tests because they were gay and that their straight work-mates were not subjected to the same.[25]

Thirty-one-year-old Leo related his experience of being gay in the workplace in the context of being bullied by his manager. As mentioned above (social or political change), Leo worked as an organisational psychologist in a large, Sydney-based company. He believed in social justice and devoted a lot of his working time to convincing employers that outlaying resources to assist injured workers to return to work was mutually beneficial: 'My motivation is probably more about helping people restore their quality of life … Workers compensation is a government scheme … [and] the more efficient and more effective it is [the] … better'. Leo, like Noah, the teacher discussed under social or political change was assumed by work colleagues to be straight. When speaking about his coming out, he said:

I used to find it difficult early on coming out … because we always are constantly coming out to new people we meet all of the time and because people generally assume I am straight unless I say that I am gay. Initially … I was a little bit clunky and awkward … [and] felt it was this really big deal when I needed to tell people, and of course they were just work-mates or people I barely knew and it was a non-issue for most of ... [them] but I would make this really awkward big issue out of disclosing [*laughs*] that I was gay and that would create a bit of an awkward situation for a minute.

Leo's experience was different from that of the gay teenagers Ritch Savin-Williams interviewed in Manhattan who did not know what coming out meant and was more in line with the results of a recent study of Australian workplace cultures conducted by Lloyds of London, the shipping underwriters. The Lloyds study showed that almost half of LGBTI workers keep their sexuality a secret at work and that 60% had received verbal abuse in the workplace.[26] Because the study looked at the workplace experiences of members of the five sexual minorities represented by the acronym LGBTI, it would be unwise to generalise its findings to all gay male employees. What it does suggest, however, is that sexual difference continues to be a distinguishing marker in the workplace, that the heterosexual assumption still predominates, and that gay people and other sexual minorities still have to carefully consider whether or not they reveal their sexuality to work-mates. It provides also the context for understanding Leo's account of his initial reticence about coming out and then the awkwardness that accompanied doing so with work-mates.

The manager who bullied him was, according to Leo, 'quite authoritarian and hierarchical in the way he managed the project' they worked on. But it was not until Leo's work-mates alerted him that he was aware of the bullying:

I had never even thought that it was really bullying until a couple of my colleagues in my team actually said I really should address this because it definitely constitutes bullying and it is quite unreasonable.

This is not the first time I have read accounts of gay men's willingness to accept unusually high levels of emotional stress or abuse before acknowledging it as such.[27] Whether it is a consequence of encountering homophobic taunts when children and teenagers or the general level

4 Working Lives of Men Aged 45 and Younger   153

of homophobia in sports broadcasts, graffiti, the internet, or from members of the public and parliament (under privilege), is difficult to say.

There are no doubt psychological theories that would help explain Leo's apparent blindness to what his manager was doing to him. I would argue, however, that having to endure low-level homophobia over several decades before coming out and then after one has come out is wearing and could have the effect of dulling gay men's awareness of abusive behaviours or willingness to retaliate. But retaliate Leo eventually did. The bullying came in two forms. First, his manager would belittle him in front of other team members, some of whom worked to Leo. Secondly, he would draw attention to Leo's sexuality in belittling ways:

> He did not e-mail things around but he would look at something on the internet and say, 'Oh look at this guy in the lycra pants! Is that what you wear on Saturday night, Leo?' I mean it was pretty harmless stuff but it just gets annoying and he was applying ridiculous stereotypes.

Anyone who has observed bullies or been bullied will identify with Leo's predicament. Often bullies' behaviour is childish but it can be relentless. And applying logic to the situation rarely helps the victim understand the motivations of the bully, which are to humiliate and dominate; and logic rarely helps the victim cope with the bullying. In the end, Leo did speak to his superiors who gave him the option of addressing the bully directly, which he took:

> I did have some discussions with him about his behaviour and how I felt his management style was impacting on me. In fairness to him, he did modify the way he dealt with me and it was a good outcome, a good resolution.

While the experience for Leo was initially distressing, there are two important differences between his experience and how it would have played out 15 or 20 years ago. The differences concern how homosexuality and homophobia are now understood. First, in many western countries there are now legal sanctions against sexual discrimination that gay people can rely on when bullied. Secondly, public opinion is now more tolerant if not supportive of sexual minorities.

Both of these structural changes ought to make life easier for gay people in the 2010s. Fifteen or twenty years ago, it is unlikely a gay employee would have raised the matter with his superiors or received the same support from his work-mates. In the situation Leo described, the more likely response 15 or 20 years ago would have been a sniggering from the work-mates when the manager made fun of something gay he saw on television in order to mock the employee's sexuality.

The youngest man in this group was Jarrad, a 23-year-old university student from Melbourne. His experience of homophobia in the workplace was similar to Leo's except that it occurred when he was overseas on a university internship. When working for a company of industrial designers in North America, he was invited to a sports game and it was there that his mentor, whom he liked, disappointed him:

> He was maybe 54 and because of him I got invited to go to the ... [game] in a box with all the managers and our clients as well. And one of the things that upset me when I was there ... were the homophobic jokes he made.

From what Jarrad said, his mentor's jokes made him uncomfortable because he was not out to him, which underlines the difficult truth of the gay libbers: that coming out is political. Perhaps if Jarrad's mentor had known he was gay he would have refrained from making homophobic jokes, perhaps not; it is difficult to know. Jarrad's expectations—of a workplace free of discriminatory language or behaviours—could say a lot about his generation's beliefs in justice and equality and that they could find themselves disappointed by a reality that does not always reflect them.

Jarrad's disappointment was compounded by expectations of his mentor as his 'leader', which underlines a long-standing argument about dominant masculinities and men's expectations of those in positions of leadership. 'It [homophobic joking] was light hearted, it was not anything really bad but I ... do not know how the workplace is going to change', said Jarrad, 'when these are the leaders'. He had no

4 Working Lives of Men Aged 45 and Younger 155

such difficulties with people his own age, however: 'Two or three of the younger people I worked with knew I was gay and went out with me … had no problem with it at all'. Much of this was in the context of how optimistic he felt about a career in a fairly masculine dominated profession and why he was prepared to persist—in the hope that the small changes he knew were occurring would continue: 'it is good it [workplace culture] is changing and that is why I am happy to go in there and work: because it will change'.

Conclusion

Stronger evidence existed in the work histories of these men of a secondary narrative emphasising individual choice than in those of other men from this or the other age cohorts. A tendency to stress individual choice when discussing their work history was more apparent in the stories of the six men from non-government schools and this went hand-in-hand with their statements about creativity and the creative.

There are three observations I would make here. First, post-industrial societies have seen an expansion in the newer creative industries such as web-page design, internet content and design, and computer-aided-design as well as in the established creative industries such as advertising, graphic art and fashion. Secondly, stronger evidence of interest in 'the creative' among young men who had been to non-government schools supports the argument of Norbert Elias that changes in taste and social practices begin in the upper classes and then over time are disseminated among other classes.[28] Thirdly, youth might explain this cohort's interest in or emphasis on creativity or desire to work in a 'creative' field, that is, an argument can be made that, since mass advertising's appropriation of youth and youthfulness in the 1960s, the so-called 'Creative Revolution', creativity is now associated with the young and seen to be more appropriate in them than in middle age or older.[29] The fallacy that creativity resides in the young or is an attribute of youthfulness is revealed, however, in the fact of Margaret Drabble's or Patrick White's continued writing until old age, its ailments or death prevented them.

The two work histories considered for the care narrative highlighted two very different meanings of care work. The first one, Callum's, conveyed a traditional approach to care but with certain qualifications. The jobs he had before immersing himself in higher education studies involved conventional care of people with disabilities. He enjoyed interacting with the residents and his co-workers but had reservations about the domestic side of the jobs because they were in his eyes 'women's work'. His real interest—in working-class work and education—became apparent when he worked with a group of male trade teachers at a TAFE. Its connection with his early work history (as a disability care worker) was that both were in the field of working-class occupations. The 'women's work' that he disliked—possibly because of the link in his teenage mind between effeminacy and gayness—is integral to disability support work and which for a time he enjoyed because of the relations he developed with residents and some of the workers. Gavin's work history focused on a very different aspect of care work which in the jargon of human-resource management is known as 'customer focus'. His very brief homily on what he enjoyed about work stood out because he had worked in male-oriented, working-class jobs and had appeared to approach work fairly matter-of-factly. And then, toward the end of his interview he let down his guard—remember he was a young Maori talking to an older, white academic from another country—and admitted that he enjoyed helping people move to a new point in their life and, on reflection, wondered if his motivation came from childhood when because of family circumstances he had had to be self-sufficient.

Unlike the previous cohorts, the social or political change narrative was not strongly present in this cohort. There are a number of possible reasons for this. First, their generation had less to fear from HIV-AIDS which preoccupied so much of the time and energies of the middle cohort and which was the location of so much of their social and political activity. Second, a larger proportion of men from this cohort came from privileged backgrounds and in some cases their commitment seemed light or in word only, perhaps a screen for more materialistic work aspirations. Third, a large minority from this cohort were university students and so, while their work histories contained evidence of part-time jobs, there was less evidence of permanent engagement with the world of work and their work narratives tended to be shaped by aspirations rather than achievement.

Notes

1. See Chap. 1 for more details.
2. See Chap. 1 for the reason why 21 is used as a marker for adulthood.
3. For discussion of casualisation and its effects, see R. Sennett (2006) *The Culture of the new Capitalism* (New Haven: Yale University Press), pp. 48–54; I. Watson, J. Buchanan, I. Campbell and C. Briggs (2003) *Fragmented Futures: New Challenges in Working Life* (Sydney: The Federation Press). For the place of casualisation in labour-market reform 1985–2000, see M. Pusey (2003) *Experience of Middle Australia: the Dark Side of Economic Reform* (Cambridge University Press, Melbourne), pp. 50–52 (Sennett 2006; Pusey 2003; Watson et al. 2003).
4. R. Jones (2010) 'Were you a victim of the dot.com bubble?', *The Guardian*: https://www.theguardian.com/money/2000/jul/15/personalfinancenews. Accessed 25 July 2016 (Jones 2010).
5. See Appendices 1–3.
6. Expressed in US dollars for 2010; see Appendix 3. Five men earned more than US$100,000; nine US$50,000–10,000; eight US$25,000–50,000; and seven US$25,000 or less.
7. School of Arts, Social Science and Humanities, Swinburne University of Technology, Melbourne.
8. See here for USA census data on household incomes: https://www.census.gov/newsroom/releases/archives/income_wealth/cb11-157.html. Accessed 6 September 2016.
9. See Appendix 5.
10. Findlay (aged 33) New York; Eamon (aged 28) London; Denis (aged 27) Melbourne; Bailey (aged 26) London; Garth (aged 23) Melbourne; Zane (aged 22) Melbourne; Jamie (aged 21) Melbourne; Todd (aged 21) Melbourne.
11. Eamon (aged 28) London; Denis (aged 27) Melbourne; Garth (aged 23) Melbourne; Zane (aged 22) Melbourne; Jamie (aged 21) Melbourne; Todd (aged 21) Melbourne.

12. Since 1989, tertiary students are charged fees (higher education contribution scheme or HECS) to attend universities in Australia. They or their parents may opt to pay the fees at the beginning of their studies, otherwise the students are required to repay the debt after graduation and once their income exceeds a certain amount. In 1988/9, for example, the income threshold was AU$22,000 while in 2002/3 it was AU$24,365. The salary deductions continue until the HECS debt is repaid. For more information on the scheme, see: http://www.aph. gov.au/About_Parliament/Parliamentary_Departments/Parliamentary_ Library/Publications_Archive/archive/hecs. Accessed 29 July 2016. In Jamie's case, he will have incurred debt for the subjects he completed while enrolled in business and will then incur similar fees for subjects he enrols in interior design.

13. Garth (aged 23) Melbourne; Zane (aged 22) Melbourne; Todd (aged 21) Melbourne.

14. An Australian interviewed for a previous book (Nigel, aged 49, Canberra), who had been active in the far left of the union movement in Melbourne in the 1970s, said his sexuality barred him from inner circles of the union and close friendships with other left-wing unionists. Not a lot of work has been done on homophobia in unions or boards of companies in pre gay-liberation decades. For Nigel's story, see P. Robinson (2008) *The Changing World of Gay Men* (Basingstoke and New York: Palgrave Macmillan).

15. Callum (aged 43) Melbourne; Gabriel (aged 43) Auckland; Liam (aged 37) Sydney; Gavin (aged 31) Auckland; Leo (aged 31) Sydney.

16. TAFE is the acronym for the 'technical and further education' sector which is vocational and trade education for post-secondary students in Australia. Traditionally state funded and provided, private providers have entered the market in some Australian states, namely Victoria and Queensland, and achieved considerable presence. For more information, see: http://www.tafecourses.com.au/resources/what-is-tafe/. Accessed 11 August 2016.

17. A. Hochschild (2003, 1983) *The Managed Heart: Commercialization of Human Feeling* (Berkeley: University of California Press) (Hochschild 1983).

18. Robinson *The Changing World*, pp. 57–60.

19. Noah (aged 42) Auckland; Guy (aged 38) London; Dylan (aged 32) Sydney; Leo (aged 32) Sydney; Hayden (aged 21) Melbourne.

4 Working Lives of Men Aged 45 and Younger   159

20. The old cohort had at least three men who had had working-class occupations whereas there were none in the young cohort. The working-class men from the old cohort: Lucas (aged 75) Auckland (railways); Jeffery (aged 72) Auckland (railways); Baden (aged 65) (skilled worker). See Appendix 2.
21. Kyle (aged 40) Auckland; Evan (aged 35) Los Angeles; Findlay (aged 33) New York; Dougal (aged18) Melbourne.
22. See P. Robinson (2013) *Gay Men's Relationships Across the Life Course* (Basingstoke and New York: Palgrave Macmillan), pp. 101–102, 118–120, 127–128 (Robinson 2013).
23. R. C. Savin-Williams (2005) *The New Gay Teenager* (Cambridge, Mass.: Harvard University Press) (Savin-Williams 2005).
24. Jonathon (aged 44) London; Kendall (aged 44) New York; Leo (aged 31) Sydney; Jarrad (aged 23) Melbourne.
25. See http://www.abc.net.au/news/2016-10-09/allegations-of-homophobic-bullying-at-newtown-police-station/7916186. Accessed 9 October 2016.
26. See http://www.abc.net.au/news/2016-09-28/lgbti-australians-hide-identity-at-work-ethnic-discrimination/7884752. Accessed 29 September 2016.
27. Robinson *Gay Men's Relationships*, pp. 148–149.
28. N. Elias (2000, 1939) *The Civilizing Process: Sociogenetic and Psychogenetic Investigations*, trans. E. Jephcott with some notes and corrections by the author, ed. E. Dunning, J. Goudsblom and S. Mennell, rev. edn (Oxford: Blackwell Publishers Ltd), pp. 142–160 (Elias 2000, 1939).
29. For discussion of advertising's appropriation of the 1960s youth movement and meaning of the Creative Revolution, see T. Frank (1998) *The Conquest of Cool: Business Culture, Counterculture and the Rise of Hip Consumerism* (Chicago: University of Chicago Press) (Frank 1998).

References

Australian Broadcasting Corporation. http://www.abc.net.au/news/2016-10-09/allegations-of-homophobic-bullying-at-newtown-police-station/7916186. Accessed 9 Oct 2016.

Australian Broadcasting Corporation. http://www.abc.net.au/news/2016-09-28/lgbti-australians-hide-identity-at-work-ethnic-discrimination/7884752. Accessed 29 Sept 2016.

Australian Parliament. http://www.aph.gov.au/About_Parliament/Parliamentary_Departments/Parliamentary_Library/Publications_Archive/archive/hecs. Accessed 29 July 2016.

Elias, N. (1939) 2000. *The civilizing process: Sociogenetic and psychogenetic investigations*, trans. E. Jephcott with some notes and corrections by the author, ed. E. Dunning, J. Goudsblom, and S. Mennell, rev. ed. Oxford: Blackwell Publishers Ltd.

Frank, T. 1998. *The conquest of cool: Business culture, counterculture and the rise of hip consumerism*. Chicago: University of Chicago Press.

Hochschild, A. (1983) 2003. *The managed heart: Commercialization of human feeling*. Berkeley: University of California Press.

Jones, R. 2010. 'Were you a victim of the dot.com bubble?'. *The Guardian*. https://www.theguardian.com/money/2000/jul/15/personalfinancenews. Accessed 25 July 2016.

Pusey, M. 2003. *Experience of middle Australia: The dark side of economic reform*. Melbourne: Cambridge University Press.

Robinson, P. 2008. *The changing world of gay men*. Basingstoke: Palgrave Macmillan.

Robinson, P. 2013. *Gay men's relationships across the life course*. Basingstoke: Palgrave Macmillan.

Savin-Williams, R.C. 2005. *The new gay teenager*. Cambridge: Harvard University Press.

Sennett, R. 2006. *The culture of the new capitalism*. New Haven: Yale University Press.

Watson, I., J. Buchanan, I. Campbell, and C. Briggs. 2003. *Fragmented futures: New challenges in working life*. Sydney: The Federation Press.

5

Old-Age Fears or Concerns

As the gay population ages and there is a larger proportion of gay people at the older end of the spectrum with the baby boomers, I think that more services are going to be available for gay people and gay men but unfortunately I think it is going to be targeted because there is a perception that all gay men are … rich and I think that is going to impact on gay men that are still living in poverty.
(Jacob, aged 42, Melbourne)

Introduction

This chapter examines the stories that the 82 men from the international sample told of fears or concerns they held in relation to old age. The expectations ranged from the grievous about, for example, the loss of a life-long partner or having to return to the closet because of homophobia to milder concerns about, for example, having to rely on neighbours for home help or having an unwanted sibling at their death bed. The stories are examined by cohort, beginning with the oldest. The stories fell into three very broad categories—those relating to home care,

© The Author(s) 2017
P. Robinson, *Gay Men's Working Lives, Retirement and Old Age*,
Genders and Sexualities in the Social Sciences,
DOI 10.1057/978-1-137-43532-3_5

aged accommodation and social isolation. I did not use these terms when interviewing the men but simply asked them what worries old age held for them. The names for the three principal narratives in the men's accounts emerged from analysis of the data.

Home-care concerns included any reference the men made to the practicalities of living at home in old age. Accommodation concerns included any reference to an institutional setting, whether a hostel where residents have limited independence or a low-level care facility which permitted greater independence. What these accommodation settings have in common is that they are not the residents' private residence. An institutional setting is never quite as reassuring as one's home, no matter how luxurious its furnishings or facilities. Social isolation included any reference to being alone or lonely as a result of the absence of partner, friends or family—as a result of death—or because of reduced interest or ability in socialising. On the whole, the men's fears or concerns were not markedly different from those of the general population. Some were related to heterosexism or homophobia in supported-care or aged-accommodation settings. These are considered when they arise.

An individual's material resources or social class is important in determining how well and how long s/he will experience old age and applies as much to gay men as it does to the rest of the population. Other difficulties that gay men and lesbians can experience in old age concern formal and informal care networks and social connections. An assumption exists that the presence of children explains why heterosexuals are likely to enjoy an easier old age than gay men, lesbians or other sexual minorities. What this assumption overlooks is that not all heterosexuals have children, not all children and parents have caring relationships, and not all parents want to be cared for by their children or children can or want to look after their ageing parents. Where drawing attention to the absence of children in the lives of most gay people is useful is in underlining the importance to them of friendship networks as an antidote for imagined or real fears of social isolation in old age. While for some interviewees relations with family could be troublesome, nearly all of them had stories to relate of regular outings or meetings with friends and acquaintances, which suggested that in the absence of familial bonds fraternal ones were a more than satisfactory substitute.

The distinction between fear and concern is important. A fear is here understood to be something that affects a person's sense of belonging, disturbs their peace of mind and can, for example, disrupt their sleep. And a concern is here understood to be something that while vexing does not cause distress or sleeplessness. Universal fears or concerns about ageing were those that are regarded as fairly common in the general population, that is, relating to home care, aged accommodation or social isolation. Gay-specific ones almost entirely related to being marginalised in aged-care facilities because of one's sexuality. This finding reinforced other research into the ageing needs of gay, lesbian, bisexual, people (GLB) which has argued that gays and lesbians are wary of moving into nursing homes because they fear heterosexist assumptions or homophobia from staff or residents.[1]

Fears or Concerns by Age Cohort

The following section is divided into discussion of interviewees' responses by cohort. In each of the age-cohort sections, there are subsections on home care, aged accommodation and social isolation. 'Home care' is understood to refer to home-based care provided by local councils or private operators and 'aged accommodation' to refer to residential care facilities for elderly people who have legal capacity and require only low-level care; 'social isolation' is self-explanatory.

When the men spoke of aged accommodation, they were understood to be referring to the first stage of managed care in an institutional setting, such as in a nursing home, retirement home or village or a facility offering ageing in place. Each subsection and age-cohort begins with a brief outline of the principal characteristics of the men in it, namely, their race and ethnicity, class background, relationship status, and when they came out, the latter being a useful, very general indicator of the level of social acceptance each might have experienced as a young man.

Old Cohort

The old cohort comprised 25 men over 60. Six were in their 80s, nine in their 70s, and ten were in their 60s. As mentioned in Chap. 1, with two exceptions, the majority of interviewees were Anglo Saxon or Anglo Celtic. The two men who were not were a South Asian in his 60s from London and an African American from New York, also in his 60s.[2] Almost half of the interviewees had university degrees and for a little more than one-third of the men secondary school was their highest education qualification. Thirteen men or slightly more than half this age cohort were retired when interviewed.

Most of the men from this age cohort worked in white-collar jobs before retirement. The exceptions were two men in their 70s who had been railway workers. Of the men who were still employed when interviewed, all had jobs in white-collar occupations such as education or small business. On the basis of their education and very approximate indications they provided regarding their income, seven men had lower-class or lower-middle-class backgrounds, 16 had middle or upper-middle class backgrounds and two belonged to the upper class. Fourteen men were in relationships, 13 of which were long-lasting. And 11 men were single at the time of interview. Five of the interviewees had been married. One man was HIV positive.[3]

Home Care

Seven men or slightly less than one-third of men from the old cohort were concerned about the sort of care they would receive.[4] Analysis of the interviews revealed a mixture of concerns ranging from one man's wish not to burden his friends to another's reliance on an informal care-relationship built up over years with his neighbour. Two representative extracts are considered here.

Hugh and Lucas were aged in their 60 and 70s and were from Australia and New Zealand. Hugh was 62 and lived in Melbourne with his older partner of 37 years. When interviewed, Hugh's partner, who was in his late 80s, needed full-time care, most of which Hugh and his

5 Old-Age Fears or Concerns   165

partner's children were able to provide. Hugh's views on care were therefore both immediate and practical but despite the full-time load he carried domestically as principal carer and socially, his concerns about old age from personal observation of his partner's experience were that it carried no fears for him: 'old age doesn't worry me. I hope that I remain in reasonably good health'. He noted, however, that their extensive friendship network had been invaluable: 'it is a great help to know that there are people out there who really do care and support ... we're both very fortunate I think to have this support group'.

In Auckland, retired working-class Lucas (aged 75) explained why he was doing his very best to resist the good intentions of government workers who were doing their very best to persuade him to accept domestic help. He was keenly aware that if he were to accept their offer of help, it would be the beginning of a life of dependency.

> I am being pushed to some degree by the Health Department to have somebody come around and look after me ... if I give into that, I am losing my independence far more rapidly than I want to, so yes, things are going to get a bit difficult ... If somebody says 'I will give you a hand to put your shoes on' ... I would not start to put them on in the first place, so I would slowly have my independence eroded.

Lucas allowed his neighbour to mow their common nature strip for him but refused to let her take charge of his kitchen when invited into have coffee after the mowing. Various interpretations of Lucas's fierce independence are possible but the most persuasive is that like most people his age Lucas was aware that increased dependency would mean loss of control and as Norbert Elias observed when he himself lay dying the loss of control was for many old people the loss of the last vestige of their humanness.[5]

Aged Accommodation

No one looks forward to moving into aged-care accommodation. According to Sara Arber, most elderly Britons wait until the very last moment before relenting and accepting the inevitability of life in a nursing home, while according to Hal Swerissen and Stephen Duckett the majority of Australians want to die at home but only 14% are able to do so.[6] Of the 25 men from the old cohort, 14 raised concerns about accommodation in old age. Most did not look forward to aged accommodation, although one did say that he was looking forward to it because it would be like university life all over again. At least one was aware of the costs, and some raised the issue of gay nursing homes.

This section focuses on extracts from three men's transcripts that are representative of the 14 interviewees' concerns about life in aged accommodation or nursing homes.[7] All three men were in their 70s. One was from Sydney, the remaining two from Auckland. Their concerns chiefly related to marginalisation on the basis of sexuality.

The first interviewee was Christian who was 72 when interviewed in Sydney and before formal retirement had been a senior member of the Australian legal profession. He was fully occupied working for national and international bodies. He was critical of a system where large numbers of nursing homes in Australia are run by religious organisations, not all of which welcome GLB people.

> Nursing homes in Australia are often run by church organisations. Some church organisations, though not all, are not particularly welcoming to gay residents. They are not particularly understanding of the diversity of human relationships and of their needs ... [We need] to make retirement homes more welcoming ... but because of the age of people in nursing homes they will have grown up in Australia in a time when there was not great knowledge and even less sympathy for gay people.

Basil, the second interviewee, was 75 and lived in Auckland. He had had a long, continuous job in administration and been married with children. Not until relatively late in life had Basil come out, which could explain why in the following extract he said that he feared being singled out if he had to move into aged accommodation. Such a fear is neither unreasonable nor overstated given that many men from this generation, who were born in the 1930s and came of age in the 1950s, had to carefully manage their identity in times of marked hostility

5 Old-Age Fears or Concerns   167

toward gay men and lesbians and other non-conformists. As well, Basil explained in his interview how he had agonised over coming out and the effect it would have on his wife and children, a point also related to his generation.

> I feel that when you go into [a nursing home] ... you've got to get back in the closet. I am not going back into the closet for anybody. I'm out and ... would like to walk down the road with my partner, not necessarily holding hands, but at least [so] I don't care if we're seen together. Some of those people [in nursing homes] couldn't cope with that and I think it is possible that if I was in a retirement village that there is a potential for us to be treated differently if people know I'm gay. I would feel initially ... that I would need to be closeted. I would need to keep my sexuality very close to myself. I don't know how I would do it because ... while I'm not flamboyant, I'm out.

While Basil spoke about the fear of being ostracised because of his sexuality, there was an aspect also of the general in his complaint. He was worried about having his identity denied in the same way an elderly woman who all her life has been used to being called by her married surname when speaking to strangers might feel her identity denied when she is called 'love' by staff in a nursing home. What Basil was asking for was to be known and accepted for who he was—an elderly gay man in retirement.[8]

The third interviewee, Lucas had been employed in a number of different blue-collar jobs after he left school. Also from Auckland, he was 75 and retired at the time of interview. Lucas was slightly more optimistic than the two other men about life in a nursing home, fantasising about an idyllic setting where the staff would be young, attractive males. In the second half of the extract, however, he raises very real concerns about having to live in a 'heterosexual situation' and a female-dominated setting.

> Greatest thing would be to go into a retirement home that was particularly made for gay people. That would be great because then if I want to say something about the young boy who walked past delivering the

168   P. Robinson

papers to somebody, I am not going to offend anybody, but if I was in a heterosexual situation, I could not say that and I am thinking, 'Well, would that be even lonelier?'

There seems to be a preponderance of women in nursing homes.

Well, because they live longer than the guys. I can't think of anything worse because they tend to be a little bit cliquey, so if you're a gay, or if they ever find out you are gay ... you have got to be ever so careful about what you say ... [in case it] send shivers through other people's eyes.

While the elderly heterosexual woman might dread the small, verbal signals that she has lost her individual identity and is just another old love in the institution, she is at least a 'love' and not 'one of them'. Ostracism is the largely unspoken, big, fear that helps explain why so many interviewees said they did not want to move into aged accommodation or would prefer not to think about the prospect of doing so.

In addition to the story of how similar and different to the heterosexual experience of ageing is the gay experience, an important observation to draw from these extracts is that, as Chris Phillipson argued, class has a crucial influence on how an individual can expect to experience old age.[9] This was evident in the lived experiences of at least two of the three men whose views on aged accommodation were just considered.

Christian was aware of the inequalities and the potential for discrimination that can exist in some Australian nursing homes run by some religious organisations and because of some residents' views of GLB people but it was a situation he was not likely to experience:

I am not particularly worried about 'straights-ville' in the nursing home. I have made enough money in my life to make appropriate arrangements in my own case for my old age. I can understand that that could be a problem. Therefore, when I have gone to conferences on aged care and age organisations, I have emphasised the need to address the issues that have been pointed up in inquiries into the conditions of nursing homes and their treatment of older gay people.

Lucas was the only one with relatively optimistic expectations of life in a nursing home. He was also the only one of the three most likely to spend a fair part of his old age in one and the only man from a working-class background. I would argue his accepting attitude could be explained by a fatalistic approach to life gained from having to make do with precarious, insecure blue-collar employment over the course of his working life. Just like Christian and Basil, he was aware of how other residents' homophobia could affect him but unlike Basil he did not frame it in terms of having to return to the closet and seemed to accept its possibility without complaint.

Social Isolation

Twenty-two men, that is, a significant majority of the 26 men from this age cohort said that they were frightened of being socially isolated in old age.[10] Being alone or feeling lonely are experiences that can occur at any time in life. And I would argue that they are more potent in old age because of the proximity of death. When the men from this age cohort and the other cohorts spoke of their fear of social isolation in old age they were articulating a widespread, general fear, the gravity of which was underlined by both the nearness of death and that they would have to face it themselves or experience the death of their partner and friends before their own.

Fears of social isolation the men expressed concerned those two sets of circumstance—loneliness on the death of their partner and loneliness on the death of friends. The first group comprised men who were mostly in relationships: they were concerned about social isolation when their partner died. The second group of mostly single men was concerned about social isolation when their friends died. At the end of this section is a more detailed discussion of the link that I argue underlines the proximity of death and the men's fear of social isolation.

Representing the group who were concerned about being left alone after the death of their partner were two men. Separated in age by only a year, they spoke quite differently about their expectations. Alfie, aged 63, was from Manchester and Hugh, aged 62, was from Melbourne. Alfie had spent life after school working in clerical jobs in Manchester. He and his partner had been together for almost 40 years. They were

170   P. Robinson

close in age and lived in an upper-middle-class suburb of Manchester. University educated, Hugh's working life was in education and, as mentioned earlier, he was the principal carer for his older partner of more than 35 years. They lived in a well-to-do suburb in Melbourne.[11]

When asked about how he would cope if his partner died before him, Alfie replied, 'I'm scared stiff of being left on my own ... He can't go. I've got to go first. It's a done deal [*laughs*]'. When reflecting on how he would manage his own old age, Hugh in contrast said the following.

> I have got the inner resources to cope with being on my own as an older person ... There's no dementia in my family so, if genetics is part of it, I don't think there is much chance of my becoming demented ... But I think also with my interest in the arts I think that would always be a stimulation, particularly music, that contributes to a sense of wellbeing.

There are a number of possible explanations for the men's responses to the prospect of a life alone if their partner were to predecease them. The fact that Alfie and his partner were close in age whereas Hugh and his partner were not might explain Alfie's more clearly stated fear of being 'left alone'. Hugh, by comparison, seemed more removed from the effect of his partner's departure, which could be understood in light of his role as his partner's principal carer and that his partner was more than 20 years his senior and had been married with children. It is possible therefore that there was an element of the paternal in their relationship together with the fraternal. Caring for a partner day-to-day and being bedside as the other's body declines can give a person time to reflect on the likely shape of life after the partner's death.

Representing the group of men who referred to being left alone when their friends died was Jeffrey, a working-class New Zealander who lived in Auckland and was in his early 70s. He had spent his life working in the transport sector and was relying on the old-age pension when interviewed. He had considered the possibility his friends might die before him—'I maintain reasonably good health, expect for mental health sometimes ... and then [I worry that] I might lose all my friends and then what?'—and had resolved to cultivate younger friends. But this was not without its difficulties.

They're not in the same position as I'm in as far as age goes. They don't think about it the same way as ... friends of my generation do. We look out for each other ... And the whole world is young compared to us ... There are some wonderful young people here. But they still have their own lives ... Most of them are in relationships and I'm jealous of that too. It's quite sobering and saddening to go home alone when they're going home in love and all the things that go with that.

Among difficulties Jeffrey experienced when socialising with younger gay men was that they did not understand it as he and his friends did for whom it was their lived experience and in his view the young men's approach to friendship was not the same as how men his age expressed theirs: 'We look out for each other'. As well, the young men fell into relationships more easily and were not interested in having an intimate/sexual relationship with him. Including younger men in one's friendship circle might partly solve the problem of feeling alone when one's contemporaries died but only as long as the older man was clear that he sought friendship and was not looking for a relationship with a younger man, which is something else entirely.

Death as Social Isolation

Underpinning the men's grave fears of being left alone when their partner died was the deeper, more universal fear of death as personal annihilation, which everyone must face if their partner dies before them. Contemporary fear of death has been a source of historical, literary and sociological interest since at least the end of World War II. British novelists Jessica Mitford and Evelyn Waugh mocked the American 'way of death', sending up the vast cemetery lawns with sickly sweet names like 'fields of contentment', and while these might raise a laugh I would argue that beneath the class-based mockery lies a concern about death and how to die and whether the American attempt at the 'painless' death was preferable to the repressed approach with which the British establishment dealt with the end of life.[12]

French historian Philippe Ariès argued that a painless death was impossible because western society had banished death.[13] In medieval

172 P. Robinson

times, by comparison, death was 'tame' he said because humans lived with death and death lived with us. Cemeteries, charnel houses and public executions Ariès argued were a more common feature of lived experience and urban landscape and because life expectancy for ordinary people was so much less then, they lived in closer proximity to their own death. His views were shared by German sociologist Norbert Elias who in a remarkable account of his own death reflected on why twentieth-century society consigned the dying to hospital wards and a lonely death.[14]

Despite technological advances in science and medicine, argued Elias, western society had not conquered death. And despite increasing longevity, people from advanced western economies had not reacquainted themselves with the social aspect of death which wrote Ariès was normal in Europe before World War I and more common in less developed societies. Fear of what Ariès called the 'wild' death—'wild' because western society is so removed from death that it now terrifies—is not peculiar to gay people, is a common experience and a grave fear.[15] Both the reality of death and terrors associated with it lie behind some aspects of the social isolation the men from this cohort and the younger cohorts feared they would experience when their partner or friends died.

Middle Cohort

The middle cohort comprised 28 men aged 45–60. Born between the early 1950s and early 1960s, they belonged to the 'baby boomer' generation. As mentioned in Chap. 1, 18 of the men from this age cohort were in their 50s and 10 were in their 40s and the majority were white.[16] As 'boomers', these men came of age at a time of considerable social change in western countries. Not all of them were involved in social protest movements or even in their local gay liberation group or similar when they were young men but the times were momentous for the changes they created in how camp, gay or homosexual men were regarded and sowed the seeds for a sexual rights movement, which continues to effect change in the 2010s.[17] More widely, the socio-political agendas of this period reshaped how the individual was understood and laid the foundations for identity politics that continue to influence how other ethnic/religious minorities, genders and sexualities are understood.

Twenty-four (or 85%) of the men had university degrees. Of the four who did not, two left school when legally able to do so and got jobs; the other two went to trade schools. The men from the middle cohort were middle class or upper middle class, which as an age cohort only slightly sets them apart from the men from the old cohort where there was stronger evidence of men whose working lives had entirely been in blue-collar jobs.

Eleven of the men were in long-lasting relationships and another four men were in relationships of between three months and seven years.[18] Thirteen or almost half the men were single. Five men were in civil unions and four men were 'gaily' married.[19] In terms of previous heterosexual relationships, three of the men were divorced from former wives, two of whom had children with them; one man had an adopted son. Six men were HIV positive—the largest group of positive men from the international Anglophone sample where the total number of HIV-positive men was eight. It is not surprising that the largest cluster of HIV-positive men should be in the 45–60 age cohort. The baby-boomer generation experienced very high rates of infection and mortality in the first decade of the epidemic and until the mode of transmission was identified in the late 1980s and the triple-therapy treatment was discovered in the late 1990s.[20]

As explained in Chap. 3 on the working lives of this cohort, none of the men was retired when interviewed. Their occupations were varied and included nine who worked in business, either in the corporate world or small business, seven who worked in education, and twelve who worked in middle-class jobs such as media, public service or welfare agencies. In the sections that follow, the fears or concerns of the middle cohort are analysed in the same way they were for the old cohort, that is, in relation to home care, aged accommodation, and social isolation. The subsection on social isolation is slightly different this time because it includes a separate discussion on the intersection between identity, sex and class—the reason being that it is in this cohort that links were most clearly seen between class and coping with social

174   P. Robinson

isolation of ageing through sexual encounters. There is a subsection also on family and friends in the section on social isolation.

Home Care

A quarter of the men from the middle cohort raised the matter of care when discussing their old age fears or concerns.[21] Their home-care concerns comprised in order of importance: cost of services; quality of care; relationship status, that is, whether single or coupled; and the influence of religious organisations. The last three concerns are discussed in the sections on aged accommodation and social isolation where they are relevant. In this section, discussion centres on the men's concerns about the cost of paying for services in old age either for themselves or their partners, understandings about which were often formed from the experience of caring for parents or elderly relatives.

A number of interviewees raised the cost of services or the 'cost of old age' in the context of home care. Among those who did were two men who spoke at some length about it and in relation to continuing to exercise 'control' in their lives. All were earning relatively high incomes or from well-off families. When interviewed in 2010, two of them had annual incomes in excess of US$135,000.[22] Duncan, who lived in Hong Kong, and was earning a very substantial income in 2010 of approximately US$200,000, had the least to say on the subject but raised the matter of 'control', observing that: 'financial security is incredibly important because … it allows for a certain freedom and control'.

The two other men were in their 50s and lived in London. Each had parental experience to draw on, one more positive than the other. Ryan (aged 53) drew on experience with his elderly mother, saying: 'My mother … has had various problems. Sometimes it's been difficult to find out what happened to her and she's not particularly connected to people and so all these things are an issue'. During his interview Ryan was not asked if his mother's being 'not particularly connected' was a life-long personal trait or something that had developed with age. Nor was he asked what he meant by the phrase and whether it meant she

5 Old-Age Fears or Concerns   175

was an isolated individual or did not socialise easily and again whether she had always been this way or if it were a recent development. When Ryan said that 'it's been difficult to find out what happened', I assumed that either his mother was unable or unwilling to tell him about her problems or that the staff caring for her were not particularly communicative and that either way there was a communication breakdown and he was left not knowing. While concerned that he might experience old age as was his mother, Ryan was fairly certain that he would not be helpless: 'I think I will be able to control the environment in which I live and die'.

In a similar way to Duncan from Hong Kong, Ryan used the word 'control' to describe how he imagined ageing, that is, that he hoped or expected not to lose control of his life. Control in a rich person's vocabulary usually means having sufficient financial resources to ensure s/he can continue to direct how s/he is being cared for. Ryan's life story suggested a well-to-do background: a British public-school education and considerable social capital both inherited and self-made, which I would argue carried over into his use of the importance of having 'control' in old age just as in every other aspect of life and the life course. Whether his material capital matched his social capital was not clear.

If a Nordic welfare system were in place in countries like Australia, England, New Zealand or the United States, control would be an ordinary right of every elderly citizen.[23] In Anglophone countries, where the last 30 years have seen considerable policy change in the area of old age pensions and superannuation, control is increasingly tied to an aged person's financial resources. And those with more resources at their disposal have greater ability to 'control' their material and therefore their health environment. 'The extent to which people have confidence about planning the direction of their lives ... is geared around the resources they are likely to have at their disposal.'[24] As old age has become more costly, those with abundant material resources can expect a better experience of it, a fact that some sociologists have been warning about for more than 30 years.[25]

The second man with parental experience to draw on was Tate, a 51-year-old who lived in London. Single at the time of interview but aware of the possibility in the offing of a sexual/social relationship with a younger man, Tate was fairly confident that his old age would not be taxing: 'until my brain starts going and I need support ... I think I will be happy'. He was alive to the fact that his material resources would affect the quality of his life in old age:

> as long as I have a reasonable amount of money ... why should I not be happy about being old? You read, you listen to music, your friends come to visit you.

His material resources were considerable so he could contemplate old age not as a time of privation but as one of continued sociability and cultural fulfilment. Like the other two men whose accounts were considered above, Tate was aware that ageing costs money and that he expected to have sufficient to enjoy a good old age. To me, it seemed his comments about what he expected from old age were based on what he had observed in his father's experience, for, later in the interview, Tate related more intimate details of his father's old age, which spoke to concerns some people have about ageing and institutional ageing.[26]

> My father and I talk about sex a lot ... We are very good friends. He finally confessed ... three or four months ago that he had not fucked his girlfriend in two years. But he said, 'I was worried about not having a girlfriend to fuck when I was 80 but now [I am 80] I do not want to fuck'.

His father's account of his erotic imaginings and reality were instructive in Tate's view, touching as it did on the fleeting nature of sexual desire and satisfaction. For Tate, who admitted to a similar, strong sexual need, his father's confession said a lot about 'the other things that drive you, the habit of living' that are unrelated to sex or erotic desire and possibly even more sustaining in the long run.

Home-care issues for the men from the middle cohort concerned quality of care and the importance of not losing control of life in old age or becoming too dependent or prematurely dependent on others. For these men, who were still some years from being old, their knowledge of the importance of having good quality care or keeping control

Aged Accommodation

Slightly more than half the men from the middle cohort raised the matter of aged accommodation, citing two fears and two concerns.[27] The two fears related to anti-homosexual discrimination (homophobia) or loss of independence. These I regarded as fairly serious because of the impact they could have on a person's identity and self-esteem. The first was gay-specific, the other a universal fear. The two concerns related to the quality of care in aged accommodation or the loss of male company (homo-sociability). Both of these were universal concerns. Quality of care is self-evident and while the loss of company of men might appear gay-specific it is likely to be a concern for men generally. These fears and concerns are discussed in order.

Two men's views were representative of those afraid of anti-homosexual discrimination. Ward (aged 59) was from New York. He had lived with his partner for 15 years and said that they would like to move to a warmer location when they retired but were aware of homophobia in 'southern states' of the USA: 'The only southern state that doesn't really have any hostile legal environment is New Mexico'. The other man who noted anti-homosexual discrimination was Ben, a 52-year-old from Manchester. His concerns touched on the various forms this could take:

> I also fear deep old age ... because of the loss of physical autonomy and ending up in a care home where my sexuality is not erased per se but any sexual history might either be rewritten as a presumed heterosexual or, even if my sexual difference is acknowledged, I might still risk covert homophobia.

This observation suggested a strongly informed, nuanced understanding of how anti-homosexual discrimination or prejudice can operate, which is firstly through heterosexist assumptions and/or secondly as a result of what he called 'covert homophobia'. It is notable that Ben referred to these as being likely in 'deep old age' when perhaps he expected he would have less control over how he was treated, regarded or understood. Whether or not this fear was one other gay men or same-sex attracted men shared would depend on how integral their homosexuality was to their sense of self. For Ben, it was so central that in his early 50s he was worried about the possibility of losing it in deep old age.

The men who were worried about loss of independence were in their 50s and 40s and from London, Los Angeles, Manchester and New York. In the section on home care, three men with material capital referred to keeping 'control' of their environment in old age, which was understood as doing their best not to lose control of things as they aged. Other men were more direct. For example, Ben from Manchester, already noted as concerned about discrimination in aged care, said he was afraid of deep old age because 'of the loss of physical autonomy'. And Alvin, a 47-year-old from New York said: 'I would not want to be institutionalised. I would like to have someone take care of me'.

Quality-of-care concerns are represented here by the accounts of two Aucklanders in their 50s. Both were concerned about the quality of care which they might have to rely on when in aged accommodation or hospital. Their concern was a generalised one about the chance nature of receiving good quality care in state funded hospitals or low-cost, aged accommodation. The men were neither poor nor likely to have to rely on a state pension in old age. They were concerned, however, about an old age when they would have limited control over decisions concerning their conditions of life and the sort of care they could expect from staff looking after them. The first man, Austin, was 57 and had spent a great deal of his working life in education. He saw a connection between quality of care and financial resources: 'I will want to grow old, be cared for by good people but [there is] lots of stuff centred around finances and quality of care'. Austin belonged to a gay aged-care interest group, the purpose of which was to raise awareness of old age issues in middle-aged and older gay men. One of the topics they had discussed before his interview was the variability of care in aged accommodation and hospitals. The second man, Nathan (aged 50) was also from Auckland and he too belonged to the aged-care interest group. He appeared to have gained some hearsay knowledge about gay men's experience of care but its reliability was not tested in the interview: 'We do hear every now and then of older gay men being treated rather badly by nurses in hospitals'. The fact that this man held such a belief and relayed it is significant because of its power to contribute to and influence fears that men in the interest group or his friendship circle might already have about old age, even if they recognised it as hearsay, not based on a reliable source.

Two men represented those who were concerned about loss of homosociability in aged-care accommodation. Each said that he would only move into an aged-care facility if it were gender segregated, that is, gay only or male only. Danny (aged 48) was an expatriate who lived in Hong Kong. He said it would not affect him because he would not live in non-gay, aged accommodation: 'Living in a straight environment does not scare me because I won't [*laughs*]. I refuse to'. And Eddie from Manchester, who was 45 when interviewed, also said that he had no intention of moving into what he called a 'mixed home':

> I want to be in a gay home. I do not want to go into a mixed home. I avoid mixed bars so why would I want to go into a mixed home? ... I enjoy men's company ... I can go out on my own, speak to nobody, stand in the company of gay men and I am fulfilled. I feel like I am at home.

Eddie's comments are a good representation of the views of a subset of gay men who actively pursue the company of other men and who understand gay men's society and culture as being exclusively masculine. As I have argued elsewhere, same-sex sexual attraction in men and gay or homosexual identity are neither homogeneous nor synonymous.[28]

The 'mixed' nature of socialising and ageing that Eddie mentioned referred to settings or facilities that allow for both homosexual and heterosexual clients or residents. While some same-sex attracted people have welcomed the evolution of mixed bars and clubs, there are also gay men like Eddie who prefer the company of their own and have no wish to socialise with heterosexuals. Not all the men interviewed for this research favoured gay nursing homes or other forms of gay aged accommodation. Eddie was one who did and said so unambiguously:

180   P. Robinson

> When you go into a home ... the smell of some women is horrible ...
> The smell of a man is fine ... I want the smell of a man [around me] ...
> I am a bit of a gay separatist to be honest. I see the importance of community and for community you have got to exclude as well as include. If you do not exclude, it is not your community; it is this mass of people just doing things.

This view might distress gay-friendly women who like to think homosexual men are empathetic, cuddly, versions of their husbands or male partners. It was a frank explanation for not wanting to share a communal living space with women. It is reminiscent also of the views that 1970s, separatist, feminists held who refused to associate with men intellectually, sexually or socially.

Norbert Elias might not necessarily have had Eddie's preferences for an all-male environment in mind when he wrote *The Loneliness of the Dying* but one of the signal points he made in that work was that among the disjunctions that occur for elderly people when they move from the relative independence of living at home to institutionalised living in aged-care accommodation is enforced sociability with strangers. 'There is an increasing number of institutions in which only old people, who did not know each other in their earlier years, live together.'[29] Men like Eddie might avoid what Elias noted if all-male or exclusively gay aged facilities were established, affordable and available in their neighbourhood and if their friends also became residents. Gay men who did not have this option could find themselves having to move into mixed nursing homes and for at least some of the men from the middle cohort their fear was that enforced sociability would include cohabiting with women and homophobes.

Institutional accommodation is a universal fear among elderly people, only slightly mitigated by class. No one, rich or poor, wishes to move from home to an aged-care facility and class mitigates the experience only in terms of better accommodation facilities available to people able to afford them—such as private room, en-suite bathroom, private dining. Few people welcome the prospect of communal living in old age. For the men from the middle cohort, the prospect of moving into aged accommodation held additional fears and concerns. They feared the prospect of anti-homosexual discrimination or losing independence. The first was a gay-specific fear that varied according to the importance men placed on their sexual identity. The second was a universal one associated with life in an institutional setting. I would argue that class would mitigate these fears also because there is already evidence of high-end accommodation providers using diversity as a marketing strategy,[30] and abundant resources will always enable a high level of independence even in an institutional setting, until, that is, physical dependency becomes the person's daily norm. Concerns expressed by the men from the middle cohort related to quality of care, again a universal concern and something that is mitigated by class and then to the loss of the company of men, which could be avoided if all-male or gay-only nursing homes were established and the men were willing and able to afford them.

Social Isolation

Social isolation was the most important of the three old-age fears or concerns in the eyes of the men from the middle cohort. Twenty men (or 80% of the group) referred to it.[31] Their views are discussed in relation to, first, their fears about the role their partner would play in their old age and, second, their thoughts about how they would adapt and build social connections in their old age.

The connection the men made between social isolation in old age and the role of their partner centred on expectations or hopes about the longevity of their relationship. Not surprisingly, this was associated with fears about who would predecease whom and how the survivor would manage his social/emotional life after his partner's death. Of the twenty men from the middle cohort who discussed the matter of social isolation, eight specifically did so in the context of the role their partner would have in their old age. Six of these men were in their 50s and two were in their 40s. Four were from Hong Kong, two were from New York, and there was one from each of London and Sydney. Having a younger partner and how they imagined it would affect their old age was raised by two men, both in their late 50s and both from Hong

Kong. Bernard, whose partner was almost 20 years his junior, said about him, 'he is very accepting of my age and [that] helps me deal with ageism'. Raymond, also from Hong Kong, explained why he enjoyed life with his partner who was 20 years younger:

> I have an amazingly enjoyable life [with him]. I do things now which I would never have dreamed of doing in my younger days and I am so much happier now than I was in those younger days.

Both men recognised an emotional debt to their younger partner. Bernard saw a link between his partner's acceptance of their age difference and his own self confidence and Raymond appreciated the vitality his younger partner brought to his life.

The presence or absence of a partner in old age was raised by six men. Two of them were from Hong Kong, two from New York, one from London, and one was from Sydney. Their views varied from quite intense fear to moderate concern. The men who were frightened about the absence of a partner in old age included those who were in long-term relationships and worried about their partner predeceasing them. Most people in couple relationships fear how they will cope if their partner predeceases them—a reality mostly experienced by women in heterosexual relationships because of men's shorter life expectancy.[32] Ever since same-sex attracted men began to feel safe and confident to create their own relationships, however, this has been a fear they have felt and a reality they have experienced also, even if the relationships have not been publicly acknowledged. A 48-year-old man from Hong Kong said he was worried about life in old age if his partner predeceased him. Danny, already noted as being wealthy, was an expatriate and was in a long-standing relationship with a partner seven years younger. For a man in the prime of life with a partner he loved, the idea of not being together with him was something he did not wish to contemplate:

> Do I check out first or does he check out first or what happens after that? You try not to go there [i.e. think about it] too much because you could take yourself down a dark hole.

Based on his response, it is unlikely Danny will be discussing death with his partner until it is imminent, which is usual for some couples. A second man with fears of being single in old age was Everett who lived in New York and was 49 at the time of interview. Everett had been gaily married but was single at the time of interview:

> My greatest fear is not having a partner. Nobody wants to be alone and it is definitely one of my biggest fears. I have a choice. I can either grow old or I can die. I have a choice so I choose to grow old and I choose to live out my life but one of my greatest fears is that I will grow old alone and I really would not like to do that ... I would love to be able to share my life with someone. It is very important to me.

Everett was not asked what he meant when he said, 'I can either grow old or I can die' and the sentence sits somewhat anomalously in the extract. Putting it to one side, Everett held intense fears about the prospect of being single in old age. As mentioned, these feelings of loneliness and aloneness could be connected with the fact that he had once been married and had been single for 2 years.

A third man never referred to life without his partner. Also an expatriate living in Hong Kong, Zachary (aged 52) expounded on the importance to him of his couple relationship with his partner of 22 years suggesting it was the central mandala of his life:[33]

> I am very fortunate in the relationship I am in. And, touch wood, we are comfortable. That brings me a lot of comfort and in that sense ... [if we were] poor together, we would be fine. We'd figure it out together.

As an afterthought, Zachary added: 'But at the back of my head, I still know we should be planning better [for retirement]'. Both he and his partner had well-paid jobs in Hong Kong and it is possible that given that, as each was in his early 50s, retirement and its financial demands were still some way off.

The central importance of the couple relationship in the lives of the two people it comprises has been written about at length.[34] For

184   P. Robinson

heterosexuals, it has a long history. Now, as gay men are willing and able to speak more freely and openly about their intimate lives and in an increasing number of countries able to get married, its similar centrality is more in evidence and obvious.[35] A fourth man in his late 50s said that he and his partner were talking about where and how they would share their retirement together. Two assumptions underpinned the certainty with which this 59-year-old New Yorker explained his old-age plans. The first was that he and his partner would remain together and the second that they would spend their old age together: 'We own a home in Long Island and so we have been planning for retirement all along through savings'.

The dread that being alone in old age holds for some people was underlined in the accounts of two men in their 50s. Ryan, already noted as being well-connected, was a 53-year-old who lived in London. He was acutely aware of how alone was his single life:

> I am alone now and I am constantly having to face my age every day and it is a problem. It is boring. I never had it before because for some reason it did not seem to be that important.

Like Everett from New York, Ryan had been in a long-term relationship until relatively recently. After 14 years with his partner, they had separated around four years before his interview. He continued his account of what being alone in old age could mean to him.

> I am sure that if I was in a relationship, some of this stuff would come up as well. It is not a question of whether you are alone or in a relationship but it is more difficult when you are alone. Yes, I am afraid of being lonely. I often wonder if I remain single when I am in my 80s what I will be doing. What will my life be like and whether I will accept it ... I am doing pretty well for somebody my age but I lie about my age.

The fact that Ryan admitted to lying about his age in the context of what fears or concerns he had about old age could suggest that he hoped to remain young-looking or youthful for as long as he could. Later in the interview, he expanded on his sex life and how he was still sexually attractive to younger men and that he found it easier to lie about his age:

> Sometimes, I lie to people partly because I do not want to put them through the embarrassment. And that sounds like a delusion but it is a truth actually. Other times, I lie because I simply do not want them to know that I am 53. If I can get away with being seven or eight years younger, why not?

Being still immersed in the social/sexual gay scene, Ryan rationalised his lying as a simple strategy to maximise his sexual attractiveness and chances of finding a sexual partner when he was feeling sexually adventurous. What Ryan revealed was a fairly long-standing approach for sexual adventurers on the gay scene.[36]

The sixth man was Isaac (aged 56) who lived in Sydney and had a long-standing relationship of more than 30 years with a partner who was over 20 years his senior. Isaac was frank about the likelihood his partner would predecease him and that the strategy he had adopted, with his partner's agreement, was to widen his circle of gay friends and acquaintances by actively engaging in casual sex at beats. This strategy was his way of preparing for life after his partner's death and the story that he told of being, 'out there and going to beats again', leads into considering the various strategies some of the men from the middle cohort adopted to deal with the prospect of social isolation in old age.

Identity, Sex and Class

Elsewhere, I have argued that certain gay men in their 40s and 50s showed no inclination to reduce their involvement in the gay scene as they moved through middle age and headed toward early old age.[37] Their attachment to the gay scene can be understood as a set of practices developed over three decades or more and enforced by routine, which they are either unwilling or unable to change. As mentioned in Chap. 1, one of the central arguments in this book builds on the work of Georges Bataille in proposing that sex and work are bound together, representing twin poles of human-ness.[38] One of the more important observations Bataille made regarding the relation between sex and work is that because the dominant class have more leisure time at their disposal, they have greater opportunity to devote more time to the enjoyment of sex.[39] A man from the middle cohort reported a sex life that supported Bataille's claim regarding the sexual activity of the dominant classes. Like other interviewees, he was asked a question about his use of the Internet.[40]

The men did not understand the question uniformly. Some assumed I was asking them about their use of Facebook, others as to whether they used it to talk with other people in chat rooms. And a small, third group assumed I was asking them if they used the Internet for making sexual arrangements on, for example, a smart-phone application like Grindr or a gay website like Gaydar.

Fifty-one-year-old Tate who lived in London belonged to the third category and assumed the question referred to using the Internet to arrange sexual encounters. When I asked the question, he said, 'that's a euphemism if I have ever heard one', and then elaborated, saying that his experience had begun some years before in France where he tried using a computer application, which was fairly basic and for that reason unsatisfactory. 'It was a time when there were no pictures and was just people saying how long their dicks were. I developed a block to any kind of online cruising.' As mentioned, Tate was one of the richest men in international sample. He stated his income in 2010 as being in excess of US\$130,000. His aversion to online cruising changed when he was in Egypt, however, as is suggested in the following extract.

> By accident, I found myself in Cairo for ten days and I knew that I was going to be in Cairo for ten days so I used Gaydar to organise a different fuck for each night of those ten days that I was in Cairo. And the first fuck showed up the first evening and I fell in love with him and I cancelled all the others.

Unfortunately for Tate, the man with whom he fell in love when he was in Cairo was not free to return his love in the way that suited Tate because as a Muslim from an upper-class family, he was obliged

5 Old-Age Fears or Concerns 187

to marry and have children. Tate's next experience was with the smart-phone application, Grindr, which gave him access to men looking for casual sexual encounters. In the following extract, he describes the appeal of Grindr.

> [You] go on [your smart phone] and you see a list of the 20 or 30 people nearest to you who are also either online or recently have been online and you can have free chat with them. You can exchange photos, you can exchange locations and so on ... Grindr ... was so successful that I wound up meeting a string of men one day.

When telling the story of his ill-fated love affair in Cairo, Tate said that he believed he had, 'this terrible propensity for falling in love', which continued as he explored the social/sexual possibilities available on Grindr: 'I liked these guys so much that one out of two wound up not just being one night stands but more'. In line with Bataille's argument about the ability of the dominant class to enjoy greater sexual encounters, I would argue that the principal reason Tate was able to enjoy sexual relations with so many men was because he was rich and not tied down to conventional daily routines of work and on holidays. Some of his casual sexual partners became boyfriends, which made for a busy if not complex private life until he and one of them fell in love.

> There was this great accumulation of ... fuck responsibilities that people were expecting me to ...
>
> *Take them out for dinner?*
>
> No, fuck them. No it was just sex. There was nothing else. And ... I had five or six steady boyfriends here which I have now had to drop one by one ... and tell them that I am now in ... my monogamous phase and I will let them know when I am available again.

Tate was a middle-aged man with a young man's appetite for sex and romance. His sexual adventurism could be understood first, as mirroring approaches other men from this cohort said they were using now as a defence against loneliness or, second, as a man with a strong sexual desire making use of the free time his wealth allowed him and the opportunities available to him because of gay sexual practices and new technology. The extent to which frequent, anonymous, sexual encounters can provide protection from social isolation in early old age is not clear, but the stories discussed in the previous section of men from the old cohort who sought relationships with younger men suggest it is unlikely.

Accounts from men in their 50s of sexual adventurism and the benefit of having younger partners related to approaches that some people use—gay and straight, male and female—to avoid thinking about or being alone in old age. Other strategies men from the cohort discussed in relation to this included closer ties with family and friends and continued contact with the gay scene. And these are considered next.

Family and Friends

Maintaining close ties with family and friends was recommended by two men as an antidote to social isolation in old age. The first was a man in his 50s from Melbourne, the second a 45-year-old from Manchester. Fifty-one-year-old Calvin moved back to Melbourne to be closer with his sister and cousins after spending much of his 40s elsewhere for work. His large, well-connected, middle-class family provided sociability that was important for Calvin:

> I am lucky that I have a close ... supportive relationship with my sister and I have a lot of cousins that I have close, friendly relationships with. I go to a lot of extended family activities so in that regard I am lucky.

Calvin had extensive knowledge and experience of gay scenes in Melbourne, Sydney, and Hong Kong. His familial activities seemed to counter-balance his involvement in the gay scene, its parties, dances and festivals: 'I am included in extended family activities ... and that is good for me in terms of my social network'. Suspicious of the claims of social media to 'connect' people, Calvin here explains what connectedness meant to him:

5 Old-Age Fears or Concerns   189

> I think the Internet is a double-edged sword. You get this remote connectedness with Facebook which I think is rubbish ... It is amusing but it is not connecting with people really and ... when you go to the bars and you go around, you look at some people and you think, 'You probably do not have many close friends' ... I think it is important ... to keep a broad range of contacts in your life.

Calvin's understanding of connectedness shows a strong preference for practical, visceral connections with people over the virtual connections of social media, which could be explained by a combination of factors including his class, age and grounded knowledge of the bars and clubs that comprise the gay scene.

Forty-five-year-old Eddie expected his long-standing friendships as well as his relationship of more than 18 years to continue for the rest of his life and into old age. 'I have old friends,' he said, 'friends of all ages and they seem to get on quite well so I do not have this stereotype of [being] old and decrepit in old age'. He expected also to enjoy old age, saying: 'I think old age is the start of something. I have no idea what to expect ... I am not feared of it and I am quite looking forward to it', especially, he observed because of his middle-class life:

> Fortunately, I am not digging roads. I am not being a chef. I am not driving vans. I have got a reasonably middle-class job now. I will bet you if I was digging roads I would be a bit fearful of being old but, because I am not, I am not.

Perhaps no other social group knows better than those who work with their body—whose body is their tool of trade—the effect a lifetime's physical labour can have on the body and afflict it in old age. Eddie was born into a working-class family and had worked digging roads, as a restaurant chef, and driving vans and so knew what it meant to have to use his body to earn his pay. For this reason, he was very aware, as he said in his interview, of the better life he expected to lead in old age since beginning work in the higher education sector more than 10 years ago.

A third man, Marvin, was 59 and from Los Angeles. He was concerned about family members being involved with his end-of-life care, in particular a sister, about whom he said: 'I absolutely can't stand [her] and she's the one who is going to stand by my bedside and talk shit as I'm trying to die'. Marvin's frank comment about the distress of not being able to prevent an annoying sibling from being by his bedside was both a familiar concern and a reminder of what many gay men experienced during the HIV-AIDS crisis in the 1980s when hospital staff could exclude partners from being at their dying lover's bedside in favour of family members.[41]

His concern was less about the quality of staff care than how to exercise control over the circumstances of his dying. He was taking legal steps to prevent his sister being present when he was dying: 'When I put that clause in my advance directive it was with the understanding that I did not want to face that inevitability [his sister's presence at his bedside]'.

Gay men are generally no more likely than anyone else to experience family difficulties that continue to play out when they are old or dying. Where their experience can be more intense or long lasting is when family difficulties relate to parents', relatives' or siblings' rejection of them because of their sexuality. This is different from relationship breakdowns caused by disagreements over birthday presents, finances, football teams, property, wills or any other difficulties that affect family members because whether or not they are aware of it the person who rejects another because of their sexuality is rejecting the core of that person's being and, if they cannot make peace with their GLB relative, the wound is unlikely to heal. One relationship breakdown which is similar to what occurs when a GLB relative is rejected because of their sexuality and that is when families or family members fall out or feud over religious conversion or change of religion. Because coming out can be understood as being born again, it, like religious conversion or change of religion, results in the re-formation of the self. And any breach caused by rejecting someone for who they are or have become is not easily repaired.[42]

Young Cohort

This age cohort was the largest of the three age cohorts used for this study, comprising 29 men aged 45 and younger. Eight of the men were in their 40s, ten were in their 30s, nine were in their 20s, one was aged

19 and one 18. All but one of the young men were employed and had white-collar jobs including business, education and retail. There was also a group of university students comprising eight undergraduates and one postgraduate. More than two-thirds of the young men had university degrees and the remaining one-third trade or secondary-school qualifications.

More than half of the men from this cohort had partners. Two were in long-lasting relationships, that is, had been with the same partner for ten years or more.[43] Men whose relationships were between three and ten years' duration were in their 30s or 40s and most of the men in relationships of 12 months or less were in their 20s. There was no particular pattern for the single men: they were spread across all three deciles. In the next section, the men's responses are discussed in relation to home care, aged accommodation and social isolation.

Home Care

The men from this age cohort believed that gay men had a harder time in old age because they did not have children to take care of them and because of insufficient or inadequate gay community interest and/or awareness of gay men's old age needs. Almost all the young men who raised the matter of home care in the context of old-age needs ($n = 7$) referred to the heterosexual assumption that children ease the burden of old age when discussing how gay men could expect to experience old age.[44] And because gay men are generally childless, the young men spoke of old age as likely to be more difficult for gay men. A small group referred to what I have called 'communal absence' or a lack of interest in or awareness of old age issues in the gay community. When they did so, however, they voiced strong views about what was not being done by the gay 'community' and what needed to be done, that is, what they regarded as weaknesses in the gay men's communal response to ageing issues.

Caring for family members shaped the views of two men who considered home-care needs in the context of gay men's absent children. The first was a 44-year-old Londoner called Jonathan, the second a 32-year-old Sydneysider called Dylan. Both were university-educated and had

192   P. Robinson

white-collar jobs. Jonathan had a high-paying job in an international corporation and Dylan worked in finance. Jonathan expressed a strongly reflexive understanding of older person's care needs in the context of looking after his parents, which he did with his brother's help:

> I have got five god children who I fully intend to keep close relationships with partly because I want to make sure that at least one of them looks after me in my old age ... My brother and I are geared up to look after our parents who are still very lively and do not need any kind of care but they will do one day. We are gearing ourselves up for providing that role. And [as we do this] I think, 'Who is going to do it for me?' It does not make any difference how much money you have got, you come to a point in your life where you are old and you need someone to look after you or to help you do things and I think, 'Who is it going to be?'

Jonathan's account is instructive for a number of reasons. First, his strategic decision to keep close relations with 'at least one' of his god children suggests a strong belief in the role and usefulness of being able to maintain a quasi-familial bond with people from a generation younger so as to be able to rely on them to care for him in his old age. This might change in time as gay relationships become more recognised and therefore normalised and acquire the same generational bonds that already exist in heterosexual families.

At the moment, most gay men are born into heterosexual families and grow up forming relationships as someone's child, grandchild, cousin, or sibling. While some gay men form alternative families, others do not and instead maintain conventional relationships with their birth family and wider family. As Jonathan made clear in the extract above, however, he has planned to make use of something like a kin relationship—with his god children—so he will be in a position to draw on what he regarded as the traditional familial support that elderly people would draw on when they needed help because of infirmities brought on by old age. This decision might reflect a distrust in the informal care networks that exist between gay men or unfamiliarity with them. For whatever reason, Jonathan spoke of the more binding relationship he believed existed when relatives or quasi-relatives were involved.

5 Old-Age Fears or Concerns 193

Decisions such as these, taken by gay men like Jonathan could change as the idea and practice of gay families become more common.[45]

Preparations that Jonathan said he and his brother were making to care for their parents when elderly appeared to be practical expressions of their family's beliefs about the role of children in parents' old age— which are also widely held beliefs in most human societies. One point worth making in regard to how Jonathan explained these roles and responsibilities relates to his use of the verb 'to gear up', which has two meanings in this context. The first is as a synonym for 'to prepare', the second as a synonym for 'to borrow money'. While what he meant was not clear from the interview, it is likely he meant it in both senses, that is, that he and his brother were preparing to work together in caring for their parents and that to do so they were acquiring funds to provide for them, which could include paying for in-home care or aged-accommodation bonds and fees.

The other man with awareness of home-care needs gained from familial experience was Dylan who had been one of his grandmother's carers. He observed that, even though or perhaps because she had three generations to look after her, her care needs were 'still an issue'. This group comprised also men with backgrounds in gay activism including Gabriel, a 43-year-old from Auckland. Reflecting on his role as a health manager with the GLB communityin New Zealand, he said that he believed the work he did in the area was one means of, 'insulating myself from the fear of old age'. The other means was in the form of a child he had had with a lesbian couple, about which he said the following.

> I have someone behind me that is probably going to generate his own kids and I'll have an extended family. So my support is not only going to be reliant on my peer group. It's kind of an insurance policy I guess in a perverse kind of way. It does make a difference. I am conscious of the fact that as a gaycommunity in general we do not have what I refer to as an infrastructure of care behind us, having multiple children and multiple grandchildren and stuff and that familial responsibility.

Gabriel shared Jonathan's understanding of the importance for old people of being able to rely on familial bonds for their care needs. His plans for home care in old age included his biological son with a lesbian couple and his friendship network. In his view, his son would provide him with a blood bond to successive generations of relatives and thus an extended family, the absence of which he argued means gay men cannot rely on what Gabriel calls an 'infrastructure of care'. Like Jonathan, Gabriel's beliefs regarding the care needs of old people were based on the heterosexual assumption that it is children's responsibility to look after their parents in old age. More clearly than Jonathan, Gabriel appreciated the role that gay men's friendship networks can play in providing supported aged care, although, when he spoke of his so-called 'insurance policy' for old age, he was referring to his son, not his friendship group.

The remaining men who raised home-care concerns in the context of absent children were in their 30s and from Sydney and London. Two of the men said that they were not interested in having children and the third expressed no view either way. All stated, however, that they believed the absence of children was a handicap or disadvantage for elderly gay men. Aiden, a 33-year-old from London said the following about the absence of children in old age: 'Things I worry about: that I won't have children around me, although I don't want children really'. Liam (aged 37) from Sydney voiced similar concerns: 'We don't have children. We're not going to have children and so who's going to look after us?' He then touched on thoughts similar to Jonathan about whether to draw on a younger generation for support in old age:

> It is going to be people that we have to pay to look after us [that] is the reality of it. There are our nieces and nephews ... but there is a sense of not wanting to be a burden on them. And visiting my grandmother in this retirement village ... I had thoughts that this ... might happen to me one day and who's going to do the stuff that needs to be done and who's going to get me in there? [*Laughs*] Who's going to organise all this for me? And that's something I am concerned about.

Liam seemed to think it a burden or unusual that he and his partner might have to pay carers to look after them when they are old, which suggests he believed it to be a familial responsibility and not one to

5 Old-Age Fears or Concerns 195

leave to strangers. In contrast to Jonathan, Liam was unwilling to call on support from a younger generation—in his case his nephews or nieces—and his account suggested a degree of uncertainty about how he and his partner would manage old age. But in their defence, it was still a long way off for them. Also, like Dylan and Jonathan, Liam's awareness of the home-care needs that can accompany old age was awoken or accentuated by experience with an ageing relative, his grandmother.

The third man in his 30s who referred to absent children was Leo. He lived and worked in Sydney and in the following extract revealed an astute appreciation of the social settings in which gay men have to shape their lives.

> We do not build those structural family kind of things around us ... the marriage and the kids. If you do not get married and you do not have kids, then it is a concern that when I am 70 or 80 or even younger, I might look back and feel alone or unfulfilled ... so that is maybe a concern if I do not go ahead with the marriage or the kids.

Leo was single at the time of interview but it was clear he included gay marriage and having children in future projections he had for himself. He was not asked if he would have children as a single father or whether having children would be a point of agreement he would require from a potential partner but from this extract of interview either would seem possible.[46] Like Gabriel from Auckland, Leo focused on what he believed were structural weaknesses in the gay world, that is, the absence of support for homosexual relationships and families. He made no mention, however, of the alternative family and relationship structures that groups of radical, queer and left-wing gay men and lesbians have been experimenting with for some time.[47]

Together with the effect of the absence of children on gay men's old age, young men raised also the matter of communal absence or what they regarded as an apparent lack of interest or awareness in ageing issues on a gaycommunity level. Their views are here represented by Gabriel (aged 43) from Auckland. His views reflect both a personal reflexivity and the professional knowledge gained from being a GLB health manager in New Zealand.

196 P. Robinson

> I am conscious of the fact that as a gay community in general we do not have … that familial responsibility … to elders within our community. My biggest concern is how are we … as a community going to provide and take responsibility for making sure that we have the right access to services and support mechanisms and support people—from acute care right through to social care, social support, and networks.

Gabriel seems to suggest that an 'infrastructure of care'—which he associated with, 'having multiple children and multiple grandchildren and stuff'—exists only when a community of individuals has children and grandchildren in its midst, which is not yet the case with gay communities. I have argued elsewhere that the absence of what Gabriel called 'responsibility to elders' is a result of the exaggerated regard for youthfulness and youthful display and the distrust of inter-generational relationships—whether intimate, sexual or social—among gay men and in gay communities.[48] Excessive emphasis on youthfulness in gay relationships and practices as well as the relative absence of children and grandchildren are likely to lessen as the gay world becomes more integrated, which it is likely to do as gay marriage and the preponderance of gay families become more common.

Aged Accommodation

The seven men from the young cohort who spoke about aged accommodation were well informed about issues facing elderly people who have to move out of home and into an aged-care facility.[49] Some referred to the absence of gay community interest in aged accommodation and other matters affecting old gay people such as the effects on poor men of transition from home to aged accommodation. Others saw gay, aged accommodation as a fruitful investment opportunity. The views of each group, the politically aware and the young entrepreneurs are discussed next.

The politically aware men were those who either discussed aged accommodation fears in the context of gay men experiencing prejudice in care facilities or who saw aged accommodation in terms of communal absence. The views of the men who raised anti-homosexual prejudice in aged accommodation facilities are here represented by the views of Liam, as 37-year-old from Sydney. Earlier in this section, his views were considered in relation to how gay men would navigate old age in the absence of children to help them. His understanding of the sort of prejudice gay men might experience in aged accommodation facilities was informed by an interview he had held with an elderly gay man who was living in a self-care retirement village:

> I asked him about being 'out' there and he dodged the question in a way that made it clear that he wasn't out and really couldn't be. He was a man who had been in the closet for a lot of his life into middle age and had a really difficult time because of that and now here he was in his 80s back there [in the closet] again. To find any kind of gay connection he had to leave the village and wasn't willing to tell [other residents] ... because they all gossip. I was quite affected by that ... I don't know if my generation will deal with it in the same way. I think he accepted that this is the way it has to be because that's what happens, that's what we have to deal with.

For many years, GLB activists have warned that gay men and lesbians could face returning to the closet when they move into retirement settings because of prejudice against same-sex people.[50] Liam's account of what his interviewee told him confirmed activists' and some gay people's worst fears about life in aged accommodation. It also showed, however, that old gay men are capable of making strategic decisions in response to risks they suspect might accompany coming out to strangers in a new setting. Liam's interviewee was not prepared to take the risk because he judged gossip between other residents would be used against him.

Over time, and as the makeup of the residents' population changes, it is possible that Liam's interviewee would find the risk less acute. For example, he might review his decision if more accepting residents replace the homophobes when they move on. It is possible also that, having decided on the basis of first impressions not to trust his fellow residents, he continues to live in the closet. Liam was in his late 30s when interviewed and said that by contrast gays from his own generation would neither hide nor expect to hide their sexuality when they moved into aged care.

The views of the politically aware men who raised communal absence in relation to aged accommodation are here represented by Callum, a 43-year-old from Melbourne who worked in the education sector and had a partner of 6 years. In his view, the baby-boomer generation was responsible for the plight of the elderly in contemporary society, gay and straight and the communal absence was broader than the gay community.

> I think that the culture movements of the 1960s and 1970s ... [brought] into being this individuality that is actually quite corrosive and poisonous.
>
> *Your parents' generation were communal because of the Depression and WWII?*
>
> And they looked after each other. There was a regard for the other. They were not self-centred. My thing about ageing is that I do think it is going to be a little bit different to how it is now. I think locking people in nursing homes is bad news. But I also too think leaving people to their own devices is equally bad.

At the time of interview, Callum was becoming more involved in looking after his elderly parents. His chief complaint seemed to be that the so-called 'ageing problem' was related to the break down in traditional community and the neighbourhood and other communal bonds that accompanied them and increasing individualisation, an argument that Ulrich Beck and Elizabeth Beck-Gernsheim, among others, have been making since at least the late 1990s.[51]

There were two young entrepreneurs who regarded the increasing demand for specialised gay aged-accommodation as a possible investment opportunity. Both men were from London and in their late 30s and early 40s. The first man, Connor (aged 41), was single, university educated and worked in retail. In the following extract from his interview, he remarked first on how he imagined himself as an old man and then responded to a comment about specialised nursing homes for gay men.

5 Old-Age Fears or Concerns   199

I think if I did end up in a home, I would be one of those incredibly difficult, belligerent, argumentative, old men ... I'd be a really grumpy old man.

In Australia, New Zealand, and the USA, there is talk of gay nursing homes. What are your thoughts on these or the possibility that you might end up living in one?

I think they are an absolutely brilliant idea. I cannot believe that nobody has actually invested in producing one over here yet. But it may be that we're not quite at the point where a generation would want to go into one but I would think that the generation that is heading for nursing homes in about ten years would leap at the chance. And if I had cash to invest, I would invest in one, certainly. I think it could only be an absolute winner.

While Connor was not convinced the time was yet right for segregated, gay, nursing homes, he did observe that there was likely to be greater demand for them in 2020 or thereabouts, which would be when the first born of Generation X and Y would be in their mid 50s. He was not asked to explain his reasons but from his response it seemed he had thought at length about gay nursing homes or that gay men and lesbians were already taking up residence in them in other countries.[52]

Thirty-eight-year-old Guy who was also from London shared Connor's view that the time was not yet right for the opening of or, from his point of view, investing in gay nursing homes. In the extract from interview that follows, Guy outlines his views of ageing in the context of the gay community, hinting at communal absence, and what he knows of how other minorities in London manage their elderly citizens.

Perhaps that we really ought to try to integrate more with the ageing population because when you think about it, every other community, whether it is religious or ... you do look out for your neighbours and ... the older generation.

Australian gay men in their 20s I interviewed for an earlier project said it was a pity there were no social spaces where people of different ages could mix and so many gay social spaces are scene related.[53]

Old people are covered by plenty of organisations and you could argue why make one specifically for gay older people ... but it would be intriguing to know whether older gay men and women would like to go to somewhere that is segregated.

They tend to be worried about having to go back into the closet if they go into a nursing home.

In the past, I have thought about a business proposition—to open a gay nursing home, but only if there is a need for it and I am not sure if there is one yet.

Guy's observations about integrating with the older generation of gay men echoed similar views discussed earlier in this section when other men from the young generation spoke about communal absence, which occurs both structurally, as in an absence of gay institutional involvement in ageing and socially, as in the ageism that results from undue emphasis on youthfulness in the gay world and resulting absence of spaces for people from different generations to socialise in non-sexualised settings. As well, his ruminations on whether gays and lesbians would want to live in segregated, aged-accommodation facilities mirrored similar concerns some men from the other cohorts expressed about the desirability of gay nursing homes.

Social Isolation

Fear of being alone or lonely in old age attracted most attention from the young cohort. Sixteen men or more than half the young men referred to it in their interviews.[54] They referred to social isolation brought about by the absence in old age of children, partner or friends, as well as communal absence. In addition, two men referred to work as a possible antidote to social isolation. Both were Londoners and anticipated working into late old age. In the next section, these are discussed in order.

The social isolation that the young men expected to come with old age chiefly concerned absence of relations with children and friends. This view is represented here by Callum, a 43-year-old from Melbourne.

5 Old-Age Fears or Concerns 201

As mentioned above, he argued in his interview that old age was often miserable because people were either institutionalised or left on their own. His intention was to avoid both pitfalls so common in old age and instead to age disgracefully. In his answer, Callum began by nominating 70 as the age when he would accept death without too much dissent and the sort of retirement he imagined for himself.

> Ideally, 70 would be nice … with at least 15 years of not really doing full time work, just listening to music, reading books, having fun with people, drinking, sitting around … I don't want to be poor and old and I want to have paid off my house by then … I want to see my nieces and nephews living their lives. I want to see that.

Callum's picture of his old age is based on retiring at 55 in order to have 15 years free of work commitments. In the following extract, he reflects on how in the 1980s he had not expected his friends to survive the dark years when gay men were being overwhelmed by the HIV-AIDS epidemic.

> I think now that in my 60s I will be hanging out with more gay men who are in their 60s than I thought I would have been … I did think in the 1980s that … we were all going to die but I don't think that now. I also think that there will be a lot of men that I hang around with and I don't think we are going to do those stupid things like going to lawn bowls or the movies with our nice tweed jackets on. I don't think we're going to be doing that. I think we're going to get pissed in pubs and fall over. And I think we're going to have fun.

Compared to the fears held by other men from the young cohort, Callum was not concerned about being alone or lonely in his old age. On the contrary, he was certain he would be enjoying the company of other men like him and that they would be misbehaving themselves. Callum's self-image as proud and defiant youngest child of a family of eight children partly helps explain his rejection of the image of the old gay man as tweedy like the character from the film *Four Weddings and A Funeral* or cultured and genteel like the central character in the film, which was adapted from Thomas Mann's novella,[55] that shaped many people's views on the life of an old gay man, *Death in Venice*.[56]

Communal absence or lack of ageing interest or awareness in the gay community was also raised in the context of social isolation in old age. Extracts from the interviews of two men represent the views of those who raised communal absence. The first man was Gabriel, the 43-year-old from Auckland who had strong, clear views on this matter. As mentioned, he was involved in gay ageing activism in the New Zealand context.

> The most critical thing is about social connection and social interaction because that is what gives people a sense of life, purpose. My goal would be to see that we had opportunities and avenues so that people don't become isolated, that they're not house-bound and that the activities … [are] not just a care giver going in there and saying hello and having a cup of tea in a semi-patronising kind of way. It's about people getting out into communities and … feeling empowered and supported and nurtured within an environment. And not necessarily exclusively an older environment either but making sure that we take better care of our community in the wider sense.

The strength in Gabriel's view of the solution to social isolation lies in its universality. He believes that gay communities need a serious injection of communalism, that the weak supports that bedevil gay old age are a symptom of a wider lack of connection and interaction between gay men. And he is not the first to observe such serious, structural weakness in gay communities. Gay men have been expert at arranging social/sexual venues for nights of endless pleasure or taking advantage of latest information technology to arrange for sexual connections on-the-go. They have been less expert, however, at creating the means or settings for genuine, non-sexualised connections and interaction. Gabriel argued for more of the latter in his interview and linked the loneliness and isolation some elderly gay men experience with the absence of an ideology and the practice of good care in gay communities and more widely in the general society.

The second man to raise the matter of communal absence was Leo, the 31-year-old from Sydney. In the following extract, he explained the effect continued immersion in the scene can have on gay men.

> People that want to keep engaging with the bars and clubs and that scene, if that's their way of interacting with the gay community or that's really central to their lives, then that's going to be a big loss as they get older. Or they're going to find it difficult because they will continue to go out there but they won't attract as much attention or people will see them in a particular light that they weren't seen in when they used to go as a younger person.

Leo's observation about gay bars and clubs related to Gabriel's view on structural weaknesses in gay communities. While not wowser-ish, his judgement concerned the limited support he believed ageing gay men could expect to find in bar life when they ceased to be of interest to other patrons. This was at odds with Callum's view (above) of how he thought he and his friends would enjoy themselves in old age: 'I think we're going to get pissed in pubs and fall over. And I think we're going to have fun'. Leo then argued that 'most people' would move away from the bar and club scene as they become more conservative with age.

> But I think for most people they will grow beyond the bars and clubs and they might attend certain specific venues or events occasionally but they will find other outlets and activities to come together with other gay men and continue a social and full life without needing to access that, they won't mourn the loss of that as much as those people where it's really central to their existence.

For Leo, the bar and club scene was a stage in the life of gay men like himself, the well-educated and well employed. His observation that not all gay men were like him and his social network was astute, for there are gay men who will continue to shape their social life around regular visits to the public bar of their gay 'local'.

Conclusion

The stories the men from the old cohort told in relation to home care were a combination of universal and gay-specific, emphasising as they did, first, the care role that men can take on for ageing partners and, second, the importance of informal neighbourhood relations in the context of domestic care. Gay-specific concerns or fears were most strongly evident in regard to aged accommodation and mostly concerned heterosexist assumptions the men anticipated they might have to overcome or more seriously homophobia from other residents. They were not so serious, however, that any man said that he would refuse moving into a nursing home.

Their reluctance seems to me to be similar to the reluctance that old people in general hold for the transition from family home to aged accommodation. The stories those from the old cohort told touched on three universal experiences. The first, which is common to people in couple relationships was how they would cope if their partner predeceased them. The second, which is common to everyone, was how social life in old age would change when friends died. The third was how they would manage the loss of identity that comes with becoming a 'resident' of an aged-care facility and an 'old person'. As mentioned, for those aged 60 and older, the loss of identity they feared was to have their gayness forgotten or ignored as they transformed into a resident who lived in a numbered room. For straight men and women, the loss of identity that ageing brings is to be transformed like gay men into a homogeneous mass known simply as 'the residents' or 'the oldies'.

A relatively small number (one-quarter) of the men from the middle cohort were concerned about home care. Their concerns related to its cost and the importance of keeping control of life in old age. The latter point is a concern for all people but in this sample it was men with high incomes or from upper-middle-class backgrounds who most emphatically expressed the concern. Aged accommodation was raised by half the age cohort. Fairly grave fears were recounted in regard to aged accommodation and these related to homophobic discrimination or loss of independence—the latter being similar but not identical to the concern of losing control of life. Two concerns were raised as well and these were quality of care or loss of male company (homo-sociability) on having to move into a female-dominated environment.

Of the aged accommodation fears or concerns for the middle cohort, I would argue that three were universal and one was gay specific. Fear of losing independence and concerns about quality of care or losing the company of men were universal because they would apply to the rest of the population. Not all women would be troubled at the prospect of losing men's company but it is a concern that would affect some men, gay or straight.

The predominant old-age fear for middle-aged interviewees was social isolation and 80% of the cohort referred to it. Most people are aware of or fear social isolation in old age and it is not gay specific. What was novel about some of the discussion in relation to it was the solution that some men from this age cohort openly spoke about, which was to continue sexual adventures for as long as they were able to do so. Sexual activity in older people is not uncommon.[57] What was notable, however, was the men's announcing it as a strategy to overcome social isolation.

Many of the young men argued that the absence of children from the lives of old gay men explained why old age was so hard for them. What they overlooked was that many old gay men have children from previous marriages or heterosexual relationships and that children are not always present when elderly parents need support or help and that, of course, the absence of children in the lives of old gay men will change as more gay couples have children. At first, I was surprised at the knowledge and concern the young men showed in relation to the lives of old people, that is, until I listened more carefully to their interviews and realised that they were often raised in the context of experiences the men had gained from looking after their grandparents.

Some of those who spoke about the absence of children in gay lives mentioned strategies that they had adopted which, in the case of one man, was to establish close ties with his godchildren and, for another, to have a child with a lesbian couple. Absence was raised a second time when they discussed home-care concerns—in relation to what they

206 P. Robinson

regarded as the absence of gay-community interest in or action to support elderly GLB people. This was repeated in the views they expressed on aged accommodation and social isolation. They were the only age cohort to raise gay-community inaction regarding old age and to do so in relation to each of the three principal narratives, namely, home care, aged accommodation, and social isolation. And I would argue that close relations with grandparents, which is generally a feature of people their age and at their stage in the life course, could explain this heightened awareness and concern which they then use to imagine their own old age.

Aged accommodation was raised in the context of two contradictory narratives, communal absence and entrepreneurial opportunities. Men who had a relatively high level of socio-political awareness spoke about accommodation for the elderly in the context of the absence of both mainstream and gay community interest or action. At the other end of the political spectrum, was a small group of men who saw the likely growing demand for gay-specific nursing homes as a potential investment opportunity for them or their friends. These men were either rich or socialised with gay men with money. As was the case with the men from the older cohorts, a predominance of young men feared social isolation in old age or understood how frightening it would be for the elderly.

The quotation that heads this chapter was included because it helps explain what the men from the old cohort might have experienced, which could give carers and policy makers some idea of the emotional background of this group of men, some of whom are in deep old age while others are just entering early old age. I raise this because it emphasises why some men from the old cohort hold grave fears about homophobia in care workers or residents of aged facilities.

Notes

1. See for example A. Cronin (2006) 'Sexuality in gerontology: a heteronormative presence, a queer absence' in S. O. Daatland and S. Biggs (eds) *Ageing and Diversity: Multiple Pathways and Cultural Migrations*

5 Old-Age Fears or Concerns   207

(Bristol: The Policy Press), pp. 107–122; B. Heaphy (2009) 'The Stories, Complex Lives of Older GLBT Adults: Choice and Its Limits in Older Lesbian and Gay Narratives of Relational Lives', *Journal of GLBT Family Studies*, 5: 119–138; M. Hughes and S. Kentlyn (2011) 'Older LGBT people's Care Networks and Communities of Practice: A Brief Note', *International Social Work*, 54(3): 436–444 (Cronin 2006; Heaphy 2009; Hughes and Kentlyn 2011).

2. Four were from Auckland, one was from London, three were from Manchester, nine were from Melbourne, two were from New York, and six were from Sydney.

3. A shorter, less detailed version of the discussion of old-age fears or concerns of men aged 60 and older appeared in P. Robinson (2016) 'Ageing Fears and Concerns of Gay Men Aged 60 and Over' *Quality in Ageing and Older Adults*, v. 17, n. 1, pp. 5–15 (Robinson 2016).

4. Amery (aged 82) Sydney; Godfrey (aged 81) Sydney; Lucas (aged 75) Auckland; Ashton (aged 70) Sydney; Parry (aged 63) New York; Hugh (aged 62) Melbourne; Arthur (aged 62) London.

5. N. Elias (1987) *The Loneliness of the Dying* trans. E. Jephcott (Oxford: Basil Blackwell) (Elias 1987).

6. S. Arber (2006) 'Gender trajectories: how age and marital status influence patterns of gender inequality in later life' in S. O. Daatland and S. Biggs (eds) *Ageing and Diversity: Multiple Pathways and Cultural Migrations* (Bristol: The Policy Press), pp. 71ff; H. Swerissen and S. Duckett (2014) *Dying Well* (Grattan Institute: Melbourne) (Arber 2006; Swerissen and Duckett 2014).

7. Herbert (aged 82) Melbourne; Godfrey (aged 81) Sydney; Clancy (aged 81) Melbourne; Drake (aged 77) Melbourne; Lucas (aged 75) Auckland; Basil (aged 75) Auckland; Christian (aged 72) Sydney; Ashton (aged 70) Sydney; Arran (aged 70) Melbourne; Sean (aged 67) Auckland; Parry (aged 63) New York; Fergus (aged 63) Manchester; Bryce (aged 63) Manchester; Anselm (aged 61) Melbourne.

8. Former Australian High Court judge, the Hon Michael Kirby AC CMG touched on this topic in an interview shown on the Australian Broadcasting Corporation's television news, 3 March 2016: http://www.abc.net.au/news/2016-03-03/lgbti-people-face-coming-out-all-over-again-in-aged-care/7217260. Accessed 3 March 2016.

9. C. Phillipson (2013) *Ageing* (Cambridge: Polity), pp. 66, 68 (Phillipson 2013).

208 P. Robinson

10. Randall (aged 87) Melbourne; Herbert (aged 82) Melbourne; Amery (aged 82) Sydney; Hector (aged 81) Melbourne; Godfrey (aged 81) Sydney; Clancy (aged 81) Melbourne; Drake (aged 77) Sydney; Ambrose (aged 77) Melbourne; Lucas (aged 75) Auckland; Basil (aged 75) Auckland; Jeffrey (aged 72) Auckland; Colin (aged 72) New York; Christian (aged 72) Sydney; Ashton (aged 70) Sydney; Arran (aged 70) Melbourne; Sean (aged 67) Auckland; Baden (aged 65) Melbourne; Bryce (aged 63) Manchester; Alfie (aged 63) Manchester; Hugh (aged 62) Melbourne; Arthur (aged 62) London; Anselm (aged 61) Melbourne.

11. For more on the relationship narratives of gay men in long-term relationships, see P. Robinson (2013) *Gay Men's Relationships Across the Life Course* (Basingstoke and New York: Palgrave Macmillan), pp. 62–82 (Robinson 2013).

12. J. Mitford (1963) *The American Way of Death* (New York: Simon and Schuster) (Mitford 1963); E. Waugh (2010, 1948) *The Loved One* (London: Penguin Books) (Mitford 1963; Waugh 2010, 1948).

13. P. Ariès (1975) *Western Attitudes toward Death: from the Middle Ages to the Present*, trans. P. Ranum (Baltimore: The Johns Hopkins University Press) (Ariès 1975).

14. Elias *The Loneliness of the Dying*.

15. Ariès *Western Attitudes toward Death*.

16. Four were from Auckland, six were from Hong Kong, four were from London, three were from Los Angeles, two were from Manchester, two were from Melbourne, six were from New York, and one was from Sydney.

17. In Melbourne, for example, a social organisation called the Alternative Lifestyle Organisation (ALSO) was established in the late 1970s with a focus on legal rights and relationship recognition. Its members tended to aver the radical politics of gay liberation, which was established in Sydney and then spread to other Australian capital cities. For more on the genesis of gay liberation in Australia and the earlier, locally based Campaign Against Moral Persecution Inc. (CAMP Inc.) see P. Robinson (2008) *The Changing World of Gay Men* (Basingstoke and New York: Palgrave Macmillan), pp. 37–43 (Robinson 2008).

18. See Appendix B.

19. For more on gay marriage and civil union, see Robinson *Gay Men's Relationships*, pp. 100–120. 'Gaily' married is not common usage but

an invention of the author which might or might not catch on. It is not meant to disparage straight marriage or suggest the heteronormative marriage is by comparison a 'sad' marriage.

20. For a summary of the period, see Robinson *The Changing World*, pp. 55–62.

21. Ward (aged 59) New York; Marvin (aged 59) Los Angeles; Austin (aged 57) Auckland; Ryan (aged 53) London; Tate (aged 51) London; Ethan (aged 49) London; Duncan (aged 47) Hong Kong.

22. Chosen as a marker for a high income in 2009 when the research for this book began, it now seems quite modest.

23. G. Esping-Andersen (2015, 1990) *The Three Worlds of Welfare Capitalism* (Cambridge: Polity Press), pp. 48–54 (Esping-Andersen 2015, 1990).

24. Phillipson *Ageing*, p. 95.

25. See, for example, similar arguments in C. Phillipson (1982) *Capitalism and the Construction of Old Age* (London: Macmillan) (Phillipson 1982).

26. For more on the sexual needs of residents of aged-care facilities, see, for example, M. Bauer, D. Fetherstonhaugh, L. Tarzia, R. Nay and E. Beattie (2014) 'Supporting residents' expression of sexuality: the initial construction of a sexuality assessment tool for residential aged care facilities', *BMC Geriatrics*, 4:82. doi:10.1186/1471-2318-14-82 (Bauer et al. 2014).

27. Ward (aged 59) New York; Marvin (aged 59) Los Angeles; Raymond (aged 58) Hong Kong; Ryan (aged 53) London; Hilton (aged 53) New York; Zachary (aged 52) Hong Kong; Mike (aged 52) Melbourne; Ben (aged 52) Manchester; Nathan (aged 50) Auckland; Carl (aged 49) Auckland; Danny (aged 48) Hong Kong; Fred (aged 47) London; Duncan (aged 47) Hong Kong; Alvin (aged 47) New York; Eddie (aged 45) Manchester.

28. Robinson *Gay Men's Relationships*, pp. 3–4, 6–7.

29. Elias *The Loneliness of the Dying*, p. 74.

30. This page from the website of a high-end accommodation provider referred to diversity and community which from the author's informal discussion in 2015 with the company's 'relationship manager' meant GLB people were welcome and already in residence: http://arcare.com.au/arcare-values/. Accessed 13 April 2016.

31. Ward (aged 59) New York; Bernard (aged 59) Hong Kong; Raymond (aged 58) Hong Kong; Austin (aged 57) Auckland; Isaac (aged 56) Sydney; Logan (aged 56) Auckland; Cam (aged 56) Los Angeles; Ryan (aged 53) London; Hilton (aged 53) New York; Zachary (aged 52) Hong Kong; Mike (aged 52) Melbourne; Tate (aged 51) London; Earl (aged 51) New York; Calvin (aged 51) Melbourne; Buck (aged 51) Hong Kong; Everett (aged 49) New York; Danny (aged 48) Hong Kong; Fred (aged 47) London; Jude (aged 46) Los Angeles; Eddie (aged 45) Manchester.

32. Phillipson *Ageing*, pp. 66–67.

33. Image for entwined relationships, see P. White (1966) *The Solid Mandala* (London: Eyre & Spottiswoode) (White 1966).

34. U. Beck and E. Beck-Gernsheim (1995) *The Normal Chaos of Love*, trans. M. Ritter and J. Wiebel (Cambridge: Polity Press), pp. 86–101 (Beck and Beck-Gernsheim 1995). On its importance for gay men, see Robinson *The Changing World*, pp. 115–133 and Robinson *Gay Men's Relationships*, pp. 37–82.

35. For more on the nature of gay men's relationships in Australia, see Robinson *The Changing World*, pp. 115–133 and on long-term gay relationships (based on the study of an international sample of 97 gay men) see Robinson *Gay Men's Relationships*, pp. 62–82.

36. See, for example, J. Rechy (1977) *The Sexual Outlaw: A Documentary* (New York: Grove Press Inc.); E. White (1986) *States of Desire: Travels in Gay America* (London: Pan Books Ltd.) (Rechy 1977; White 1986).

37. See, for example, Robinson *Gay Men's Relationships*, pp. 40–48.

38. G. Bataille (2001, English translation 1962, orig.1957) *Eroticism*, trans. M. Dalwood, London: Penguin Books (with introduction by C. McCabe) (Bataille 2001).

39. Bataille *Eroticism*, pp. 159–161.

40. All interviewees were asked this question: 'Do you use the Internet to supplement your social life?'

41. For more on this and its contribution to the marriage rights movement, see Robinson *Gay Men's Relationships*, p. 101.

42. Robinson *The Changing World*, pp. 44.

43. For more on long-lasting gay relationships, see Robinson *Gay Men's Relationships*, Ch. 3.

44. Jonathon (aged 44) London; Gabriel (aged 43) Auckland; Jacob (aged 42) Melbourne; Liam (aged 37) Sydney; Aiden (aged 33) London; Dylan (aged 32) Sydney; Leo (aged 31) Sydney.

5 Old-Age Fears or Concerns   211

45. For more on gay families, see Robinson *The Changing World*, pp. 143–150.
46. For details of the type of fatherhood arrangements gay men make, see Robinson *The Changing World*, pp. 145–148 and Robinson *Gay Men's Relationships*, pp. 87–91.
47. See, for example, K. Plummer (1992) 'Speaking its name: Inventing a lesbian and gay studies' in Ken Plummer (ed.) *Modern Homosexualities: fragments of lesbian and gay experience* (London: Routledge), pp. 20ff; J. Weeks (2007) *The World We Have Won: The Remaking of Erotic and Intimate Life* (Oxford: Routledge), p. 20 (Plummer 1992; Weeks 2007).
48. Robinson *The Changing World*, pp. 161–165; P. Robinson, (2011) 'The Influence of Ageism on Relations between Old and Young Gay Men' in Y. Smaal and G. Willett (eds) *Out Here: Gay and Lesbian Perspectives VI* (Melbourne: Monash University Publishing), pp. 188–200 (Robinson 2011).
49. Callum (aged 43) Melbourne; Gabriel (aged 43) Auckland; Jacob (aged 42) Melbourne; Connor (aged 41) London; Guy (aged 38) London; Liam (aged 37) Sydney; Dylan (aged 32) Sydney.
50. See, for example, this warning about homophobia in old age from long-time, gay activist, Peter Tatchell in *The Guardian*, 21 January 2015: http://www.theguardian.com/society/2015/jan/21/lesbian-gay-bisexual-seniors-face-old-age-homophobia. Accessed 16 April 2016 (Tatchell 2015).
51. E. Bech-Gernsheim (2002) *Reinventing the Family: In Search of New Lifestyles*, trans P. Camiller (Cambridge: Polity); U. Beck and E. Beck-Gernsheim (2008) *Individualization: Institutionalized Individualism and its Social and Political Consequences* (London: Sage Publications) (Bech-Gernsheim 2002; Beck and Beck-Gernsheim 2008).
52. For example, in Sweden: E. Margolis (2014) 'LGBT retirement home: the end of the rainbow', *The Guardian*: https://www.theguardian.com/society/2014/jul/27/lgbt-retirement-home-sweden. Accessed 5 January 2017 (Margolis 2014).
53. Robinson *The Changing World*, pp. 161–173.
54. Gabriel (aged 43) Auckland; Callum (aged 43) Melbourne; Noah (aged 42) Auckland; Jacob (aged 42) Melbourne; Connor (aged 41) London; Liam (aged 37) Sydney; Evan (aged 35) Los Angles; Anton (aged 35) London; Finlay (aged 33) New York; Aiden (aged 33) London; Jackson

212   P. Robinson

(aged 32) New York; Dylan (aged 32) Sydney; Leo (aged 31) Sydney; 31Gavin (aged 31) Auckland; Eamon (aged 28) London; Denis (aged 27) Melbourne.

55. T. Mann (1975, 1902, 1903, 1912) *Death in Venice, Tristan, Tonio Kröger*, trans. H.T. Lowe-Porter (Harmondsworth: Penguin Books) (Mann 1975, 1902).

56. M. Newell (dir.) (1994) *Four Weddings and A Funeral* (PolyGram Filmed Entertainment, Channel Four Films, Working Title Films); L. Visconti (dir.) (1971) *Death in Venice* (Alfa Cinematografica) (Newell 1994; Visconti 1971).

57. See, for example, M. Gott and S. Hinchliff (2003) 'Barriers to Seeking Treatment for Sexual Problems in Primary Care: A Qualitative Study with Older People', *Family Practice*, 20: 690–695 and Bauer et al. 'Supporting residents' expression of sexuality', *passim* (Gott and Hinchliff 2003).

References

Arber, S. 2006. Gender Trajectories: How Age and Marital Status Influence Patterns of Gender Inequality in Later Life. In *Ageing and Diversity: Multiple Pathways and Cultural Migrations*, ed. S.O. Daatland, and S. Biggs, 61–76. Bristol: The Policy Press.

Ariès, P. 1975. *Western Attitudes toward Death: from the Middle Ages to the Present*, trans. P. Ranum. Baltimore: The Johns Hopkins University Press.

Bataille, G. 1957/2001. *Eroticism*, trans. M. Dalwood, introduction by C. McCabe. London: Penguin Books.

Bauer, M., D. Fetherstonhaugh, L. Tarzia, R. Nay, and E. Beattie. 2014. Supporting Residents' Expression of Sexuality: The Initial Construction of a Sexuality Assessment Tool for Residential Aged Care Facilities. *BMC Geriatrics* 4: 82. doi:10.1186/1471-2318-14-82.

Bech-Gernsheim, E. 2002. *Reinventing the Family: In Search of New Lifestyles*, trans. P. Camiller. Cambridge: Polity.

Beck, U. and E. Beck-Gernsheim. 1995. *The Normal Chaos of Love*, trans. M, Ritter and J. Wiebel. Cambridge: Polity Press.

Beck, U., and E. Beck-Gernsheim. 2008. *Individualization: Institutionalized Individualism and its Social and Political Consequences*. London: Sage.

Cronin, A. 2006. Sexuality in Gerontology: A Heteronormative Presence, a Queer Absence. In *Ageing and Diversity: Multiple Pathways and Cultural Migrations*, ed. S.O. Daatland, and S. Biggs, 107–122. Bristol: The Policy Press.

Elias, N. 1987. *The Loneliness of the Dying*, trans. E. Jephcott. Oxford: Basil Blackwell.

Esping-Andersen, G. 1990/2015. *The Three Worlds of Welfare Capitalism*. Cambridge: Polity Press.

Gott, M., and S. Hinchliff. 2003. Barriers to Seeking Treatment for Sexual Problems in Primary Care: A Qualitative Study with Older People. *Family Practice* 20: 690–695.

Heaphy, B. 2009. 'The Stories, Complex Lives of Older GLBT Adults: Choice and Its Limits in Older Lesbian and Gay Narratives of Relational Lives'. *Journal of GLBT Family Studies* 5: 119–138.

Hughes, M., and S. Kentlyn. 2011. Older LGBT People's Care Networks and Communities of Practice: A Brief Note. *International Social Work* 54 (3): 436–444.

Mann, T. 1902/1975. *Death in Venice, Tristan, Tonio Kröger*, trans. H.T. Lowe-Porter. Harmondsworth: Penguin Books.

Margolis, E. 2014. 'LGBT Retirement Home: The End of the Rainbow', *The Guardian*: https://www.theguardian.com/society/2014/jul/27/lgbt-retirement-home-sweden. Accessed 5 Jan 2017.

Mitford, J. 1963. *The American Way of Death*. New York: Simon and Schuster.

Newell, M. (dir.). 1994. *Four Weddings and A Funeral* (PolyGram Filmed Entertainment, Channel Four Films, Working Title Films).

Phillipson, C. 1982. *Capitalism and the Construction of Old Age*. London: Macmillan.

Phillipson, C. 2013. *Ageing*. Cambridge: Polity.

Plummer, K. 1992. Speaking Its Name: Inventing a Lesbian and Gay Studies. In *Modern Homosexualities: Fragments of Lesbian and Gay Experience*, ed. Ken Plummer, 3–25. London: Routledge.

Rechy, J. 1977. *The Sexual Outlaw: A Documentary*. New York: Grove Press Inc.

Robinson, P. 2008. *The Changing World of Gay Men*. Basingstoke and New York: Palgrave Macmillan.

Robinson, P. 2011. The Influence of Ageism on Relations between Old and Young Gay Men. In *Out Here: Gay and Lesbian Perspectives VI*, ed. Y. Smaal, and G. Willett, 188–200. Melbourne: Monash University Publishing.

Robinson, P. 2013. *Gay Men's Relationships Across the Life Course*. Basingstoke and New York: Palgrave Macmillan.

Robinson, P. 2016. Ageing Fears and Concerns of Gay Men Aged 60 and Over. *Quality in Ageing and Older Adults* 17 (1): 5–15.

Swerissen, H., and S. Duckett. 2014. *Dying Well*. Grattan Institute: Melbourne.

Tatchell, P. 2015. 'Lesbian, Gay and Bisexual Seniors Face Twin Fears of Old Age Homophobia', The Guardian: http://www.theguardian.com/society/2015/jan/21/lesbian-gay-bisexual-seniors-face-old-age-homophobia. Accessed 16 Apr 2016.

Visconti, L. (dir.). 1971. *Death in Venice* (Alfa Cinematografica).

Waugh, E. 2010, 1948. *The Loved One*, London: Penguin Books.

Weeks, J. 2007. *The World We Have Won: The Remaking of Erotic and Intimate Life*. Oxford: Routledge.

White, E. 1986. *States of Desire: Travels in Gay America*. London: Pan Books Ltd.

White, P. 1966. *The Solid Mandala*. London: Eyre & Spottiswoode.

6

Old Age Plans

We have been very bad about it. Although we have tried to have common savings accounts at different times in our relationship, we still have not managed that. We keep our financials separate ... I have not been very good about planning for retirement and I know neither has he. Neither of us has done much about it and we need to start being realistic.
(Zachary, aged 52, Hong Kong)

Introduction

This chapter analyses the plans and preparations which the men from the international Anglophone sample had made or, in the case of younger men, believed they would make for their retirement and old age. All the interviewees were asked the same question: 'What preparations or plans have you made for your retirement and old age and when did you begin to make them? If you have not, do you think you will and, if so, when?' For many but not all of the men in their 20s, retirement and old age were too distant for them to contemplate seriously and they laughed when I asked them the question.

© The Author(s) 2017
P. Robinson, *Gay Men's Working Lives, Retirement and Old Age*,
Genders and Sexualities in the Social Sciences,
DOI 10.1057/978-1-137-43532-3_6

215

At the other end of the age spectrum, I also found men in their 80s who said they had made no such plans, with the exception, perhaps, of owning part or all of the house in which they were living. These tended to be an exception to the approaches related by the men from the old cohort (aged 60 and older); more about this below. As well, those men who said they had no plans were not answering the first part of the question—because at age 80 or more they were in what is known as 'deep' old age—but the second part, relating to when they had prepared for retirement and old age or made their plans. The circumstances of the men who said they had made no plans are examined in more depth later in the chapter.

In this chapter, the stories told from all three age cohorts are examined—starting with those from the old cohort followed by those from the middle and young cohorts. There is a strong link between the discussions in this chapter and those in the previous chapter where the men's old-age fears or concerns were examined by age cohort.

Finally, a brief word about the historical context of their old-age 'plans'. The history of pensions and the provision of state benefits for workers at the end of their working life began in Britain, Europe and the British Dominions in the decades prior to the outbreak of World War I. Before the state became involved in providing old age pensions in the late nineteenth and early twentieth centuries, relatively small numbers of employees received retirement pensions, limited to 'a select band of (mainly salaried) employees, notably civil servants, those working for the public utilities, and armed services officers'.[1] Germany introduced pensions for male workers over the age of 70 in 1889.[2] Queensland and New Zealand were the first colonies in the British Empire to introduce the old age pension, which they did in 1891 and 1898 respectively,[3] a decade or more before similar legislation was introduced in the Commonwealth Parliament of Australia and the British Parliament (1908).[4] In Canada and the USA, pension schemes were introduced in 1927 and 1935 respectively.[5]

State-funded pensions were meagre in scope and value until the 1950s. In Britain and North America, for example, pensions varied from between 17 and 20% of the average wage.[6] In the decades following the end of World War II, however, the expansion of the welfare state in many advanced western democracies saw an increase in the proportion of people receiving pensions and moderate increases in their value.[7]

In the Australia context, the old age pension—funded from government taxation revenue—was introduced in 1908, during the decade after the proclamation in 1901 of the Commonwealth of Australia, when signal legislation shaping the structure of the new nation was being passed: immigration legislation in 1901 to safeguard a white Australian population; legislation in 1904 for the systematic determination of wages and salaries; and trade legislation in 1908 to introduce tariffs to protect fledgling manufacturing.[8] The old age pension was introduced in the aftermath of the decision of the newly created Commonwealth Court of Conciliation and Arbitration to create what became known as the 'basic wage':

> The basic wage was understood as the primary means of delivering wage justice and hence economic security. Welfare payments, as they were introduced, were always designed in the knowledge that it was there. Hence Australia did not opt for the compulsory insurance model being adopted in many European nations, in which workers, employers and government were all called upon to make a contribution. Nor did it embrace the concept of universal benefits built upon a notion of citizenship rights. Rather, it chose a residual system, means-tested, moralistic and funded from general taxation.[9]

And it was to be available only to white males aged 65 or over:

> The Bill provided for the payment of £26 per annum to be paid fortnightly. Men were to receive the old age pension at the age of sixty-five: the Governor-General might declare by proclamation that the pension could be paid to women at the age of sixty. Pensions were not to be paid to Asiatics (except those born in Australia) or aboriginal natives of Australia, Africa, the islands of the Pacific, or New Zealand.[10]

Since their inception, the old age pension and other forms of welfare payments in Australia have been understood as a form of state charity for the deserving poor, not as a basic right for citizens as was the case in, for example, France and other European countries. The concept of the basic wage continued as the context in which pension and other welfare payments were provided until the radical economic reforms of the 1980s.

The post-war welfare-state experiment continued in the West till the 1980s when proponents of radical economic reform found support in conservative governments in Britain, the USA and elsewhere to introduce programmes to privatise state-owned utilities and broader neo-liberal fiscal and monetary policies. By the 1990s, many western governments had embarked on what was known as 'welfare reform' which according to Richard Sennett and Loïc Wacquant, among others, had the effect of victimizing the poor—by removing or reducing state-funded services, increasing statutory requirements for unemployment benefits and/or rates of imprisonment for minor crimes.[11]

In Australia, the impetus at government level was, according to historian Shurlee Swain, 'to limit welfare expenditure and combat what they increasingly saw as the problems of welfare dependency'.[12] The context for this was in her view the 'inroads made by neoliberal economics':

> The neoliberal emphasis on the freedom of the individual undermined notions of the collective good, positioning welfare recipients as a danger to their dependants and a strain on the national economy, while introducing generous benefits and tax concessions for those who can be constituted as trying to help themselves ...

> While this new understanding of welfare may sit comfortably with an overwhelmingly middle-class electorate, it leaves those who had placed their faith in the older notion of social security as the safety net preserving the notion of Australia as the land of the 'fair go' feeling lost.[13]

In 1992, a national superannuation scheme was introduced in Australia which required employers to make payments to their employees' superannuation account. Its unstated purpose was, according to Swain, to reduce reliance on the old age pension and 'provide generous tax benefits to those who through private savings were able to fund their own retirement'.[14] In the broader, global setting, encouragement for individualised pension schemes, initially the agenda of the World Bank and International Monetary Fund, was later taken up by trans-national bodies such as the International Labour Organisation and the Organisation for Economic Cooperation and Development.[15]

The men from the three age cohorts whose life histories are the subject of this chapter were born between the mid 1920s and the mid 1990s, during which time each one of the three systems of old age pension operated. The original, mean and market-oriented system was replaced after World War II with a more generous, state-oriented one, which lasted 30 years until a return in the 1980s to the mean, marketised scheme that is now in place in most western advanced economies.

In the case of the men from the old cohort, who were born between 1924 and 1949—the Lucky generation with some from the Baby boomer generation—their working life and old-age expectations would have been shaped by the existence during those decades of an old-age pension system that was generous in neither payment nor scope. By contrast, the men from the middle cohort who were born between 1950 and 1964—all 'boomers'—lived in a time when the welfare state was being extended and there was no serious thought of dismantling it. And the young generation who were born between 1965 and 1993—the X & Y generation with some i-Generation—grew up as the welfare state was being dismantled and privatised welfare was becoming the norm in the West.

Old-Age Plans by Cohort

Plans for old age I broadly defined to include anything from highly structured financial plans that included ownership of residence(s) and a self-funded superannuation fund, to sketchy plans such as an awareness that taking in boarders and relying on the pension would suffice for the owner of a three-bedroom house in the suburbs of Auckland or Manchester. The men's replies were then analysed and sorted according to whether their retirement plan was structured or sketchy.

In the case of the young cohort (men 45 or under) retirement plans were divided between those who had a plan or had thought about planning for retirement and those who had a sketchy retirement plan or had no idea and had not thought about retirement. In each of the cohorts, the men's old-age plans are discussed in that order. The exception is the

220 P. Robinson

old cohort where I begin by discussing a small group of men who said they had no plans to retire and in their interview explained why they would not stop working and had no interest in watching the roses grow or the paint peel.

Old Cohort

As mentioned, the 25 men from this cohort were born between 1924 and 1949 and thus belonged to what the Australian Bureau of Statistics (ABS) defined as the 'Lucky' generation (1926–1946) with a few men also from the 'Baby Boomer' generation (1946–1966).[16] They were born into a world and grew up during a time when many could count on receiving a government-funded old age pension. In Australia and New Zealand the pension was means-tested, represented only a fraction of the full-time wage, and was funded from taxation revenue.[17] In Britain and the USA, old age pensions then were similarly modest if not meagre.[18]

In the following section, the men's accounts of their retirement plans are organised according to the answers given by three groups. The first group said they had no plan to retire. The second group comprised men who, while retired, had only sketchy plans for their retirement. And the third group consisted of men who had retired and had well-organised, structured retirement plans.

No Plans to Retire

Seven men from this cohort said that they had no plans to retire, by which they meant they had no intention of ceasing work. These men had interpreted the question—'What preparations or plans have you made for your retirement and old age and when did you begin to make them?'—to concern whether or not they would retire. Mostly they admitted that they had retired from their career's work and then declared that they were nonetheless still working. As interviewer, I had not anticipated this ambiguity in the question. It was only the men from the old cohort who interpreted the question thus, largely I think because retirement was their present experience. For the younger age

6 Old Age Plans 221

cohorts, it was something yet to occur and for many from the young cohort too far off to contemplate.

Two of the group were in their 60s, four in their 70s, and one was in his 80s.[19] Some had retired from a lifetime's work but continued to do paid work of one sort or another and, in one case, to work as fully as he did when he held high legal office:

> I come to work every day. I come seven days a week. I have so much work, I am flat out. Therefore, my life is very busy, very intense, unbelievable if you looked at it rationally. But interesting and arguably important things come up. They ask me to be involved and it is a compliment. I feel an obligation to do what I can, especially if it is a human rights issue or an issue to advance equality for all people, not just gays but for all people in society.[20]

Two explicitly stated that they wanted to work till they could work no longer or till they died, the remaining men implied as much in what they said.

The men who said they would work till they 'dropped' were from London and Sydney. Lucas was 62, lived in London, and worked in HIV-AIDS policy development. He said about retirement: 'I have made no plans because I do not intend to retire'. His decision was made easier because in the last 20 years, his work had changed from hands-on direct training of educators in South Asia: 'now my work is around management and around policy development'. Being active was a prime motivation for him:

> There are a lot of other things I want to achieve before I 'kick the bucket' so to speak. We have made no plans at all other than I am maybe writing my will in the next few years.

Lucas's partner was a younger man from a poor background and Lucas wanted to ensure he would inherit his property, 'because I do not want any fights when I am gone … My family have been very supportive of my partner but money is money'.

Ashton, the 70-year-old from Sydney was born brought up in New Zealand and moved to Sydney 30 years ago. His attitude to work and retirement was straightforward: he had no intention of retiring despite his partner's injunctions, and felt fit and able to continue working. About these, he said:

> I will retire when I want to ... I am capable of staying on working till I am 75 which I have always planned to do ... My partner's always saying to me I should retire. I said, 'Look I do not want to bloody retire. What would I do?' I work between half past six and half past ten in the morning, 25 hours a week, and I am quite comfortable doing that. I will carry on as long as I am able to.

In his opinion, retirement led to premature death: 'People should be able to work for as long as they are possibly able to. Too many people retire and they are dead within six months of retirement age'. If forced to retire, his intention was to keep active and fit:

> One of the things that saved me over the last few years from heart problems and from cancer is the fact I have been so superbly fit. And you look at people ... and you think (a) physically they are not fit and (b) mentally they don't ... seem to be fit ... I still ride horses ... [not] as much I used to. I read a lot and am interested in all sorts of things. Politics I cannot stand, religion I do not get involved in but I like to think I have got an enquiring mind. You have got to be active, even if it is voluntary.

Included in the men whose views on old age and retirement implied a belief in the 'work till you drop' approach was Fergus, a 63-year-old from Manchester who retired from academia when he was 52: 'I had just got to so hating setting and marking exams, I really detested it with a loathing and thought I could do other things'. Like a number of other men from the old cohort, he engaged in voluntary work: in the interview, he explained that he did not like using the word 'retire':

> I was working all day yesterday on a new web page and I was giving a talk the day before to schools ... There is a network of teachers up here that wants to get me involved in some new syllabuses. I am happy I can do the work I want now though I am not paid.

There was also Lucas, a 75-year-old from Auckland. He stopped working two years ago because of illness but, like others in his family, did not believe in retirement: 'my grandfather and my mother and probably the people before them just worked till the day they died and I intended to do that'. Such an approach to work and retirement is not uncommon and is a well-known means of postponing the inactivity that is associated with deep old age and death, about which Simone de Beauvoir wrote the following:

> Apart from some exceptions, the old man no longer *does* any thing. He is defined by an *exis*, not by a *praxis*: a being not a doing. Time is carrying him towards an end—death—which is not *his* and which is not postulated or laid down by any project. This is why he looks to active members of the community like one of a 'different species', one in whom they do not recognise themselves.[21]

A desire to keep working or to find a paid or unpaid activity once a formal working life comes to an end is not strongly class-based, except that factory workers and office workers—more than those who work in professions or who are self-employed—do have to retire when they reach retirement age and have no choice than to cease a life time's work. In the case of some who began their working life at an early age and for whom work was plain hard labour, its end is welcomed. The fact of forced retirement is not to say, however, that retirees cannot continue paid work in a different field—depending on their fitness and interest in doing so—or voluntary work which was included in the repertoire of work activities of the men who intended to work till they dropped. Part of the explanation for which could be a desire to remain active members of society with something like the kind of identity they once had as butcher, baker or high court judge.

Also notable about Lucas's account was his belief in 'work till you drop' as an inherited trait. While it is unlikely to be a genetic disposition, I would argue that individuals form views about work and the work life at a very early age: observing the practices of their parents, relatives, friends, and other working people in their neighbours, they adopt them as the norm.

224   P. Robinson

Retired with Sketchy Plans

Because ageing populations will be the hallmark of advanced economies until the mid twenty-first century, the goal of policy makers since the 1980s has been to encourage the baby boomers and following generations to take greater responsibility for their financial and material security in old age, the privatisation of the old age pension. Recent data, however, from an Australian study which found that up to one-third of people living on the old age pension were living in poverty would suggest two things: that privatising the pension has not succeeded and that the pension in Australia is still manifestly inadequate.[22] Insofar as qualitative research of the kind undertaken for this book can be generalised to the rest of the population, given the finding of poverty in one-third of Australian pensioners, it might not be coincidental that just under a third of the old men from the sample had only sketchy retirement plans, had not prepared for their old age, and would have to rely on the pension.

The eight men with sketchy plans for retirement lived in Auckland, Manchester, Melbourne and Sydney. Two were in their 60s and three in each of their 70s and 80s.[23] Among everyday Australians, no matter what class, home ownership has been the critical element in their approach to old age: 'What matters for a tolerable retirement (far more than superannuation) is owning the home in which you live. If you do, the age pension is enough to get by on. If you don't, you have to pay rent'.[24]

The truth in this was borne out in the lived experience that Australian and New Zealand interviewees revealed when discussing their retirement plans. The men who explicitly stated that home ownership meant old age was manageable or that they were relying on it to make theirs manageable were 81-year-old Godfrey from Sydney, 75-year-old Basil and 72-year-old Jeffrey from Auckland.

Godfrey had worked in local government before retiring at 60 when he was offered an attractive redundancy payment in the 1990s when councils were being restructured:

> I never set out to make plans. It just happened. I thought that I would automatically work until retirement age which is 65 for men but the local

government I worked for decided to offer some of the oldies a redundancy and I thought, 'here I go; I am 60 and I might as well take it'.

He lived on his redundancy until he turned 65 and applied for the pension. When asked if home ownership was part of how he managed his retirement, he replied: 'Oh yes, an important factor was that I do own my own house':

> I have great sympathy for people who are on the pension and have to pay exorbitant rents … That is part of my family background. We were independent land owners. I grew up with that sort of ethic. And my family encouraged it too, my father particularly.

The two Aucklanders in their 70s related similar stories and from similarly straightened emotional and material circumstances. Each referred to a recent breakdown of their couple relationship as the context for having to re-evaluate their living and financial arrangements.

Basil (aged 75) had been married and had adult children with their own families. His working life had involved a lot of travel in Melanesia and he said that when he and his partner separated, his family advised him to move closer to them: 'I have just bought a unit … around the corner from my daughter … so that is one aspect of preparation [for retirement]'. Unable to buy the property outright, he had taken out a reverse mortgage:

> I did not have enough to buy the place so I borrowed from this company and I do not pay anything back and every month the interest is added on … so that at the end … I am guaranteed a place to live as long as I am alive.

He received the pension and supplemented it with occasional odd-jobs for neighbours:

> I still go out and do gardening, do housework for people to help with my pension because that is the only income I have got. I do not have any cash in the bank of any consequence, hardly enough to pay my funeral expenses.

Because of his impecuniousness, Basil did not expect to leave his children anything of real value: 'if when I die, there is no equity in that house, then nobody gets anything apart from the goods and chattels inside'.

Seventy-two-year-old Jeffrey, also from Auckland said that he had no retirement plan because, 'my partner was my plan'. And then his partner left him which was a cruel twist because of the loose arrangements they had made: 'He had a good job. We had worked to get him up to that position and he was supposed to be my bank roll'. This sort of arrangement is not uncommon among gay couples where there is an age difference: the older agrees to support the younger while the latter gets established in his career and in return the younger agrees to support the older when he retires. After his partner's departure, Jeffrey was moving into a three-bedroom house and making use of practices from an earlier more communal time to make ends meet: 'I will next week be in a three bedroom home [with] one boarder, a very good fellow. And that and the pension and perhaps another boarder I can almost cope with my reduced expectations'.

Some old men with less serious upheavals in their personal lives also found it difficult to plan their future. The sort of predicaments they faced are represented here by accounts from an Aucklander in his 60s and a Melbournian in his 70s. Sean (aged 67) from Auckland said that he could not see or plan clearly because of his partner's alcoholism:

> I think if he does not do anything about it, he could well die before me … On one level, you have got to leave stuff to somebody but I think I may need some option than leaving … everything to him. Or maybe when he dies then I can revise the will.

Sean's focus on his will could be explained by an experience he recounted earlier in the interview about his parents' deaths. A working life that took some time to lead to a fulfilling career—factory work, teacher training, arts management, then retail sales—had not left him with material assets of any significance. And the inheritance he received when his parents died allowed him to reduce some of his debt: 'After the death of my parents and difficulties with wills and also I did a little bit of travelling and I thought it was time to get my will in place'. More than a decade after his parents' deaths, the matter of his will was still playing on Sean's mind, complicated by the uncertainties of his partner's life path.

Seventy-year-old Arran from Melbourne was restricted in what he could do because of the role his partner's wife and daughter played in their lives. His partner who was 81 had never divorced his wife and all three shared a large house in leafy suburb. They had an investment property and his partner owned part of a house, both of which they wanted to sell.

> However we do have a wife and she has this huge apartment which is filled with furniture and ... she thinks that the three of us could live together and rent a house. She imagines that we will be able to rent a house somewhere nice and big enough to live independent lives. I am not easy about that ... I do not agree with renting particularly. I have always owned and I do not like the idea of spending a thousand dollars a month as my share ... That is a lot of money wasted.

Arran's plan was to buy a flat closer to the central business district for him and his partner but things were not quite so straightforward: the impression I left with was that any solution would involve his partner and his partner's wife. And after a serious culling of 'the wife's' possessions, all three of them would most likely move into another rented property.

Retired with Structured Plans

The ten men with retirement plans that appeared highly structured and organised were mostly in their 60s and came from Manchester, Melbourne, New York and Sydney.[25] The stories of their retirement plans fell into two groups. The first were those that emphasised financial organisation as central to their other retirement plans. The second were those whose health circumstances had forced on them a need for high-level plans. These are discussed in order.

Men who emphasised the importance of the financial in their retirement plans had worked in a variety of occupations, including in education, journalism and media. They were living on incomes ranging from between the equivalent in 2009 terms of US$20,000 and

US\$65,000, which meant that their standard of living varied between relative poverty and relatively comfortable.[26] The financial arrangements the men revealed in their interviews included income from investment properties and supplemented with part-pension, income from stocks and shares or from a formerly organised superannuation scheme or privately funded pension. Despite the relative poverty of some of the men, with one exception they owned their own residence and all would be described as middle class.

The men with the most organised plans were often those in their 60s or 70s and in relatively long-term relationships, between 25 and 37 years for example. Their experiences are represented here by the accounts of two men, Drake, a 77-year-old Sydney-sider and Bryce, a 63-year-old Mancunian.

Drake and his younger partner had been together for more than 30 years, during which time they had bought investments, 'that put us into joint financial arrangements which inevitably through the years just become massively tied up'. Complicating their financial arrangements further was the fact that Drake had two children from a previous marriage and, while juggling his emotional obligations to his partner, his daughters, and his partner's siblings was not easy, his intention was that their wills reflected their regard for them:

> We have done what we can to make it easier for the surviving one and fair for those people like offspring and rellies [relatives] to whom we do have great affection and we want to benefit in various ways. We are trying as hard as we can to make it right.

Bryce and his partner who were both the same age had been together for almost 40 years. They had worked in Manchester or nearby and had retired for different reasons in their 50s. At 63, they were used to retirement and organised their lives around frequent holidays abroad, by sea and by air, though their preference was for cruise holidays:

> We are going on a cruise in September, so we drive to Southampton on the Thursday, stay at a hotel, get on the boat, sail off for a month to the Black Sea and then get back and there are no howling kids, there is no long wait in aeroplane queues, whatever.

Although his immediate answer to the question was, 'No we have not in a sense',[27] Bryce then explained what plans he and his partner had made, which centred on the financial: 'we did make reasonably sound financial provisions ... so that we did not think we would be hard up [in old age]'. Bryce said they had not made plans because although they were extremely secure financially, there was one question they had not resolved, which was whether to remain in their house:

> We have made wills. We have talked at length about whether or not to leave this area. We have sometimes said it is perhaps not the best area to grow old. But then what we inevitably keep coming up is we are not sure where is the best place to grow old, not in a nursing home ... We have made no plans ... other than financial and I guess that is an important lynchpin in making plans for growing old. It might be sensible possibly to try and find a house that is on the level, not two floors.

Later in the interview, Bryce outlined the virtues of living where they were—a house with two floors notwithstanding—and these included good public transport and good neighbours: 'We are fortunate we have very good neighbours and you might say it is better to have good neighbours and grow old with good neighbours you know'. Even though Bryce averred that he and his partner had not 'in a sense' made retirement plans, his awareness of their present house and its location to amenities showed thought and care and considerable insight into their future needs.

The well-made retirement plans of two men were shaped by the condition of their health. The first was Randall, a man in his 80 s who suffered from dementia and was cared for by his long-term partner. The second was Parry, who was in his 60s, HIV positive, and in a long-term relationship with another man with HIV.

Randall had worked in human services and was long retired by the time of our interview. He shared a house with his younger partner, Hugh, also interviewed for this book, who was 62 and had worked in education before his retirement. Because of Randall's poor cognitive health, it was largely Hugh who explained their living circumstances and retirement plans. He began the story of their well planned retirement by emphasising how frugally they lived:

I think we have always planned for the future so we have never been extravagant in the way we have spent money. We have always lived simply. So when we used to do a lot of entertaining we much preferred to entertain at home rather than meeting at a restaurant. Neither of us really particularly enjoys going to a restaurant because of the ambiance or the noise or the expense. So we have actually lived very simply. And the last time we were overseas was 1983, just after Randall retired.

Hugh then explained that one reason for their austerity was because they did not want Randall to go into a nursing home: 'I would want to care for him at home, and when I cannot do it on my own, as I am doing it now, I would want to pay for domiciliary care'. Apart from their frugal predispositions, I would argue that Hugh's and Randall's financial arrangements were forced on them by Randall's illness and Hugh's determination to avoid Randall moving into a high-level care facility.

Parry lived in New York and was HIV positive. This was fortunate because local government in New York had special welfare arrangements for people living with HIV-AIDS:

In New York, if you have less than 200 T cells, you were entitled to go on disability … I never had that capability but at one point I had an opportune infection, an ulcer … and so I qualified for being retired under the AIDS denomination and … [could] retire.

As well, Parry was living in subsidised accommodation, so his financial circumstances were both organised as a result of his illness and provided him with a relatively good standard of living. The effect of HIV on the lives and retirement plans of other men from the sample are discussed later in the chapter.

Middle Cohort

The 28 men from this cohort were born in 1950–1964, a time of general rising prosperity in the West—when the welfare state was being extended and strengthened. Many of them took part in or were influenced by the youth movement and then the liberation movements of the late 1960s and 1970s. This was a generation that believed it could change the world and would never grow old. Now they are growing old and the evidence from this non-representative sample is that while many of them were careful in making plans for their old age many were reckless also and will live out their 70s and 80s in receipt of the old age pension.

Sketchy Plans

More than a third of the men from the middle cohort ($n = 11$) showed evidence of having sketchy plans for their retirement.[28] Included in this number were four men who were HIV positive. The presence of these men in the cohort (aged 49–59) is significant because, until the mid 1990s, those living with HIV-AIDS assumed they would die prematurely. With the release in 1996 of a new triple-therapy drug treatment for HIV, accounts began to circulate in gay and mainstream media of men adjusting to 'life after death', that is, to having a future when before they had none and where they could expect to live a relatively long and healthy life. The effect of the new drug treatments, then, was to restore longevity to men who had previously assumed they would not live to middle age, let alone old age.

The four men living with HIV were from Auckland, Los Angeles and New York and were aged in their 40s and 50s. One was black-skinned, the others white-skinned. Two of the men were in full-time employment and two were casually employed when interviewed. The two men from Los Angeles, both in their 50s, were precariously employed and had no retirement plans; as well, both had problems with their families with which to contend. The first one, aged 59 recounted how until quite recently he had lived and why he had no retirement savings:

> I am going to have to work forever. I am not going to have a retirement plan that sweeps in and I am not going to be able to 'retire' [his emphasis] and live on the money I have saved or anything like that because I spent it as fast as I got it … I had the best time with no expectations of

being older because I thought I was going to die of HIV. I am not saying that was the catalyst but ... as a 60-year-old person, everybody I know, everybody I cared about died. They were all dead, so why wouldn't I? ... I did not think that far ahead.

His calm, clear account of his life as a man living with HIV included an admission that he spent money when he got it but not because he was going to die. And yet, expecting not to live to old age, he had made no plans for retirement, and this, together with his spend-thriftiness, meant he was destined to work till the end of his life in a neo-liberal society with no compassion or belief in safety nets for people living in poverty.

The other man from Los Angeles was aged 56. His life was affected by troubles with his sibling, which got worse after the death of their father. Nonetheless, his tone was relatively positive:

I found myself in my retirement suddenly and I made it up as I went along. I am in it now and now it is working okay. I was living with my late father ten years ago in Arizona, in his house, when he suddenly passed away. I always thought that when he was gone that I would find myself living in his house, with a little money in the bank. Well, thanks to my brother, I was railroaded out of the house and found myself back in Los Angeles, with a little bit of money and a bad case of depression and not knowing what to do. And living in a garage.

When interviewed, he had a casual job working as a kitchen hand in a restaurant. His HIV status appeared to contribute less to his parlous situation than the fraught relationship with his older brother.

The other two men with HIV had relatively secure jobs. One worked in human services in New York, the other in education in Auckland. The New Yorker, who was in his early 50s said that he had once made retirement arrangements but had to convert them to cash when his situation changed: 'I am sitting here with no arrangements other than social security and I make very little as a social worker so even devoting cash flow to retirement savings is not something I can do'.

The man from Auckland, who was in his late 40s explained that he had made no retirement plans because his prognoses had been extremely poor from the start: 'in 1988, I was told I probably had about two years to live and then again in 1996, I was told I had about one year to live'. He was in his late 20s in 1988s, so he spent all of his 30s expecting to die from AIDS: 'HIV has played a huge role throughout my adult life ... [and] has affected nearly everything else I have done', including making plans for the future as this extract shows:

> It has made future planning something I have not really considered. Well, I have over the last couple of years but up until recently I have worked on the assumption that I was not going to be around for all that long, so I did not need to worry about it. And I am now having to revise those plans and I am not sure what is happening for my future. I am a little bit worried about it.

Aware that he would receive an inheritance when his mother died, he was now more concerned than before about his next 15–20 years: 'I have got to focus and think actually I could be alive up to 65 may be and I need to think about retirement'. When I observed the social effect of medical research for people like him, he replied: 'Effective HIV treatments changed everything'.

Coming as they did from different backgrounds and varying levels of engagement with the world of work, what these four men had in common was no provision or extremely minimal provision for their retirement and old age. As they testified, the effect of being a PLWHA for most of their lives had been to take away their individual expectation of a long future or even a certain one.

Structured Plans

A large number of men from the middle cohort ($n = 17$) reported fairly well-organised, structured plans for their retirement.[29] Included in this number were three men with chronic health conditions, two of whom had HIV, while the other was living with a cancer in remission which if it returned could mean a major medical intervention. All were in their 50s. Two came from Melbourne, the other from Auckland.

234   P. Robinson

Their stories are considered now because they contrast with the four men with HIV whose sketchy retirement plans were just discussed. These men were financially secure and had thought about retirement, what it would mean, and old age. The two men with HIV related quite different accounts of how the disease would affect their retirement.

The Aucklander, who was in his mid 50s, explained that, like the men in the previous section, retirement was something he had only recently considered. And that for most of his adult life he had expected not to live to old age. Unlike them, he had not been forced to dispose of or reduce his material assets—'I am just really pleased I did not cash in my insurance policies or anything like that'—or leave a well-paid job. What he had in common with them, though, was the new lease of life that came with improved drug treatments:

> Now I am on a medication with heaps of other medication available to me if this one fails. And I do firmly believe probably the first time that I will live a normal life. Dealing with mortality was hard but moving from mortality to longevity has been harder.

The idea that mortality was more manageable than longevity for some PLWHA began to circulate in groups of gay men in the 1990s when more PLWHA were living healthier lives and not progressing to AIDS or death.[30] To outsiders including HIV-negative men, it seemed counter-intuitive, a bizarre set of beliefs but, as Logan explained, once someone was reconciled to it, there was something reassuring about death's fixedness:

> Mortality ... is final and you have everything put in place. You know what is going to happen. There is a defined end. You know where your will is ... Everything around your death is organised. Then all of a sudden all of that has to come undone and you have got to live. You then have to start thinking about your retirement.

He was fortunate, he explained, because he had maintained a strong, supportive relationship with his partner, who had a good salary and would keep working and support him when he retired. When they began their relationship there was an imbalance in property: 'I had most of the property and the capital' which would be redressed over time: 'by the time I am ready to retire, he will be still of a working age on a very good salary which will allow me to still have the lifestyle that I am accustomed to through him'.

The Melbournian with HIV had a successful career as a bureaucrat in Australia and also overseas. At 52, he had managed his retirement plan carefully: 'there are ways to live one's life ... that ... avoids peaks and troughs. I am very fortunate compared to many people that I have options'. He was aware also of the benefits of being single and without dependents:

> I am relatively comfortable and reasonably confident that I will not be starving [when retired] or out on the street. And ultimately it would be a great thing if with my last breath I spent my last dollar of credit.

The man with cancer in remission was also from Melbourne. He was 56 and in a relationship of more than 30 years. His partner had a family from an earlier heterosexual marriage and the two had highly structured retirement plans, partly because of the need to cater for his partner's children. They jointly owned properties and had begun thinking about the type of accommodation they might need: 'if [partner] becomes disabled ... we [will] need a house that is flat with a property that is flat with a ramp. The plan is to rent out this house and rent a property that matched what we needed'. Carefully considered, their retirement plan would preserve their chief capital asset and provide appropriate accommodation for the older partner's needs, that is, a house at ground level on levelled property and with ramp access to both.

The remaining men with structured retirement plans included four who were rich or very rich: two belonged to the international corporate or professional elite, one came from a rich family and the other was a successful publisher. The rest ($n = 10$) earned moderate, middle-class incomes. These men's stories will be examined in that order, beginning with the four men described as rich.

The international corporate or professional elite has a very long history: it could be argued that some of its earliest examples were in imperial Egypt when consuls and generals extracted vast fortunes from territories they governed or conquered. In more recent times, it is associated with staff working in finance, law, accounting for multinational corporations that have their headquarters in Europe or USA, undertaking activities in the rest of the world.[31]

Fred and Duncan were both 47 when interviewed and were employed by large multinational corporations. Fred was from London and with his partner had highly organised long-term plans. He had a pension scheme: 'having worked for 25 years solid for various companies, it is good'; and he and his partner owned properties: 'a pretty good portfolio of property in London which is valuable stuff'. He said that he and his partner planned to retire early:

> We both want to retire from full time work as soon as we can—by the time we are 50 I would say and do more portfolio and stop working. So we need to pay off our mortgages to give us complete security and then we can work in a way which suits us more than it suits the big companies out there that want us to dedicate a hundred per cent of our time to them.

While these men are likely to become the new landlord (or rentier) class, it is also clear that their superior financial situation—whereby they could buy properties in London—arose from their labour and not as a result of capital inheritance or the returns of capital, which supports an argument of Thomas Picketty about recent sources of income and the shift from capital to labour returns, which he dates from the post-war decades, when 'inherited wealth lost much of its importance, and for the first time in history, perhaps, work and study became the surest routes to the top'.[32]

Duncan was an Australian expatriate living in Hong Kong. Like Fred, he worked for a large multinational corporation and he and his partner had properties in London, also like Fred and his partner but not to the same extent: 'we wish to be … clear of mortgages and actually establish probably another home outside of London'. His long-term plan was to be able to divide the year between northern and southern hemispheres:

if I could paint an ideal scenario it would be ... either six months there and six months in Australia or six months there and six months in Asia, or a completely ideal scenario six, three, three. And for the moment I think London will remain the base. The caveats are my parents are getting older so ... and [his partner's] mother will be 80 this year.

The remaining men lived on moderate incomes.[33] Their retirement plans consisted of superannuation (or pension) accounts and property ownership, the latter on a smaller scale than the four who belonged to the international corporate or professional elite. Their stories are represented here by those from a Mancunian and a Melbournian. Eddie, 45, was from Manchester and was in a relationship of more than 18 years. His partner, who was slightly older, was in a better position: 'he is prepared because he is paying extra [into his pension] and he earns more than me so he can prepare for that'. Eddie's master plan was to reduce their debts, pay off their mortgage and then to save for their retirement:

We know we could not live on state benefits [old age pension] for example. If we got rid of all our debts so we did not have mortgages to pay and we do not get into debt so we do not have loans to pay. And that might seem a little bit far fetched about retirement but it is all part of the plan because if I do not have debts ... [and] am earning full time money then I can save a substantial amount of that and it will be saved. I am quite good at saving, so that would help the absence of a good pension.

In terms of speculative things, we own a house and we thought ... [about] these deals ... where people buy your house but you live in it and they release a substantial amount of the equity ... We have no intention of leaving anything to anyone; we intend to spend as much as possible. And [in Manchester] we have these old people's flats. We live in a house but we see these old people's flats and we think they look really nice. You have got to be over 50 and I am thinking why don't we just sell it and move into one of them.

Eddie's plans are predicated on low mortgage rates, which have been a common feature of housing finance in the West since the global financial crisis in 2008/2009,[34] and which in some large cities, such as London and Sydney have caused steep rises in house prices.[35] But underlining it was an awareness of the inadequacy of the old age pension and having funds available for living when retired—hence his speculating about a reverse mortgage or selling their house and moving into flats for old people when he was over 50.

The Melbournian's plans also centred on home ownership but with a different emphasis. Calvin was 51 and worked for a telecommunications corporation. His plan was to buy a house with enough spare bedrooms to allow him to take in boarders. An old-fashioned approach but an assured one, tried and tested by generations before him:

> I have bought a house ... which is a three bedroom property and ... and that is part of my retirement planning in the sense that I can have up to two flatmates for company and income ... It is part of my superannuation in the sense that it is bigger than I need but with the property situation in Melbourne in another ten years' time I could sell it and have enough to retire on ...

> I could buy a one bedroom apartment in the city and possibly have a place in the country or possibly live somewhere cheaper elsewhere and it will give me money and enough to live. So that is one of the factors why I bought such a big place at this stage of my life.

Calvin's plan to realise capital from the sale of his house in ten years' time and then buy a smaller residence and be left with some capital to fund his retirement, fully or partly with the pension, was a common theme in the stories from those with moderate incomes. And in some way but to a lesser degree mirrored the plans of the richer men from the international corporate or professional elite.

Young Cohort

The 29 men comprising this cohort mostly belonged to Generation X and Y with a small number from i-Generation. They grew up in a time when the welfare state was being dismantled and into a world where neo-liberalism was replacing Keynesian economic principles and practices, the state was being shrunk, and the free market expanding.

6 Old Age Plans 239

This cohort would be expected to pay for their own retirement as governments of advanced western economies were forecast by the mid to late twentieth-first century to have nil or minimal responsibilities for old age or the pension. Their retirement stories are examined from the perspective of those with sketchy or no plans followed by those with structured plans.

Sketchy or no Plans

Eighteen interviewees from the young cohort had fairly sketchy plans for retirement, no plan at all or no idea about retirement.[36] The three with some sort of plan were aged between early 30s and early 40s. Of the 15 who had no idea about retirement two-thirds were in their 20s.

Two men with sketchy retirement plans had full-time work and were aged 42. Noah, a teacher from Auckland, said his partner was encouraging him to begin planning for their retirement—'He is on my case all the time about retirement plans and saving for when that time comes … and making a will'—but that he delayed doing anything because he was unsure of his feelings: 'What is at the back of my mind is … [whether] he [is] the one for me for the rest of my life. It is a block. Is it where I want my assets to end up?' Just as heterosexuals in de facto relationships have to be aware of palimony,[37] that is, claims partners could make on their material assets in the event of a relationship break-up, gay people in relationships before the advent of gay marriage or civil union also had to be alert to the implications of sharing property, bank accounts, and other financial instruments. Noah was interviewed just as the New Zealand parliament was set to pass legislation to allow gay marriage.[38] Whether or not this was a catalyst, Noah was conscious of the fact that if he followed his partner's advice and made firm plans for retirement, his savings could become part of their joint property. And the symbolic and literal aspects of doing so seemed to trouble him.

The other 42-year-old with a loosely formulated plan for retirement was Jacob from Melbourne. He and his partner enjoyed work that allowed them to travel (see Chap. 4) but had not acquired property or accumulated much in their superannuation accounts. Their plan was to begin treating their superannuation more seriously. Interviewed two years after the global financial crisis, Jacob was still aware of its impact on his superannuation:

> One of the things that we are now focusing on now that we are middle aged is looking to top-up our superannuation ... at making voluntary contributions ... where we can, looking at jobs that pay good super. Although it is quite disconcerting that with the global financial crisis that my super fund lost 20 something per cent.

Together with increasing his contribution to superannuation, Jacob was paying more attention to the increased flexibility allowed for under changes to superannuation regulation in Australia:

> I am glad they changed the law so it makes it easier to move between super funds and move within the super fund into different programs as you get older. At the moment I have just moved everything from one of my super funds into Australian shares because they are doing so well and hopefully I will take it out quite quickly when we think that the market is going downturn.

While at the same time being aware that the greater control he could exercise over his superannuation funds and returns might be cosmetic only:

> You can try and gamble in the different portfolios for your super fund which makes it more easy because it gives you the perception that you have some sort of control over your finances when in fact you probably do not. But it is just nice to pretend to gamble with your super.

Fifteen from the young cohort had no plans or ideas about retirement. The majority were in their 20s and had been educated at non-government schools. One, Zane, a 22-year-old from Melbourne, was unimpressed when asked about his retirement plans: 'that is totally irrelevant. I have no idea. I have never thought about it'. He then revealed more about his family's financial circumstances, contradicting himself: 'I come from a generally wealthy family and there is some sort of inheritance there. I have got a superannuation fund and I am good at what I do ... I am not at all worried about my retirement'. Zane's initial indignant response to my question might have been his way of saying that no one his age could be expected to know about retirement. But then immediately admitted to having a superannuation account and being a good worker—and in the context of an inheritance which he seemed to imply would take care of everything.

Others with a similar background to Zane also referred to their family's financial situation instead of saying that at their age it was too early to have any real concerns for or know much about retirement. Garth also from Melbourne and aged 23 said the following:

> I have had money set aside since I was born like various investments. But that was done for me by my family, like a trust fund. But otherwise apart from like compulsory contributions to superannuation and stuff and like a stake in the family trust I have made no other plans.

> *Will you look after your future as your parents prepared you or spend it at once when you turn 30?*

> I am a terrible spendthrift and I have no self control with money, but I have managed to keep my hands off the money that has been set aside for me for probably three years. I think if I ever did use any it would be to set up my own business in which case at least I would have the proceeds from that and then be able to contribute to my retirement.

Both Zane and Garth were enrolled in tertiary education when interviewed, as was Todd, another Melbournian, aged 21. All three had been educated at non-government schools and came from upper-middle-class families. Avoiding any reference to retirement when he answered, Todd used the question as an opportunity to explain what he wanted from life:

> I would love to have the life that my parents have afforded me through [their] hard work and I plan on working just as hard to make sure that happens. But apart from that ... I really just want to be happy. I am not

fussed by money and, despite the fact I do fashion, I am not very material. I do not buy expensive clothes. I go to opp[ortunity] shops ... I want to be happy and surrounded by people that I love and who love me back ... The only thing I am trying to consciously prepare in my mind is friendships that last, relationships that last.

It is not clear if Todd's desire for love and for secure relationships was simply a statement of very basic human needs. That he raised it in answer to a question about retirement plans could be interpreted as either avoiding a topic about which he knew little or a self-absorbed concern of someone who will never have to worry about money, let alone in old age.

And finally the retirement plans of two which were sketchy because they depended on what their older partners decided to do about their retirement and material assets. Neither referred to joint property ownership, possibly because they were unaware of their palimony entitlements, too subordinate in the relationship to raise the matter, or the older partner was not a property owner. Thirty-one-year-old Gavin from Auckland said in relation to his partner's retirement:

He is 56, so it is not that far away ... I keep pressuring him ... to go back to Australia. I would like to go to the Gold Coast or Brisbane while I am still young enough to make some money ... He is really up there as far as he can go in his career I suppose. No we have not really talked about it as such except for ... [my] nagging him, 'Come on, let's go to Australia, let's go back to Australia or let's go somewhere else and do something'. But we have not really spoken about it too much.

Gavin's emotional dependency—perhaps also material dependency but that was not made clear—meant he could not make plans for himself. Whether or not theirs was a mutually dependent relationship, it did seem that his partner's decisions affected his ability to plan for the future and this included retirement. On the other hand, Gavin believed he stood a better chance of better employment in Australia, a belief partly influenced by the fact his partner had lived in Australia and the allure of the Gold Coast in Queensland about which I had heard before from interviewees in Auckland. Any decision concerning moving away from Auckland, however, would depend on his partner, which, as he explained, was a source of some frustration for Gavin.

Nineteen-year-old Brody from Melbourne was in a similarly dependent relationship with an older man. When asked whether he had any plans for retirement, he said that his 40-year-old boyfriend was planning to buy a house and that they hoped to live together:

> He has decided to get his own house because up until now he has just lived with other people ... And then he's decided that he wants to move closer to me ... And ... we have already ... moved on to ... that it is our house and that we are getting three dogs and two cats [*Laughs*] ... He wants to have a house by the end of the year and by the end of the year if my parents have met him and they are not too distressed about me moving out I would move in with him.

Possibly too young to have a well-formed idea about retirement, Brody's answer to the question entirely consisted of chat about his new relationship of nine months and the next big step in his life, which, with his parents' approval, would be to move in and live with his partner.

Structured Plans

Slightly more than one-third of the young cohort had structured retirement plans,[39] most of which were similar to those from the older cohorts, that is, they comprised a superannuation or pension fund and some form of property ownership.

In the case of two Australians, they and their partners had bought a house and were buying a second or third 'investment' property. Callum, a 43-year-old from Melbourne wrote about his and his partner's retirement strategy:

> We do have this plan ... I have my own house, he has his own house. I have currently rented my property out and with a view that after twelve months I will buy another property and the other property will be a country property, and eventually one of our houses ... his house or my house will be sold and that will be our retirement. So property is the way that I am kind of planning my retirement.

Callum was a university lecturer and his partner a medical specialist, so both earned above-average incomes. Working in medicine, the partner could earn three or four times the average income, which in Australia in 2016 was approximately AU$79,000.[40] The men's disposable incomes, as well as historically low bank interest rates, and the fact they have no dependents, could explain their retirement strategy to sell property when they needed funds for old age. Couples with children could be more likely to adopt a strategy that preserved capital assets to pass on to the next generation.

Liam, a 37-year-old Sydney-sider and his partner were adopting a similar but less developed plan for their retirement, involving joint ownership and an 'investment' property:

> Beyond superannuation have we made any plans? We have bought a house. My partner has an investment property as well ... Being ten years older than me [he] is much more conscious of these things than I am. And I am just ... starting to think [*Laughs*] maybe it is time to be a bit more serious ... I cannot say that I have made plans seriously but there is that niggling thought in the back of my mind of growing older and what that will be like.

The youngest of those with structured plans, 26-year-old Bailey from London said that while retirement was a very long time off, 'about 44 years away for myself', he was aware of having to make plans: 'I am starting to create a stock and housing portfolio to ensure an income in my later years'. None of these men referred to the old age pension as inadequate but all referred in their answer to superannuation or, in the case of Bailey, work pension, and then underlined their belief that unencumbered house ownership was a desirable if not essential component of a secure old age.

Conclusion

It is not surprising that those from the old cohort had the most extensive stories of plans for old age: for it was the lived experience of a great many of them at the time of interview. What was surprising about their stories, however, was that they revealed that almost one-third had no intention of *not* working, even if they had retired from their life's work, that another third had only sketchy retirement plans, and finally that a third of them had well-formed, structured plans.

Because most of those who said they had no intention of retiring were also living on incomes from self-managed superannuation or pension funds, their numbers would be added to those with structured plans to show that about two-thirds of the old cohort had made well structured plans for their retirement. This being the case for the old cohort, it was not surprising, almost to be expected in fact, that just under two-thirds of those from the middle cohort also had structured plans. If generalised to the wider middle-class population—for the bulk of those comprising this sample were middle class—findings such as these would suggest that western governments have been successful in encouraging people to contribute to their own personal superannuation or pension schemes and so too their long-term aim to privatise old age.

The fact that a significant minority of those from the old cohort had no intention of *not* working, that is, they stated that they intended working 'till they dropped' calls for some mention of voluntary work and its importance in the lives of retirees. It was important because they referred to it when asked if they were retired or intended to retire and in the answers they gave it was included in the repertoire of the work activities that they described. One explanation for its importance could be a desire to remain an active member of society with some kind of identity similar to that which they once had as a butcher, baker or high court judge. If that is the case, do those whose work is more than just a job tend to want to keep up involvement in public life through never ceasing to work? While this sample provided no evidence of workers who had been employed in factories or manual labour wanting to 'work till they dropped' and take up voluntary work in their retirement, a similar study might find evidence to contradict the link I suggest between work which is more than just a job and the desire in retirement to continue involvement in public life.

The effect of health on retirement plans, how structured or otherwise they were, varied across cohorts. In the old cohort, I would argue that ill health or chronic ill health underpinned those of two with structured plans: one man with dementia and one man living with HIV. In the middle cohort, there were four men living with HIV, two of whom were precariously employed and all of whom had nil retirement plans, mostly because for the greater part of their adult life they expected to die before they reached old age. These accounts were in contrast to those from the old cohort but also in contrast to three others from the middle cohort who, while ill or suffering from chronic illness, had well-structured plans. Two of these were PLWHA and the third was in remission from cancer. Not so surprisingly, there were no accounts from the young cohort of illness, chronic or otherwise, or its effect on retirement plans.

What the varying accounts from those interviewed for this study suggest, however, is that it is difficult to show a clear, direct link between the two. And I would argue that this is particularly important for PLWHA and their care and carers because it suggests that there is no one dominant narrative about how the disease affects men's ability or willingness to plan for their future. From the evidence provided in this chapter, four PLWHA from the middle cohort had made *no* plans for their retirement; while, on the other hand, three others, one from the old cohort and two from the middle cohort made well-structured plans for their retirement and old age.

The young cohort revealed what some might expect to hear from a group in their 20s and 30s, that is, a relatively low interest in or knowledge of old age and its material requirements. A number of those in their 20s spoke of good, continuing relations with their grandparents and, while they did not admit and I did not inquire, I suspect their interest in old age was limited to their relations with their own kith and kin. Few, if any, had experienced death at the end of life of anyone close to them or had much experience of old age as the penultimate stage of life, apart from, as I say, knowledge of what their grandparents let on about their lived personal experience of it.

Among those from the young cohort, there was some evidence of preparations or plans for retirement and along lines similar to those from the older cohorts, that is, superannuation or pension scheme plus property ownership. About one-third had structured plans while the remaining two-thirds had only sketchy plans or either no plan for or no idea about retirement. The ones with plans were doing or planning to do what those from the older cohorts were doing or had done: buying the residence they were living in and in some cases buying an 'investment property' also. Most if not all referred to superannuation or a pension fund of some sort. The majority with only a vague idea of planning for retirement or who had no idea at all included a group of young men from rich families whose *laissez faire* attitude to retirement and old age could be explained by the effect of the financial security provided by their parents in the form of trusts and other financial arrangements which were designed to take care of them for life and/or the very relaxed attitude toward finances and the future that is natural in people from their milieu.

Notes

1. C. Phillipson (2013) *Ageing* (Cambridge: Polity Press), p. 63 (Phillipson 2013).
2. Phillipson *Ageing*, p. 64.
3. For history of the old age pension in colonial Queensland, see http://www.qgso.qld.gov.au/products/reports/qld-past-present/qld-past-present-1896-1996-ch09-sec-02.pdf. Accessed 6 January 2017; and for New Zealand, see: http://www.nzhistory.net.nz/old-age-pensions-act-passes-into-law. Accessed 7 November 2016.
4. S. Macintyre (1999) A *Concise History of Australia* (Port Melbourne: Cambridge University Press), p. 151; Phillipson *Ageing*, p. 64 (Macintyre 1999).
5. Phillipson *Ageing*, p. 64.
6. Phillipson *Ageing*, p. 90.
7. Phillipson *Ageing*, p. 90–91.
8. J. Hirst (2015) 'Nation building, 1901–1914' in A. Bashford and S. Macintyre (eds) *The Cambridge History of Australia Vol 2: The Commonwealth of Australia* (Port Melbourne: Cambridge University Press), pp. 21–26, 28–31 (Hirst 2015).
9. S. Swain (2015) 'Society and welfare' in Bashford and Macintyre *The Cambridge History of Australia Vol 2*, p. 302 (Swain 2015).
10. M. Clark (1981) A *History of Australia V* (Melbourne: Melbourne University Press), p. 292 (Clark 1981).
11. R. Sennett (2000) *Respect: The Formation of Character in a World of Inequality* (London: Penguin Books); L. Wacquant (2009) *Punishing*

the Poor: The Neoliberal Government of Social Insecurity (Durham and London: Durham University Press) (Sennett 2000; Wacquant 2009).

12. Swain 'Society and welfare', p. 305.
13. Swain 'Society and welfare', p. 306.
14. Swain 'Society and welfare', p. 306.
15. Phillipson *Ageing*, p. 93.
16. See Chap. 1.
17. For details of original Australian legislation, see Swain 'Society and welfare', p. 302. For details of original New Zealand legislation, see http://www.nzhistory.net.nz/old-age-pensions-act-passes-into-law. Accessed 10 November 2016.
18. Philippson *Ageing*, pp. 89–90.
19. Amery (aged 82) Sydney; Lucas (aged 75) Auckland; Christian (aged 72) Sydney; Colin (aged 72) New York; Ashton (aged 70) Sydney; Fergus (aged 63) Manchester; Arthur (aged 62) London.
20. Christian (aged 72) Sydney.
21. S. de Beauvoir (1977/1970) *Old Age*, trans. P. O'Brien (Harmondsworth: Penguin Books), p. 244; emphasis in the original (Beauvoir 1977/1970).
22. Australian Broadcasting Corporation, 'Age pension rates leading to "profound level of deprivation"', 15 September 2016: http://www.abc.net.au/news/2016-09-15/age-pension-rates-leading-to-'profound-level-of-deprivation'/7847310. Accessed 25 November 2016 (Australian Broadcasting Corporation 2016).
23. Hector (aged 81) Melbourne; Clancy (aged 81) Melbourne; Godfrey (aged 81) Sydney; Basil (aged 75) Auckland; Jeffrey (aged 72) Auckland; Arran (aged 70) Melbourne; Sean (aged 67) Auckland; Alec (aged 62) Sydney.
24. P. Martin 'A home truth: we push up prices', *The Age*, 27 October 2016 (Melbourne: Fairfax Media), p. 21 (Martin 2016).
25. Randall (aged 87) Melbourne; Herbert (aged 82) Melbourne; Ambrose (aged 77) Melbourne; Drake (aged 77) Sydney; Baden (aged 65) Melbourne; Alfie (aged 63) Manchester; Bryce (aged 63) Manchester; Parry (aged 63) New York; Hugh (aged 62) Melbourne; Anselm (aged 61) Melbourne.
26. In November 2016, US$20,000 (2009) was worth US$22,387 and US$65,000 (2009) was worth US$72,759; source: Historical Currency Conversions, https://futureboy.us/fsp/dollar.fsp. Accessed 29 November 2016.

6 Old Age Plans   249

27. All interviewees were asked the same question: 'What preparations or plans have you made for your retirement and old age and when did you begin to make them?'

28. Marvin (aged 59) Los Angeles; Austin (aged 57) Auckland; Cam (aged 56) Los Angeles; Hilton (aged 53) New York; Ryan (aged 53) London; Zachary (aged 52) Hong Kong; Earl (aged 51) New York; Tate (aged 51) London; Carl (aged 49) Auckland; Ethan (aged 49) London; Timothy (aged 46) New York.

29. Bernard (aged 59) Hong Kong; Ward (aged 59) New York; Raymond (aged 58) Hong Kong; Isaac (aged 56) Melbourne; Logan (aged 56) Auckland; Ben (aged 52) Manchester; Mike (aged 52) Melbourne; Buck (aged 51) Hong Kong; Calvin (aged 51) Melbourne; Nathan (aged 50) Auckland; Everett (aged 49) New York; Danny (aged 48) Hong Kong; Alvin (aged 47) New York; Duncan (aged 47) Hong Kong; Fred (aged 47) London; Jude (aged 46) Los Angeles; Eddie (aged 45) Manchester.

30. The effect on some PLWHA of realising that longevity not premature death was their future was explored in the film, *Desert Migration*, written and directed by D. Cardone (Los Angeles: 13th Gen and Best Revenge Productions, 2015): http://desertmigrationmovie.com/home. Accessed 24 December 2016 (Cardone 2015).

31. See Chap. 3.

32. T. Piketty (2014) *Capital in the Twenty-First Century* trans. A. Goldhammer (Cambridge, MA: Harvard University Press), p. 241 (Piketty 2014).

33. Bernard (aged 59) Hong Kong; Ward (aged 59) New York; Raymond (aged 58) Hong Kong; Ben (aged 52) Manchester; Buck (aged 51) Hong Kong; Calvin (aged 51) Melbourne; Nathan (aged 50) Auckland; Everett (aged 49) New York; Alvin (aged 47) New York; Eddie (aged 45) Manchester.

34. See, for example, this article from *The Guardian* predicting 2017 mortgage rates in Britain of 1 per cent: Treanor, J. (2016) 'Base-rate cut could lead to UK mortgages at less than 1% interest', https://www. theguardian.com/money/2016/sep/20/november-base-rate-cut-home-loans-less-than-1. Accessed 21 December 2016 (Treanor 2016).

35. See, for example, this article suggesting it would take an 'average' couple more than eight years to save for a deposit for a house in Sydney: M. Janda (2016) 'First home buyers "locked out" of Sydney real estate, struggle in Melbourne' (Sydney: Australian Broadcasting Corporation): http://www.abc.net.au/news/2016-12-22/

250 P. Robinson

first-home-buyers-all-but-excluded-from-sydney-real-estate/8141168. Accessed 23 December 2016 (Janda 2016).

36. Jacob (aged 42) Melbourne; Noah (aged 42) Auckland; Connor (aged 41) London; Findlay (aged 33) New York; Dylan (aged 32) Sydney; Jackson (aged 32) New York; Gavin (aged 31) Auckland; Leo (aged 31) Sydney; Eamon (aged 28) London; Denis (aged 27) Melbourne; Garth (aged 23) Melbourne; Jarrad (aged 23) Melbourne; Zane (aged 22) Melbourne; Hayden (aged 21) Melbourne; Jamie (aged 21) Melbourne; Todd (aged 21) Melbourne; Brody (aged 21) Melbourne; Dougal (aged 18) Melbourne.

37. Palimony is a North American term from 'pal' or friend plus alimony or compensation after marriage or relationships break-up, usually in context of payment(s) made to the female partner or wife but now also in context of the break-up of same-sex relationships.

38. Legislation to legalise gay marriage passed the New Zealand parliament by a majority vote of 77 to 44 in April 2013, see *Sydney Morning Herald*: http://www.smh.com.au/world/new-zealand-passes-gay-marriage-bill-20130417-2i0l4.html.

39. Jonathan (aged 44) London; Kendall (aged 44) New York; Callum (aged 43) Melbourne; Gabriel (aged 43) Auckland; Kyle (aged 40) Auckland; Guy (aged 38) London; Liam (aged 37) Sydney; Anton (aged 35) London; Evan (aged 35) Los Angeles; Aiden (aged 33) London; Bailey (aged 26) London.

40. Equivalent in other currencies: AUD79,000 = GBP46,180 HKD440,050; NZD82,370; USD56,600, see: https://www.google.com.au/webhp?sourceid=chrome-instant&ion=1&espv=2&ie=UTF-8#q=1 AUD to GBP. Accessed 26 December 2016. See following Australian Bureau of Statistics report for average Australian income: http://www.abs.gov.au/ausstats/abs@.nsf/mf/6302.0. Accessed 26 December 2016 (Australian Bureau of Statistics report for average Australian income 2016).

References

Australian Broadcasting Corporation. 2016. Age Pension Rates Leading to "Profound Level of Deprivation", 15 Sept 2016. http://www.abc.net.au/news/2016-09-15/age-pension-rates-leading-to-'profound-level-of-deprivation'/7847310. Accessed 25 Nov 2016.

6 Old Age Plans 251

Australian Bureau of Statistics Report for Average Australian Income. 2016. http://www.abs.gov.au/ausstats/abs@.nsf/mf/6302.0. Accessed 26 Dec 2016.

Beauvoir, S. de (1970/1977). *Old Age, trans. and P. O'Brien*. Harmondsworth: Penguin Books.

Cardone, D. (dir.). 2015. *Desert Migration* (Los Angeles: 13th Gen and Best Revenge Productions, 2015). http://desertmigrationmovie.com/home. Accessed 24 Dec 2016.

Clark, M. 1981. *A History of Australia V.* Melbourne: Melbourne University Press.

Hirst, J. 2015. Nation Building, 1901–1914. In *The Cambridge History of Australia Vol 2: The Commonwealth of Australia*, ed. A. Bashford, and S. Macintyre, 15–38. Port Melbourne: Cambridge University Press.

Janda, M. 2016. First Home Buyers "locked out" of Sydney Real Estate, Struggle in Melbourne. Sydney: Australian Broadcasting Corporation. http://www.abc.net.au/news/2016-12-22/first-home-buyers-all-but-excluded-from-sydney-real-estate/8141168. Accessed 23 Dec 2016.

Macintyre, S. 1999. *A Concise History of Australia.* Port Melbourne: Cambridge University Press.

Martin, P. 2016. 'A Home Truth: We Push Up Prices', *The Age*, 21. Melbourne: Fairfax Media.

Phillipson, C. 2013. *Ageing*, 63. Polity Press: Cambridge.

Piketty, T. 2014 *Capital in the Twenty-First Century*, trans. and ed. A. Goldhammer. Cambridge, MA: Harvard University Press.

Queensland, old age pension, see http://www.qgso.qld.gov.au/products/reports/qld-past-present/qld-past-present-1896-1996-ch09-sec-02.pdf, Accessed 6 Jan 2017; and for New Zealand, see: http://www.nzhistory.net.nz/old-age-pensions-act-passes-into-law, Accessed 7 Nov 2016.

Sennett, R. 2000. *Respect: The Formation of Character in a World of Inequality.* London: Penguin Books.

Swain, S. 2015. 'Society and welfare'. In *The Cambridge History of* Australia, vol. 2, eds. Bashford and Macintyre, 284–307.

Sydney Morning Herald. http://www.smh.com.au/world/new-zealand-passes-gay-marriage-bill-20130417-2i0l4.html.

Treanor, J. 2016. Base-Rate Cut Could Lead to UK Mortgages At Less Than 1% Interest. https://www.theguardian.com/money/2016/sep/20/november-base-rate-cut-home-loans-less-than-1. Accessed 21 Dec 2016.

Wacquant, L. 2009. *Punishing the Poor: The Neoliberal Government of Social Insecurity.* Durham and London: Durham University Press.

7

Conclusion

This book has shown how similar to and different from the working lives and ageing concerns of everyday people are those of gay men. In the first half of the book, on working lives, there was ample evidence of the ordinariness of their life stories and a strange similarity to the lives of straight men in occupations and professions spanning a large array of jobs. Interviewees spoke of what it meant to be teachers, tradesmen and factory workers, an automobile designer, a toy seller, a television cameraman and a mortgage broker, as well as how they fared as lecturers and lawyers, clerical workers and sales assistants, rail workers and engineers. In their number were also a nationally recognised drag queen, a senior judge, a number of professors, but no hairdressers or window dressers and, to my knowledge, no spies.

To what extent they were representative of gay men in their native country or in the popular imaginary, I will leave the reader to judge. But they all defied corrupting stereotypes and reinforced arguments made over more than 30 years that gay men suffer when shut out or forced to live double lives and can yet adapt to hostile situations and survive. To work is to survive and all the men interviewed for this book had work stories to relate. Some had periods in their lives when they were forced out of the job they loved by homophobes or homophobic

© The Author(s) 2017   **253**
P. Robinson, *Gay Men's Working Lives, Retirement and Old Age,*
Genders and Sexualities in the Social Sciences,
DOI 10.1057/978-1-137-43532-3_7

prejudice.[1] These were more powerful in the lives of those from the old and the middle cohorts but were still present in the young cohort, those born after 1986, who were supposed to inherit a new world of greater social tolerance and acceptance.

Gay marriage is a nice, easy way to appease homophobes and attract the support of gay-friendly straights but the reason many gay men—mostly from the older cohorts but also from the young—are hesitant to embrace this latest push for equal rights is that it seems like just another example of having to take on the accepted ways of straights-ville instead of the straight world being asked to accept gay men and their ways. And, as I argued elsewhere, until sex education in secondary schools in western advanced countries includes detailed advice to male same-sex students about the joys and risks of anal sex, the incidence of HIV-AIDS will not disappear as a serious health risk to young, gay men, and homophobia will not disappear once and for all.[2]

To conclude, I highlight what I regard as the more significant findings from this research, beginning with the working histories and the principal narratives they provided, followed by the gay-specific experience of whether to be out in the workplace and its effect, then focusing on old age and its concerns for gay men and their accounts of preparations they plan to make or have made.

With one or two exceptions, a notable feature of the interviewees' life stories was the absence of ambition in the accounts they provided about work and its meaning. One possible reason for this could concern the modesty of successful people: after achieving greatness, they can forget the struggle involved in getting it. Or it could be associated with an ancillary argument of Michael Pollak, which was that in the 1960s and 1970s middle-class and upper-class, white, gay men tended to underachieve in their careers because of shame or difficulties controlling the tension between their public and private lives.[4] Put another way, the marginalised positions of gay men could also explain the absence of ambition in their work narratives.

If all-male workplaces operated then as many do now, where hegemonic males dominate work practices and relationships, it is possible that homosexuals did not expect to succeed and instead were satisfied with a workplace presence that avoided unnecessary attention. This could certainly have been the case for the old cohort and many from the middle cohort. Whether or not it continues more generally and continues to affect the young cohort is a moot point and, in a sense, only time will tell. When one of the young men spoke of workplace difficulties because of his sexuality, he was fairly sure that change was 'on his side' and that they would abate or disappear.

By comparing the experiences of a sample divided by age cohorts, it is possible to identify change over time in certain characteristics or preferences. In the case of the working histories of this sample, the rank order of work narratives showed the strongest evidence of generational change in the type of work to which interviewees gravitated.[5] The three principal work narratives for the old cohort were work as work followed by care or creative work, and social or political change. For the middle cohort, they were, in order, care, travel, and work as work. And for the young cohort, the three principal work narratives were creativity, care, and social and political change. The most obvious change over time was the decline in importance of the work-as-work narrative from primacy for the old cohort to negligible import for the young cohort. The next most obvious change was the primacy of care for the middle cohort and the emergence of travel for them as an important narrative. Finally, the emergence of creativity as the narrative of most importance for the young cohort was notable and is the subject of more discussion below.

Decline in importance of work as work—defined as the pragmatic, no-nonsense approach to work, the approach that men in general but also women adopt when they go about their everyday work—mirrors structural changes in western economies since the 1950s when many of the old cohort were starting out, that is, the gradual decline in manufacturing, the slow then rapid growth of casual and precarious employment. In the old cohort, those whose working lives were represented by this narrative worked in working-class and middle-class jobs such as bricklayer, electrician, librarian, photographer, psychologist, sales representative and store-man. Their jobs were no different, in other words, from the sort of jobs that the great mass of working men had during the post-war decades. Other features of the work histories represented by this narrative included men who had many jobs, moved about, enjoyed a great deal of flexibility in their career and then, by contrast, men who had only one job or a couple at most. Included in the men's narratives was the nascent concept of 'love travel' which affected a small number and which increased in importance for the men from the younger cohorts.

The middle cohort saw a quite radical shift in the rank order of primary work narratives: work as work was relegated to third in importance and care became the principal one, followed by travel. In the old cohort, the care-or-creative narrative comprised work histories of men who taught, worked for religious organisations, children's crafts, were composer, poet and retail manager. Care work and creative work were joined together on the assumption that each field of work was more accepting of gay men and women and they were less likely to experience homophobia or sexism. And as the men related, mentoring or taking care of younger people of both sexes inspired and sustained their careers. For the middle cohort, care transformed from care or creative work to become care alone. The type of stories included in this narrative moved from the very general notion of care for others—as the old cohort understood and practised it—to the specific care that men with HIV or at risk of infection required, a historically contingent form of care that answered the call for help that gay men increasingly made in the 1980s and 1990s.

Social or political change transformed also from being understood in general terms (the old cohort) to including the human rights and social needs of gay men (the middle and young cohorts). Travel was a new narrative for the middle cohort where it blossomed, not to be taken up by the young cohort. Included in this narrative, which comprised jobs in travel organisations (airlines, shipping companies, hotel chains) and taking jobs that required work overseas (trade, diplomacy, multinationals) were stories related to finding a love interest or life-time companion while travelling or leaving home and travelling with their partner. Love travel or love and travel was a new theme connected as it was to the flexibility some gay men realised they could enjoy in work when they appreciated they were not tied down in the same way as were straight, married males. Not all gay men were aware or took opportunity to enjoy this freedom or flexible arrangements it allowed them. Some followed careers that had an identical shape to those of straight men.

Individual choice was raised in the context of work in the life stories of young men from privileged backgrounds. And this tended to go together with their statements about the importance of creativity and the creative. There are three observations I would make here. First, post-industrial societies have seen an expansion in the newer creative industries such as web-page design, internet content and design, and computer-aided-design as well as the established creative industries such as advertising, graphic art and fashion. Second, the fact that there was stronger evidence of interest in 'the creative' among young men who had been to non-government schools supports the argument of Norbert Elias that changes in taste and social practices occur first in the upper classes and then over time disseminate among other classes.[6] Third, youth might explain this cohort's interest in or emphasis on creativity and or desire to work in a 'creative' field, that is, an argument can be made that creativity is a stronger impulse in the young and when young than it is for people in middle age or older: because when they settle into middle age or older they replace creativity with other desires and forget its importance. This might be the case for some but not all and does not explain why Margaret Drabble or Patrick White kept writing until old age or its ailments prevented them.

Intriguing as well was the status with which some from the young cohort endowed blood and inheritance when relating their life stories. A number of those from wealthy families stated (without irony) that they had inherited interests or in their terms, 'passions', from parents or other family members. I am not sure how widespread this thinking is in the i-Generation but, if it is, it could either suggest the triumph of scientific or medical understandings over social understandings of the self. Or it could be evidence of the dissemination of upper-class notions of family and inheritable traits: like the royal family and aristocrats more generally, upper-class families tend to explain personalities or personal traits, physical characteristics as they do their livestock, that is, as a result of breeding and bloodlines. For young men whose families were upper middle class, this tendency could help explain the decline in egalitarianism that has been a feature of social change in Australia and other Anglophone countries since the 1980s.

Whether the men could be out in the workplace affected those from the old and middle cohorts more than the young and I would argue was evidence of generational change. Three from the old cohort revealed strategies that were consistent with understandings of how same-sex attracted men managed their identities in the 1950s and 1960s.[7] One, whose career was in manufacturing, managed his by saying nothing and letting those around him form their own opinion. He was a formerly married man who did not remarry and lived with two other men. He let his workmates draw their own conclusion because he worked in 'a *very* conservative industry'. The second man worked in education and was scrupulous in remaining closeted through fear of losing his job. Both worked in occupations where they risked their reputation or livelihood if they came out or were known to be homosexual.

The third man worked in entertainment, an industry that has a long history of employing gay people, notwithstanding the purge of gay and left-wing employees that entertainment and media in the USA experienced in the McCarthy period.[8] His approach was to adopt a role that is familiar to many gay men and others in subordinate positions: to cooperate and behave. There are a number of reasons gay men adopt this approach, the most obvious being to avoid attracting the attention of dominant or aggressive males with the power to shame or humiliate them, whether or not these men are part of the formal hierarchy of the workplace. Evidence from the three men's stories suggested that within the field of work, then, a person's occupation affected whether he could be out in his workplace.

Being out in the workplace was probably hardest for the middle cohort, the baby boomers, because their adulthood coincided with the gay liberation and other social movements of the 1970s including the women's, black power, and environmental movements. While all called for personal and public change, the gay liberation movement made a particularly powerful call on same-sex attracted men: to be open and public about their sexuality and in doing so to foster change in small, neighbourhood and workplace circles. In the middle cohort was the story from a man of real savagery he experienced in response to the making public of his sexuality. Married and a resident of a small town in New Zealand, his outing was accompanied by symbolic violence

7 Conclusion 259

and the threat of real violence. Expelled from home and hearth he was denied any contact with this children until they were adults. The stories of two others from the middle cohort were comparatively mild and told of acceptance in both middle-class and working-class milieux.

In the young cohort, three men related stories of challenges they overcame in the workplace because of their sexuality. The first worked in accounting, a profession with a reputation for cautiousness if not conservatism. His record with employers was mixed: gay bosses helped, working for a homophobic union did not. He was not an activist and did not insist on acceptance but carefully assessed his colleagues and workplace on how safe it would be for him to come out. Something similar was the experience of the other two from the young cohort. The older had to deal with a homophobic manager and did so by seeking support from their superiors and then raising the matter directly. The manager ceased his homophobic behaviour when confronted. What these stories suggest is real change over time. The men from the young cohort were able to approach being out in the workplace in ways that were not available to the men from the old cohort and only some from the middle cohort. But they are evidence of important structural changes that will continue to benefit gay people.

The work of Philippe Ariès underpins my understanding of why old age is a source of such fear for twentieth-century and twenty-first-century western society.[9] Ariès argued that, because death has been banished, it is now a wild and frightening thing, which, according to Norbert Elias, now only takes place in the sanitary confinement of hospital wards.[10] This, I would argue, is why old age causes such consternation and anxiety: not only can it mean the loss of independence and relationships and contact with familiar domestic routines and neighbourhood locations, but it is also the final stage before death. And its proximity to death can arouse a very deep fear.

There were slight variations by cohort in the concerns or fears the men held in relation to old age. The old cohort understandably had the most immediate concerns or fears. They were most worried about the homophobia they might encounter in aged care accommodation, either from other residents and their families or from staff but none said he would not move into a nursing home because of it. Universal fears they reported were coping with the death of their partner, the change in their social life, and the loss of identity as they transitioned to a resident or an 'old person'.

The concerns of the middle cohort also focused on the possibility of homophobia in institutional settings. These were the baby boomers and were possibly more sensitive to such matters than those from the old cohort who had managed their sexual identities differently. The most serious fear for the middle cohort was the likelihood of being socially isolated in old age—a universal fear and one they shared with the other cohorts. As mentioned in Chap. 5, what was unique about the solution some men suggested was their intention to continue sexual adventurism for as long as they were able to do so.

For slightly different reasons, those from the young cohort were concerned also about social isolation in old age. They argued that the absence of children would be a reason gay men were likely to be socially isolated when they were old. Remember this is the generation of gay men who believe it is their right to get married and have children. And their awareness of the importance of children in old age might have been self-referential and an understanding got from their belief in the benefit they and their parents brought to the social life of their grand-parents. In contrast to those from the older cohorts, those from the young cohort were acutely aware of the inaction of their community in supporting elderly GLB people and were quite scathing of the absence of gay community interest in the matter. The other gay community absence they noted was in regard to gay-specific accommodation, which in their view was both necessary and uncontroversial.

In the previous chapter, the retirement plans of interviewees were examined by cohort. Four important findings stood out from the analysis. The first was the significant minority from the old cohort who had no intention of not working, that is, who intended to continue working in one way or another—voluntary work or a different type of paid employment than their life's work—until they could no longer work. The second was the large proportion of those from the old and middle cohorts who had well-structured retirement plans, which I argued was evidence of the success of western governments' policies since the 1980s to encourage people to take charge of their retirement or in other words to privatise old age. The third finding of significance concerned a small group of PLWHA: two from the old cohort and four from the middle. Their stories revealed two important narratives: (1) that illness can force people to take good care of their own retirement plans; and (2) that there is no single account of how PLWHA plan for their old age, for some from this sample had extremely well-structured retirement plans (from the old and middle cohorts) while a slightly larger group (from the middle cohort), who were both precariously employed and well employed, had nil retirement plans—partly because they had not expected to live till old age. The fourth significant finding related to the young cohort and the assumptions of a small group of privileged men who explained that old age held few material concerns for them because of trust funds or other financial arrangements made for them by their families.

This book has shown that many similarities exist between the lives of gay men and the general population: they hold down similar jobs; they are worried about growing old and losing their lifelong partner and being left alone in old age; and they plan well or badly for old age depending on circumstances. Where there were differences, they arose from the often prejudicial, if not discriminatory, treatment gay men received because of their sexuality. While homophobia in the 2010s is different from what it was in the past—kinder but not always, less violent but not always—it continues to affect gay men's lives. One solution is to become more like the straight majority: for some gay men being permitted to marry and have children, by adoption or surrogacy, is an ideal solution because it means they renounce their outsider status and can become pseudo-straights. Among those born after 1986, the i-Generation in this book, the appeal of designer-gaydom—marriage, adoption, parenthood etc.—was strong because, despite its limitations, a homogenised identity is preferable to a stigmatised one.[11] I heard from some in their 20s that the older generation of gays had nothing to teach them, citing ultra-conservative views that sexual excess had caused HIV-AIDS and the baby boomers had no one to blame but themselves. These men were planning their lives to be as similar as possible to those their families were mapping for their straight brothers and sisters and cousins.

For gay men who do not wish to become pseudo-straights, the path is less easy: they must seek meaning and community in a culture shaped by a long history of persecution. If they regard themselves as outsiders, from white, Anglo, straight society and from the world of pseudo-straight gays, there is a culture for them to embrace but this is not an easy choice. The alternative gay world is shaped by narratives that include ostracism because of simply who we are and have been; disease in the form of mental illness until the 1970s, sexual illnesses during the 1970s such as herpes, for example, but luckily this was a straight experience as well, and then of course HIV, from the 1980s to the present. Its notable persons are ill-fated lovers such as Alexander the Great of Macedon and his friend from boyhood, Hephaestion or martyrs such as the English monarch, Edward II, and thousands of ordinary men condemned to the flames at the hands of the Inquisition in Spain, or closeted and consumed by self-hatred such as Oscar Wilde's lover, the son of the Marquis of Queensberry.[12] And I wonder how easy it is to assume a stigmatised identity when so many of one's peers are opting for homogenisation and the apparent safety it offers. I did find evidence, however, of rebellious gays in the older cohorts but, because of the power of the homogenising push in advanced western countries, I would not be surprised if they were the last of their kind.

In some of the life stories discussed in the book, it is apparent how much easier it now is to manage workplace homophobia than it was, and for two reasons. The first and most important is that legislation is now in place in many advanced western societies to prevent discrimination on the grounds of gender or sexuality. While this is commendable, it is still the responsibility of the person experiencing homophobia to lodge a complaint and take part in often very formal procedures that the organisation's human-resources staff will conduct and which can affect working relationships and the worker's reputation. The day has not yet arrived where prohibition against homophobia is widely accepted and practised. The second reason is that, because gay people are more in evidence and more broadly accepted in any diverse workplace and are no longer hidden, it is easier for self-confident, articulate gay people to challenge homophobia when they experience it. But, as mentioned, in most cases they must still make a formal complaint—unless they do as a man from the

7 Conclusion   263

young cohort did and raise the matter informally with the homophobe's manager and then approach him unofficially and ask him to desist.

The strongest similarities between the lives of gay men and straight men was in the world of work. And here too was the strongest evidence of their capacity to manage their identity in such a way so as to protect and not jeopardise their livelihood or security. This varied by generation. The men with least to lose because they kept their sexuality a secret were those from the old cohort and some from the middle cohort. Those who were at most risk were the men from the middle cohort, who, if they followed the injunction of the gay liberationists and came out 'willy-nilly', could and often did encounter an audience unwilling to hear the story of their sexual difference. Some, but not all, the men from the middle cohort took advantage of being single, or in a couple relationship but without the financial burden of children to raise, to fully enjoy the entitlements and privilege of full-time, male employment in the 1960s and 1970s. And this was most in evidence in the stories of those who combined travel and work.

Generational change was apparent also in the approach taken to planning for retirement, with some evidence also of the effect of class. Willingness to follow the encouragement of neo-liberal policies and enrol in a private pension or superannuation fund was strongest in the middle cohort with the old cohort showing a mixed response. Among those aged 60 and over, there were men who intended to rely on the pension and to supplement it with cash from boarders or odd-jobs; there were men also who intended to live or were living on interest from capital investments and these tended to belong to the upper-middle class or upper class.

Class was an influence on the attitudes of a small group of those from the young cohort who believed that old age would not be unduly onerous because of material preparations their parents had already made for them. And finally, and again in relation to the young cohort, the fact that most of them raised the matter of how homophobia in aged accommodation could affect the well-being or self-esteem of gay men living there could be a sign of their empathy for older versions of themselves or an expression of how they expect life for them to be trouble free in a way it was not for their predecessors.

In Australia, there is a website for young gay people called Same Same that provides the sort of information that gay and lesbian newspapers provided in the last quarter of the twentieth century, that is, information about performances, clubs and bars, as well as photo galleries, reviews of films, plays, singers.[13] This book has shown the many similarities that exist between gays and straights and that these were strongest in the field of work, although being out at work was not unproblematic. This, together with the fact that retirement and old age presented similar but also different concerns for gay men, could suggest a movement towards western society transforming so that same and same are a great deal more likely to coexist with the straight world than they were even 10 years ago.

Notes

1. That gay men should be treated as 'patients' draws on a very old trope: G. Burke and K. Agius (2017) 'One Nation dumps anti-gay "ratbag" candidate Shan Ju Lin' (Sydney: Australian Broadcasting Corporation): http://www.abc.net.au/news/2017-01-08/one-nation-pauline-hanson-dumps-anti-gay-candidate-shan-ju-lin/8168388. Accessed 8 January 2017 (Burke and Agius 2017).
2. P. Robinson (2016) 'Marriage equality', *Nexus* (Melbourne: The Australian Sociological Association): http://hdl.handle.net/1959.3/431298. Accessed 8 January 2017 (Robinson 2016).
3. See Chap. 1.
4. M. Pollak (1986) 'Male Homosexuality—or Happiness in the Ghetto' in P. Ariès and A. Béjin (eds) *Western Sexuality: Practice and Precept in Past and Present Times*, trans. A. Forster (Oxford: Basil Blackwell), p. 50 (Pollak 1986).
5. Appendix 6.
6. N. Elias (1939, 2000) *The Civilizing Process: Sociogenetic and Psychogenetic Investigations*, trans. E. Jephcott with some notes and corrections by the author, eds. E. Dunning, J. Goudsblom, and S. Mennell, rev. ed. Oxford: Blackwell Publishers Ltd. (Elias 2000, 1939).
7. For discussion of pre-liberation culture and practices, see P. Robinson (2008) *The Changing World of Gay Men* (Basingstoke and New York: Palgrave Macmillan), pp. 18–35 (Robinson 2008).

8. SexTV Original Production (2005) *Gay Hollywood: The Last Taboo* https://www.youtube.com/watch?v=k1mhGDtWIHg. Accessed 8 May 2016 (SexTV Original Production 2005).
9. P. Ariès (1991) *The Hour of Our Death*, trans. H. Weaver (New York: Oxford University Press) (Ariès 1991).
10. N. Elias (1987) *The Loneliness of the Dying*, trans. E. Jephcott (Oxford: Basil Blackwell) (Elias 1987).
11. For more on the young generation's embrace of gay marriage, see P. Robinson (2013) *Gay Men's Relationships Across the Life Course* (Basingstoke and New York: Palgrave Macmillan), pp. 100–120 (Robinson 2013).
12. L. Crompton (2003) *Homosexuality and Civilisation* (Cambridge, Massachusetts: Harvard University Press), pp. 78, 375–376, 291–308; O. Wilde (2000, 1905) *De Profundis* (New York: Random House), *passim* (Crompton 2003; Wilde 2000, 1905).
13. Evo media, Same Same p. l: http://www.samesame.com.au/. Accessed 17 January 2017.

References

Ariès, P. 1991. *The Hour of Our Death*, trans. H. Weaver. New York: Oxford University Press.

Burke, G., and K. Agius. 2017. One Nation dumps anti-gay 'ratbag' candidate Shan Ju Lin. Sydney: Australian Broadcasting Corporation. http://www.abc.net.au/news/2017-01-08/one-nation-pauline-hanson-dumps-anti-gay-candidate-shan-ju-lin/8168388. Accessed 8 Jan 2017.

Crompton, L. 2003. *Homosexuality and Civilisation*. Cambridge, MA: Harvard University Press.

Elias, N. 1987. *The Loneliness of the Dying*, trans. E. Jephcott. Oxford: Basil Blackwell.

Elias, N. 1939, 2000. *The Civilizing Process: Sociogenetic and Psychogenetic Investigations*, trans. E. Jephcott with some notes and corrections by the author, eds. E. Dunning, J. Goudsblom, and S. Mennell, rev. ed. Oxford: Blackwell Publishers Ltd.

Evo media, Same Same p/l: http://www.samesame.com.au/. Accessed 17 Jan 2017.

Pollak, M. 1986. Male Homosexuality—or Happiness in the Ghetto. In *Western Sexuality: Practice and Precept in Past and Present Times*, eds. P. Ariès and A. Béjin, trans. A. Forster, 40–61. Oxford: Basil Blackwell.

Robinson, P. 2008. *The Changing World of Gay Men*. Basingstoke: Palgrave Macmillan.

Robinson, P. 2013. *Gay Men's Relationships Across the Life Course*. Basingstoke: Palgrave Macmillan.

Robinson, P. 2016. Marriage equality, In *Nexus*. Melbourne: The Australian Sociological Association. http://hdl.handle.net/1959.3/431298. Accessed 8 Jan 2017.

SexTV Original Production. 2005. *Gay Hollywood: The Last Taboo*. https://www.youtube.com/watch?v=k1mhGDtWIHg. Accessed 8 May 2016.

Wilde, O. 2000, 1905. *De Profundis*. New York: Random House.

Appendix 1

Interviewees aged 60 and over: job, income and level of education ($n = 25$)

Code name	Age	City	Occupation field	USD 000s[a]	Ed[b]
Randall	87	Mel	Human services **R**	20	U
Amery	82	Syd	Education	35	U
Herbert	82	Mel	Clerical **R**	20	S
Hector	81	Mel	Small business	62	U
Clancy	81	Mel	Retail **R**	20	S
Godfrey	81	Syd	Education **R**	20	S
Drake	77	Mel	Media **R**	45	U
Ambrose	77	Mel	Education **R**	45	U
Lucas	75	Auc	Transport **R**	25	S
Basil	75	Auc	Retail **R**	15	S
Christian	72	Syd	Law	130	U
Colin	72	NY	Education	110	U
Jeffery	72	Auc	Transport **R**	19	T
Ashton	70	Syd	Small business	50	S
Arran	70	Mel	Human services	45	U
Sean	67	Auc	Small business	20	T
Baden	65	Mel	Self employed	30	P
Parry	63	NY	Business **R**	88	S
Bryce	63	Man	Media **R**	65	T
Alfie	63	Man	Clerical **R**	55	S
Fergus	63	Man	Education	15	U
Arthur	62	Lon	Health	85	U
Hugh	62	Mel	Education	40	S
Alec	62	Syd	Research	6	U
Anselm	61	Mel	Education **R**	45	U

Occupation field: *R* retired
[a]Approximate income shown in equivalent of US dollars for 2010
[b]Education abbreviated as: *U* University; *T* Trade College; *S* Secondary school; *P* Primary school

© The Editor(s) (if applicable) and The Author(s) 2017
P. Robinson, *Gay Men's Working Lives, Retirement and Old Age*,
Genders and Sexualities in the Social Sciences,
DOI 10.1057/978-1-137-43532-3

Appendix 2

Interviewees aged 45–60: job, income and level of education ($n = 28$)

Code name	Age	City	Occupation field	USD 000s[a]	Ed[b]
Bernard	59	HK	Small business	55	U
Ward	59	NY	Education	96	U
Marvin	59	LA	Clerical	55	S
Raymond	58	HK	Business	50	U
Austin	57	Auc	Education	82	U
Isaac	56	Mel	Health	70	U
Logan	56	Auc	Business	61	U
Cam	56	LA	Welfare	10	S
Hilton	53	NY	Human services	40	U
Ryan	53	Lon	Media	50	U
Mike	52	Mel	Bureaucracy	110	U
Ben	52	Man	Education	42	U
Zachary	52	HK	Construction & bldg	110	U
Earl	51	NY	Business	25	U
Tate	51	Lon	Business	130	U
Calvin	51	Mel	Business	90	U
Buck	51	HK	Business	<10	T
Nathan	50	Auc	Small business	45	T
Everett	49	NY	Human services	25	U
Ethan	49	Lon	Clerical	55	U
Carl	49	Auc	Education	48	U
Danny	48	HK	Media	120	U
Fred	47	Lon	Construction & bldg	110	U
Alvin	47	NY	Education	60	U
Duncan	47	HK	International corporate	200	U
Jude	46	LA	Education	25	U
Timothy	46	NY	Human services	65	U
Eddie	45	Man	Education	45	U

[a]Approximate income shown in equivalent of US dollars for 2010
[b]Education abbreviated as: *U* University; *T* Trade school; *S* Secondary school

© The Editor(s) (if applicable) and The Author(s) 2017
P. Robinson, *Gay Men's Working Lives, Retirement and Old Age*,
Genders and Sexualities in the Social Sciences,
DOI 10.1057/978-1-137-43532-3

Appendix 3

Interviewees aged 45 and under: job, income and level of education (*n* = 29)

Age	Code name	City	Occupation field	USD 000s[a]	Ed[b]
44	Jonathon	Lon	International corporate	130	U
44	Kendall	NY	Finance	80	U
43	Gabriel	Auc	Health	70	T
43	Callum	Mel	Education U	68	U
42	Jacob	Mel	Research	48	U
42	Noah	Auc	Education	40	U
41	Connor	Lon	Retail	60	U
40	Kyle	Auc	Business	65	U
38	Guy	Lon	Business	90	U
37	Liam	Syd	Education U	40	U
35	Anton	Lon	Law	130	U
35	Evan	LA	IT	100	U
33	Aiden	Lon	Law	80	U
33	Findlay	NY	Clerical	25	T
32	Jackson	NY	Finance	110	U
32	Dylan	Syd	Clerical	50	U
31	Leo	Syd	Human services	90	U
31	Gavin	Auc	Retail	45	T
28	Eamon	Lon	Mechanical design	100	U
27	Denis	Mel	Entertainment	40	T
26	Bailey	Man	Education	48	U
23	Garth	Mel	Education U	25	S
23	Jarrad	Mel	Education U	<10	S
22	Zane	Mel	Education U	20	S
21	Jamie	Mel	Education U	20	S
21	Todd	Mel	Education U	15	S
21	Hayden	Mel	Education U	15	S
19	Brody	Mel	Education U	<10	S
18	Dougal	Mel	Retail	<10	S

[a]Approximate income shown in equivalent of US dollars for 2010
[b]Education abbreviated as: *U* University; *T* Trade College; *S* Secondary school; *P* Primary school

Appendix 4

Full sample: relationship data ($n = 82$)

Code	Age	Ptr age	Ptr yrs	Last ptr yrs	Relationship status, family history
Randall	87	62	37		Divorce + 4ch
Herbert	82	65	07		
Amery	82	S			
Hector	81	70	25		Married + 1d
Clancy	81	S		8	
Godfrey	81	S		0.25	
Drake	77	56	31		Married + 2d
Ambrose	77	S		17	
Basil	75	S		2.5	
Lucas	75	S			Married 52 years
Christian	72	72	42		
Jeffery	72	S			Married 24 years
Colin	72	S		9.5	
Arran	70	81	25		
Ashton	70	45	25		
Sean	67	47	16		
Baden	65	82	07		
Alfie	63	63	39		CU
Bryce	63	63	39		CU
Fergus	63	S			
Parry	63	67	25		Gay commitment
Hugh	62	86	37		
Alec	62	S			
Arthur	62	27	6		
Anselm	61	S		1.5	Married + 1 d
Bernard	59	40	12		Adopted son
Ward	59	52	15		Gay married
Marvin	59	S		10	
Raymond	58	38	11		
Austin	57	S		6	Divorced + 3 s
Isaac	56	77	31		
Logan	56	51	15		
Cam	56	S			
Ryan	53	S		14	With female
Hilton	53	S		18	Divorced + 2 d

(continued)

© The Editor(s) (if applicable) and The Author(s) 2017
P. Robinson, *Gay Men's Working Lives, Retirement and Old Age*,
Genders and Sexualities in the Social Sciences,
DOI 10.1057/978-1-137-43532-3

274 **Appendix 4**

(continued)

Code	Age	Ptr age	Ptr yrs	Last ptr yrs	Relationship status, family history
Mike	52	S		23	
Zachary	52	51	22		
Ben	52	52	20		CU
Calvin	51	S			
Buck	51	52	22		Gay union
Tate	51	25	0.16		
Earl	51	S		23	Gay union 12 years
Nathan	50	37	6		
Ethan	49	S		0.25	
Carl	49	S		4	
Everett	49	S		2	Gay married
Danny	48	43	7		Married (US)
Duncan	47	47	21		Civil p/ship
Fred	47	44	11		
Alvin	47	50	3.5		
Jude	46	S			
Timothy	46	S			
Eddie	45	51	18.5		Divorced, CU
Jonathon	44	47	10		
Kendall	44	S			
Callum	43	42	06		
Gabriel	43	35	03		CU + 1 s
Jacob	42	43	10.25		
Noah	42	36	08		
Connor	41	S		0.5	
Kyle	40	S		4	
Guy	38	S		1.5	
Liam	37	48	08		
Anton	35	S		10	
Evan	35	S		0.25	
Aiden	33	33	03		
Findlay	33	41	0.08		
Jackson	32	44	04		
Dylan	32	S		0.75	
Gavin	31`	56	03		
Leo	31	S		6	
Eamon	28	S		6.5	
Denis	27	21	0.03		
Bailey	26	37	01.5		
Garth	23	S		0.25	
Jarrad	23	S			
Zane	22	27	0.66		

(continued)

(continued)

Code	Age	Ptr age	Ptr yrs	Last ptr yrs	Relationship status, family history
Jamie	21	24	01		
Hayden	21	21	01		
Todd	21	21	01		
Brody	19	40	0.75		
Dougal	18	S		0	

CU civil union; *S* single

ch children; d daughter; *s* son

Last ptr years = length of previous relationship in years

Appendix 5

Full sample: age, year at 21 ($n = 82$)

Code name	Age	Year @ 21
Randall	87	1945
Herbert	82	1948
Amery	82	1948
Hector	81	1949
Clancy	81	1950
Godfrey	81	1950
Ambrose	77	1953
Drake	77	1955
Lucas	75	1956
Basil	75	1956
Jeffery	72	1959
Colin	72	1958
Christian	72	1960
Arran	70	1961
Ashton	70	1960
Sean	67	1964
Baden	65	1965
Fergus	63	1968
Bryce	63	1968
Alfie	63	1968
Parry	63	1967
Arthur	62	1969
Hugh	62	1968
Alec	62	1969
Anselm	61	1970
Ward	59	1971
Marvin	59	1971
Bernard	59	1972
Raymond	58	1973
Austin	57	1974
Logan	56	1975
Isaac	56	1976
Cam	56	1974
Ryan	53	1978
Hilton	53	1976
Zachary	52	1979
Mike	52	1979

(continued)

© The Editor(s) (if applicable) and The Author(s) 2017
P. Robinson, *Gay Men's Working Lives, Retirement and Old Age*,
Genders and Sexualities in the Social Sciences,
DOI 10.1057/978-1-137-43532-3

278   **Appendix 5**

(continued)

Code name	Age	Year @ 21
Ben	52	1979
Tate	51	1979
Earl	51	1978
Calvin	51	1980
Buck	51	1979
Nathan	50	1981
Everett	49	1980
Ethan	49	1981
Carl	49	1982
Danny	48	1983
Fred	47	1984
Duncan	47	1985
Alvin	47	1982
Timothy	46	1984
Jude	46	1984
Eddie	45	1985
Kendall	44	1986
Jonathon	44	1988
Gabriel	43	1988
Callum	43	1987
Noah	42	1989
Jacob	42	1989
Connor	41	1990
Kyle	40	1991
Guy	38	1993
Liam	37	1993
Evan	35	1995
Anton	35	1996
Finlay	33	1996
Aiden	33	1998
Jackson	32	1998
Dylan	32	1999
Leo	31	2000
Gavin	31	2000
Eamon	28	2003
Denis	27	2003
Bailey	26	2005
Jarrad	23	2007
Garth	23	2008
Zane	22	2009
Todd	21	2009
Jamie	21	2010
Hayden	21	2009
Brody	19	2013
Dougal	18	2014

Year @ 21 = year when interviewee turned 21

Appendix 6

Principal work narratives by age cohort

Old ($n = 25$)	Middle ($n = 28$)	Young ($n = 29$)[a]
Work-as-work ($n = 12$)	Care ($n = 14$)	Creativity ($n = 8$)
Care or creative ($n = 10$)	Travel ($n = 11$)	Care ($n = 5$)
Soc-pol change ($n = 3$)	Work-as-work ($n = 6$)	Soc-pol change ($n = 5$)
	Soc-pol change ($n = 5$)	Work as work $n = (4)$
		Travel ($n = 1$)

[a] the number of principal work narratives for this cohort were less than the number of interviewees because seven were students when interviewed

Appendix 7: Roger Horton's Article on his Time in the Australian Army

Job Description: Infantry Soldier— Australian Regular Army

The ideal candidate will be white, male and heterosexual. You will naturally be tough, stoical and self-sufficient, yet within a group, you will be self-effacing and loyal. Socially, you will enjoy drinking to excess and revel in misogyny. 'Women are really only good for one thing—that's right, fucking'. You will revile and despise weakness and vulnerability in others, above all in the effeminate soldier; the 'malinger' (the soldier who presents with various medical problems in order to avoid physical fitness training and field exercises); the over- or under-weight, especially if they can't keep up in physical exercises and training; the soldier of another racial background who represents racial impurity and a threat—'watch out he's one of them, he looks like the imagined enemy—a fucking Asian'. As an Asian-looking soldier, you may be a weak link and 'defect' to the enemy, or just desert. You will enjoy that Aussie egalitarian sense of humour that is based on the tall poppy syndrome. Achievers are to be despised and bought back into line and it is natural to put others down. 'Taking the piss' and playing on the weaknesses of others as presented in individual differences will be demanded. Being coarse, brash and speaking your mind is natural. Grossness is part of the 'levelling' experience expected. You can speak, but don't dare to think. Respecting others, being reasonably civilised and acting with sensitivity and understanding reflect effeminacy, 'girlie' behaviour, and the dreaded possibility that you're a 'poof' or a 'faggot'.

On an overcast morning not long after Anzac day in April 1989, I stepped off the bus at the 1st Recruit training battalion near Wagga Wagga, NSW. I was 19. Called Kapooka, this base is where the

---

© The Editor(s) (if applicable) and The Author(s) 2017
P. Robinson, *Gay Men's Working Lives, Retirement and Old Age*,
Genders and Sexualities in the Social Sciences,
DOI 10.1057/978-1-137-43532-3

personalties and self-esteem of new recruits were to be crushed and then moulded into those of a soldier. Individual differences in racial background, gender and sexual preference were weaknesses. These differences are seized upon, focused as opportunities to attack and abuse individuals. Verbal abuse and physical punishments prove a constant throughout the three-month training course. They are integral to the way in which racism was institutionalised in the Army. In this article, I am reflecting on my experience as an Asian-Australian who enlisted in the Australian regular army for a four-year period from April 1989 to April 1993.

Not long after arriving at Kapooka, we were assigned to platoons and were marched off to receive haircuts, dog tags, boots and kit. After a honeymoon period of less than 24 hours, the psychological and verbal abuse began. I was now Recruit Horton and labelled a 'pretty boy and mummy's boy'. Later the verbal abuse included calling me a 'gook', the derogatory term given to Viet Cong and North Vietnamese soldiers during the Vietnam War. Abuse was extended to all members of the platoon: country boys were called 'hill billies and stupid country-fucks'. Soldiers of New Zealand origin were called 'sheep fuckers', overweight soldiers 'fat fucks', and soldiers with European background 'wogs'.

Gradually and painfully, your sense of self is dissolved and eventually you learn to give up. Resisting is useless. Some recruits were psychologically damaged and broken by the experience, others stood up to it out of fear. One frightened recruit who said that our instructor reminded him of the Devil was later discharged on psychological grounds. Another soldier attempted escape from the barracks by going AWOL (absent without leave). He jumped from the second floor of the barrack block in his attempt at freedom but broke his legs on landing. There were casualties already and such recruits were labelled as 'Nancy boys' and 'weak cunts'. Instructors taunted us, asking which of us was going to be the next to crack under the pressure before packing his bags.

One month of training, of abuse and of physical punishments—endless push ups and rifle exercises, holding up rifles with arms extended for long periods. Then, the emphasis shifted to building up our self-esteem in the context of the group, and not as individuals. We were gradually praised for our efforts and achievements: 'Well done recruit

Appendix 7: Roger Horton's Article on his Time in the Australian ... 283

Horton, you are not doing too bad for a black cunt'. Peer group pressure, fear of failure, physical punishments and the scapegoating of individuals who didn't measure up were the ways that instructors kept us motivated. Steadily in this distorted and warped way, 'camaraderie' is built up by excluding those who had failed (at exercises and tests). I ended up feeling stronger and superior to civilians or what we called 'Slyvilians or civi-fucks'.

I began to feel *tough* in the sense that I represented the supreme masculine ideal. We told ourselves: 'you walked 40 kms with a pack and rifle doing it hard, no civi-fuck could do that, they are just weak as piss!' Just as football players and boxers represent extreme models of masculinity (strength and toughness), so the soldier represents another extreme model of masculinity which ultimately describes weakness in terms of femininity: 'You're a bloody Sheila, or a fucken pussy'. Instructors and trainers reinforced this *otherness* by extinguishing the differences between ourselves, we felt as one, a team united until we had little regard for outsiders. I was now a soldier not a civilian, I did not need to be civilised.

On completing my basic training at Kapooka, I felt relief, but this escape was to be short-lived. The Infantry training centre at Singleton, NSW, made Kapooka seem like a holiday. The standards of physical fitness were much higher. I was injured during a round of boxing during a week we spent at a beach rifle range. I had dislocated my shoulder and this, consequently, required two months recuperation before I could rejoin a platoon in training. I was transferred to a holding platoon for convalescence, where the morale was particularly low. The unit consisted of genuinely injured soldiers, but it also contained those soldiers in the process of being discharged for administrative problems or drug use. Some members were malingers, hoping to avoid finishing infantry training by getting either a discharge or a corps transfer. The attitude of platoons in training towards the holding platoon was that we were a bunch of 'weak cunts or bad apples'.

When I rejoined a platoon to complete my training, I was told by one member—'Make sure you keep up and put in, otherwise there'll be trouble!'. One of my new corporals said 'You know I used to fuck boys like you in Thailand'. What a warm welcome, I thought. At this time,

I considered going AWOL. That thought came just before joining this platoon in training. I had even booked a bus ticket out of Singleton. I was upset about the delays in my training, missing the mates I had trained with at Kapooka, and who were just about to march out. I was about to start week six of training while they were at week twelve and nearly at the end. I was feeling disillusioned by the alienation of this and was sitting out the back of the barracks block in tears wondering what I should do. In the end, I felt it was best to keep going and just do my time honourably and be done with the army in four years' time.

After I completed my Infantry corps training, my feeling of relief was total as I sat on the bus driving out through the gates of Singleton for one last time. I had been posted to 2/4th battalion, Royal Australian Regiment based in Townsville, Queensland. At that moment, I couldn't care less where I was going, so long as it wasn't anywhere near Singleton. The 2/4th was part of the Operational Deployment Force. We were the frontline troops on 24 h notice to move should a deployment be necessary. (Such troops have been deployed in recent years to East Timor, the Solomon Islands and now Iraq.)

In Townsville, my army life settled down to a routine but a strong racist element still sat in the background around the base. The racism was wearing me down and it is so effective because it attacks your identity and who you are. I was seen as inferior and defective from the 'normal' white soldier. The result for me was alienation and depression and the way I dealt with it was through heavy drinking and later drug use. One particularly nasty senior soldier would call me a 'weak cunt and a boy'. He was hoping I would physically retaliate so he could punch the fuck out of me, but I resisted. His attacks on me were combined with the verbal abuse from one of my platoon sergeants who liked to call me 'gook or black cunt'. I had continually repressed the feelings of anger and rage at these comments but eventually the emotional strain was too much for me. One night I broke down and became upset in the presence of another soldier in my platoon. He was very understanding and the next day bought the issue up with the platoon commander and the platoon sergeant responsible for these comments. The results were short-lived and in the long term nothing changed. Leadership was lacking in opposition to racism but would have made some difference.

Appendix 7: Roger Horton's Article on his Time in the Australian ... 285

In one incident, leadership was effective in blocking one strain of racist culture. A group of soldiers fresh from infantry corps training at Singleton had arrived and among them was a clutch of neo-Nazis. After some time, they started to verbally abuse and physically threaten some Fijian soldiers in their own rifle company. The rest of the time they were beating up civilians, local Aborigines and other soldiers. The situation could have escalated but two senior NCOs (non-commissioned officers)—one white and one Fijian—stepped in and told the neo-Nazis that such behaviour was not on, and that they would be subjected to a beating themselves if they continued their racist behaviour. Their verbal abuse and racist behaviour stopped soon after, although local Aborigines, civilians and other soldiers were still subjected to their wrath. This incident highlights the importance of leadership on the issue of racism, but also the inherent dangers of any society supporting a group of trained killers, which is what soldiers recruited become. They are a danger not only to other soldiers, but also to the community they are supposed to protect.

On one occasion I watched an effeminate pay corps corporal get harassed out of the soldiers' bar and eventually out of the battalion because he had a high voice and seemed gay in demeanour. (It was bad enough that he was in pay corps which was considered the lowest of the low. Infantry corps consist of the frontline fighting units so all other corps are considered inferior). The homophobic behaviour of various infantry soldiers towards this man was appalling. Paradoxically, this homophobic behaviour often came from soldiers who themselves often displayed homo-erotic behaviour, for example, standing on the pool table and dropping their trousers so they could swing their dicks around and show everyone how 'big', potent and virile they were—'hey look at me boys'. I felt helpless in light of this poor soldier's predicament. He had done nothing wrong but if I had come to his aid, I too would have been labelled a 'faggot' (nothing could be worse than being an Asian faggot). I would have been constantly harassed and more than likely beaten up.

This army model of masculinity is riddled with problems. Like many before me, I was drawn to the seductive idea of war as the ultimate test and proof of my masculinity. Real life requires accountability and personal responsibility, while war represents the opportunity for the ultimate form of unaccountability: the freedom to kill and murder another human being. This, I think is what often unconsciously draws men to this profession, particularly arms corps units. The chance to be violent for a living, not have to answer to anyone. The rules and laws of society are overturned in war and you have the opportunity to become a law unto yourself. The naïve sense of power and the opportunity for its abuse is very seductive to the unformed and malleable mind. Becoming a trained killer may mean that you end up in a war, or what has been called organised murder. But few realise the psychological devastation of the job specifications. Their final performance was something to which I was not subjected.[1]

Note

1. R. Horton (2006) 'Arrested Development in a man's army', *Seeing Red*, n. 5, 22–24.

Index

A

Aboriginal 10, 146, 217
Adult 8, 13, 16, 23, 39, 40, 53, 60, 66, 72, 97, 98, 104, 105, 225, 233, 234, 246, 259
Adulthood 6, 7, 39, 86, 115, 135, 258
Age, coming of 6, 64
Ageism 22, 182, 200
AIDS, *see* HIV-AIDS
Altman, Dennis 65
Arber, Sara 165
Ariès, Philippe 171, 172, 259
Auckland 10, 42, 43, 49–51, 97, 99, 103, 111–113, 135, 140, 144, 165–167, 170, 178, 193, 195, 202, 219, 223, 224, 226, 232, 233, 239, 242
Australia 5–7, 9, 15, 16, 38, 43, 45–47, 56, 57, 59, 60, 65, 67, 87, 99, 101, 107, 108, 116

Australian Bureau of Statistics (ABS) 6, 8, 10, 19, 27, 29, 30, 38, 73, 74, 110, 117, 220, 250

B

Bang (gay club, London) 16, 17
Bataille, Georges 18, 185–187
Bauman, Zygmunt 14
Beauvoir, Simone de 20, 21, 223
Becker, Howard 61, 64, 67
Beck-Gernsheim, Elizabeth 21, 198
Beck, Ulrich 21, 198
Big Brother (television programme) 65
Bourdieu, Pierre 72

C

Camp 5, 6, 38, 40, 42, 43, 61, 63, 64, 66–68, 70, 71, 172
Care work(ers), *see* old age, care work
Changing World of Gay Men, The 1
Chauncey, George, 68

© The Editor(s) (if applicable) and The Author(s) 2017
P. Robinson, *Gay Men's Working Lives, Retirement and Old Age,*
Genders and Sexualities in the Social Sciences,
DOI 10.1057/978-1-137-43532-3

288 **Index**

Civil union, civil partnership, *see* gay, marriage
Clark, Manning 247
Class 8, 21, 53, 66, 69, 173, 189, 224, 236, 254, 257
Closet, closeted 23, 24, 62, 63, 71, 95, 110, 113, 134, 135, 149, 161, 167, 169, 197, 200, 258, 262
Cold War 60
Coleherne (London gay club) 16
Connell, Raewyn 64, 113

D
Duckett, Stephen 166

E
Education
primary 69, 140
secondary 8, 10, 47, 69, 75, 87, 130, 140, 164, 191, 254; government school(s) 9; non-government (private) school(s) 128, 132, 155, 240, 241, 257; students 129
tertiary
students 6, 88, 127, 149
TAFE 136, 137, 145, 156
trade school(s), college(s) 8, 9, 173
university 5–7, 9, 10, 15, 19, 20, 40, 41, 44, 47, 51, 55, 57, 58, 87, 89, 92, 101, 103–105, 126, 128, 129, 131, 132, 136, 141, 144, 146, 173
Effeminacy 68, 156
Effeminate 51, 67, 68, 116, 281, 285

Elias, Norbert 18, 20, 95, 114, 117, 155, 165, 172, 180
Employment
blue collar 20, 167, 169, 173
casual, casualised 3, 10, 18, 50, 104, 131, 185, 187, 232, 255
corporate-professional 87, 88, 96, 104, 150
flexible 14, 15, 45, 147, 148, 256
part-time 16–18, 44, 46, 126, 127, 131, 132, 141–143, 156
precarious 13, 14, 25, 41, 169, 255
white collar 19, 115
England 14, 16, 38, 45, 48, 67, 91, 92, 95, 97, 100, 149, 175

F
Family, families
alternative 65, 262
Feminism, feminist 5, 50, 180
Forster, E.M. 15

G
Gay
community, communities 17, 19, 22, 23, 52, 53, 59, 89, 90, 94, 96, 108, 109, 116, 180, 191, 193, 195, 196, 198, 199, 202, 260, 262, 285
liberation(ists) 8, 9, 38, 39, 56, 92, 110, 114, 134, 172, 258, 263
marriage 2, 8, 9, 23, 54, 56, 61, 63, 64, 71, 107, 113, 114,

117, 148, 195, 196, 228, 235

scene 16, 96, 185, 188, 189

Gay Men's Relationships Across the Life Course 11

Generation(s)

Baby-boomer 8, 23, 38, 85, 93, 108, 110, 115, 126, 140, 146, 173, 198, 224, 258, 260, 261

i-generation 125, 126, 130, 219, 238, 257, 261

Lucky generation 38, 219

X and Y generation 10, 125, 199, 238

Gilleard, Chris 21

Grindr 186, 187

Guardian, the 65

H

Herdt, Gilbert 58, 59

Hidden Injuries of Class, The 66

Higgs, Paul 21

Hirst, John 247

HIV-AIDS 72, 73, 86, 88–92, 95, 96, 106–110, 115, 116, 125, 190, 221, 230, 254, 261

Homo-sociability 177, 179, 205

Homophobia 24, 38–40, 60, 64, 65, 73, 77, 88, 93, 111–114, 134, 140, 145, 149, 151, 153, 154, 161–163, 169, 177, 204, 254, 256, 259–263

Hong Kong 2, 3, 49, 59, 87, 88, 97, 98, 100–103, 111, 113, 174, 179, 182, 183, 236

I

Income(s) 6, 9, 14, 39, 59, 69, 87, 104, 108, 116, 126, 144, 164, 174, 186, 204, 228, 236–238

Individualisation 21, 144, 198

J

Johnson, Donald 72

Johnston, George 60

K

Kinsey, Alfred 18

L

Lesbian(s) 3, 22, 58, 71, 89, 99, 113, 145, 162, 163, 167, 193–195, 197, 199, 205

London 7, 9, 16, 17, 44–47, 57, 72, 88, 97, 98, 100, 101, 105, 106

Los Angeles 144, 178, 189, 231, 232

M

Manchester 17, 22, 42, 50, 90, 92, 108, 169, 177–179, 219, 224, 227, 228, 237

Mann, Thomas 202

Maori 10, 138, 140, 141

Marriage equality, *see* gay, marriage

Masculinity, masculinities

dominant 64, 65, 72, 131, 154, 186, 187, 205, 246, 258

hegemonic 3, 254

McIntyre, Stuart 43

McKenzie, Compton 15

290   Index

McLaren, Angus 60
McQueen, Humphrey xvi, 3, 25
Melbourne 10, 15–17, 42–51, 53,
    54, 65, 87, 88, 97, 103,
    108, 128–131, 135, 138,
    140–142
Mitford, Jessica 171
Monetarism, monetary theory (*also
    known as* economic rational-
    ism)
    economic rationalists 86
Mortgage 43, 103, 106, 225, 236–
    238, 253
Mumbai 2, 3, 11, 90

N

Narrative(s)
    narrative theory 5, 11, 12
New York 132, 164, 181, 182, 184,
    227, 230, 232
New Zealand 9, 23, 87, 97–99, 111,
    115, 138, 175, 193, 199,
    258
Nursing home(s), *see* old age, acco-
    modation

O

Old age
    accommodation 24, 162–163,
    165–166, 173, 174, 177–
    181, 191, 193, 196–198,
    204–206, 263; home care
    161–164, 174, 176, 178,
    191, 193, 195, 204; institu-
    tional, homophobia in, fear
    of 24, 206; nursing home(s),
    gay 24, 163, 166, 168, 179,
    180, 200; nursing home(s),
    homophobia in, fear of 24,
    149, 162, 254
    care work
    ; primary care work(er) 68, 212
    friendship(s), and 162, 165, 171,
    189, 194
    partner's death, and 170, 181
    pension
    ; Germany 216; privatised 219;
    Queensland 216; state-
    funded 45, 216
    privatised 219
    relationship(s), and 148, 162, 163,
    169, 170, 173, 175, 181,
    182, 184, 188, 189, 192,
    195, 204, 205, 242, 259
    social isolation or loneliness, and
    24, 162, 169, 181, 185, 188,
    200, 202, 205, 206, 260

P

Pension(s), *see* old age, pension
People living with HIV-AIDS
    (PLWHA) 56, 57, 72, 106,
    230
Phillipson, Chris 168
Piketty, Thomas 6
Plummer, Ken 22
Pollak, Michael 13, 16, 19, 254

R

Rechy, John 80, 210
Retirement
    early 3, 4, 7, 17, 22, 38, 53, 55,
    56
    premature 222

Index   **291**

Richardson, Diane 22

S

Same Same 264
Savin-Williams, Ritch 148, 152
School-of-arts, movement 53
School(s). *see* education secondary
Sennett, Richard 3, 14, 15, 41,
    48–50, 66, 103
Simpson, Paul 22
Student(s), *see* education
Superannuation 2, 147, 148, 175,
    218, 219, 224, 228, 237–
    241, 243–247, 263
Swain, Shurlee 218
Swerissen, Hal 166
Sydney 5, 10, 16, 17, 42–44, 46, 50,
    53, 55, 56, 59, 64, 87, 131,
    135, 140, 141, 151, 166,
    181, 182, 185, 188, 191,
    194, 195, 197, 203, 221,
    224, 227, 228, 237, 244

T

Terkel, Studs 3
Tourism
    'jumbo jet' 89, 97
Travel
    'love' travel 43–47, 89, 96, 100–
        102, 115, 143, 146, 256

U

Unemployment
    benefits, (*also known as* the dole)
        141
Union(s), trade 134, 149, 259

U.S.A. 6, 17, 22, 38, 47, 60, 64, 66,
    70, 90–92, 97, 103, 104,
    115, 177, 199, 216, 220,
    236, 258

V

Vietnam War 7, 282

W

Wacquant, Loïc 3, 218
Waugh, Evelyn 171
Weeks, Jeffrey 22
Welfare state 13, 86, 216, 219, 230,
    238
White, Edmund 13, 17
White, Patrick 155, 257
Wilde, Oscar 5, 15, 262
Will(s) 229
Work
    care 50, 89, 134
    creative 50
    intellectual 56, 103, 134
    sex, and, tension between 67, 254
    social/political purpose, with 55,
        106, 139
    'till you drop' 222, 223
    travel 97, 147
    work-as-work 40, 103, 143
World War I 7, 172, 216
World War II 38, 39, 42, 43, 47, 50,
    53, 54, 171, 216, 219

CPSIA information can be obtained
at www.ICGtesting.com
Printed in the USA
LVOW13*2116270717
542868LV00004BA/5/P